English in Urban Classrooms

D0217412

English in Urban Classrooms is a ground-breaking text that spans a range of issues central to contemporary school English. It attends not only to the spoken and written language of classrooms, but also to other modes of representation and communication that are important in English teaching. This includes image, gesture, gaze, movement, and spatial organization.

The team of experienced and expert authors collectively examine how English is shaped by policy, by institutions, and by the social relations of the classroom. By connecting issues of policy and social context, the book provides a detailed account of factors such as:

- the characteristics of urban multicultural schools;
- teacher formation and tradition;
- the ethos of school English departments; and
- the institutional changes that have shaped school English in urban class-rooms and students' experiences of learning.

This book offers a fascinating and enlightening read, not only to those involved in English teaching, but also to educational researchers, policy makers, linguists, and those interested in semiotics and multimodality.

Gunther Kress is Professor of Education and English at the Institute of Education, University of London.

Carey Jewitt is Research Fellow at the Institute of Education, University of London.

Jill Bourne is Professor of Primary Education at the School of Education, University of Southampton.

Ken Jones is Professor of Education at Keele University.

John Hardcastle, **Anton Franks** and **Euan Reid** are Lecturers at the Institute of Education, University of London.

English in Urban Classrooms

A multimodal perspective on
teaching and learning

Gunther Kress, Carey Jewitt,
Jill Bourne, Anton Franks,
John Hardcastle, Ken Jones,
Euan Reid

RoutledgeFalmer
Taylor & Francis Group

LONDON AND NEW YORK

First published 2005
by RoutledgeFalmer
2 Park Square, Milton Park, Abingdon, Oxon OX14 4RN

Simultaneously published in the USA and Canada
by RoutledgeFalmer
270 Madison Avenue, New York, NY 10016
RoutledgeFalmer is an imprint of the Taylor & Francis Group

Typeset in by Times New Roman by Bookcraft Ltd, Stroud,
Gloucestershire
Printed and bound in Great Britain by TJ International Ltd, Padstow, Cornwall

British Library Cataloguing in Publication Data
A catalogue record for this book is available from the British Library

Library of Congress Cataloging in Publication Data
English in urban classrooms: a multimodal perspective on teaching and learning /
Gunther Kress [et al.].
    p. cm.
    Includes bibliographical references and index.
    1. English language – Study and teaching (Secondary) – Social aspects – England – London.
    2. Urban high schools – England – London.   3. English teachers – Training of – England –
    London.   I. Kress, Gunther R.
    LB1631.E59 2004
    428'.0071'241—dc22

                                                                        2004007612

ISBN 0-415-33168-4 (hbk)
ISBN 0-415-33169-2 (pbk)

Contents

Illustrations

Contributors

Jill Bourne is Professor of Primary Education at the School of Education, University of Southampton. She writes on discourse, language and identity. Recent publications include *The World Yearbook of Language Education* (Kogan Page 2003), edited with E. Reid.

Anton Franks was a teacher of drama and English in London schools and he is now Lecturer on Drama and English in Education at the Institute of Education, University of London. Recent publications include 'Lessons from Brecht' with Ken Jones in *Research in Drama Education* 4(2) 1999 and 'Drama, desire and schooling …' in *Changing English* 4(1) 1997.

John Hardcastle is Lecturer at the Institute of Education, University of London. He taught English for fourteen years in a school in Hackney and subsequently he was an advisory teacher in East London. He has written extensively about London classrooms and he is a regular contributor to *Changing English*.

Carey Jewitt is Research Fellow at the Institute of Education, University of London, and (co)editor of the journal *Visual Communication* (Sage). She writes on visual and multimodal communication and learning. Her publications include *Knowledge, Literacy and Learning: Multimodality and New Technologies* (RoutledgeFalmer, forthcoming).

Ken Jones is Professor of Education at Keele University. He has written about English teaching (*English and the National Curriculum: Cox's Revolution?* Kogan Page 1992), education policy (*Education in Britain: 1944 to the Present*, Polity Press 2002) and is currently working on cultural histories of education.

Gunther Kress is Professor of Education and English at the Institute of Education, University of London. His recent publications include *Multimodal Discourse: The Modes and Media of Contemporary Communication* (Arnold 2001) with T. van Leeuwen, and *Literacy in the New Media Age* (Routledge 2002).

Euan Reid is Senior Lecturer at the Institute of Education, University of London. His research interests are in education in multilingual societies and his publications include *Language in Education: World Yearbook of Education* (Kogan Page 2003), co-edited with J. Bourne.

Preface

This book is the direct outcome of a research project, 'The Production of School English', conducted between 2001 and 2003, and funded by the ESRC (the Economic and Social Science Research Council). In two ways it is also the outcome of projects of very different kinds. One is the long sustained series of 'educational reforms' now in train since the late 1980s. These have affected all aspects of institutional education in all kinds of ways, yet probably no subject more so than English. While all aspects of teaching, all curriculum areas and all students, are now subject to regimes of assessment and judgements of performance not seen before, changes to the curricula of most subjects have been nowhere near as far-reaching as those in English. That alone is an issue worthy of close attention – namely, what is it about this subject, and its role in the school curriculum, that has made it the focus of such change (see Jones 2003b)?

The other project is altogether more modest in scale: it concerns the work of the SISC group (Subjectivity in the School Curriculum) over a period of about eight years, which culminated in the submission of the proposal for the 'Production of School English' project. The group – initially Jill Bourne, Roger Hewitt, Gunther Kress, Euan Reid and Janet White – had met, from 1992 on, to reflect on the effect of specific curricula on the formation of a pupil's 'subjectivity': the question, broadly framed, of what forms of subjectivity are suggested, fostered, implied, produced even, in the contents and the organizations, the deeper epistemologies as well as the implied pedagogies, of different subjects in the school curriculum. Added to this was the equally salient question of how such differences might or could play out in differential ways in the socially, ethnically and culturally deeply diverse classrooms that characterize schools in so many contemporary societies. The subjects that the SISC group had initially intended to work on were English and Mathematics – less because of the political storms in which English was embroiled during that period than because of the assumed inherent differences between them.

Two 'pilot studies' were undertaken, each tracking English in the classroom. The first was carried out over two terms in 1992, and based on detailed classroom observation and taped recordings of students' and teachers' talk. This gave the group much material for discussion about English; in part this was reported at several conferences, especially with a group of colleagues in Germany and the Netherlands (Ingrid Gogolin, Sjaak Kroon, Jan Sturm in the context of the International Mother-tongue Education Network, IMEN). A later study (supported by a small grant from the Institute of Education) involving the video-taping of three lessons, enabled the group – by this time enlarged by the addition of Anton Franks, John Hardcastle and Ken Jones – to focus very much more on the questions of methodology to be used in any research on a bigger scale. The last member to join the team, at the beginning of the project, was Carey Jewitt, as the full-time project researcher; she was, in every way, a full member of the team from the very beginning, and her work helped to ensure the success of the project in all ways.

When the project began, in 2001, it was the largest funded study on English since the major work of Barnes (1984). Hence it was also the first major study of the subject after the impact of the educational reforms of the 1990s. But given the lapse of time since 1984, it was also clear that in the intervening two decades there had been vast (social) changes affecting how English could and might be taught, a matter that was debated in the SISC group in relation to the data it had collected to work with.

The other significant fact entailed in that gap in time is of course that of technology. In 1982 television was still the new and dominant *electronic* medium, though at that time the book was still the *culturally* dominant medium in Western societies – certainly so in schools, and absolutely so in English. By 2001 this had changed profoundly. The now dominant media are the new screens: of the PC, the Playstation, the Gameboy, and the mobile phone. And by 2001 the book had been displaced by these 'new screens' as the culturally dominant medium, even though its place seemed still – ostensibly – assured in schools, and in the English classroom. One among several things that our study shows is that in reality the book's role has waned, if not collapsed, even in English. In many English classrooms texts appear as fragments, photocopied parts of larger texts. In the official anthologies in use in English classrooms, the canonical texts of the official curriculum appear as extracts, all set in the same uniform typeface; they are present as 'text' rather than as texts.

And so it was inevitable that new questions would need to be asked about English. Our first question was: 'How is English produced? What does it come to be when it is "made" in classrooms marked by such diversity?' in the environment of the pressure of new policies, in the turmoil often of the social environments of the inner city – a time now, unlike 1982, when words such as 'globalization' are part of common parlance. But the other question, suggested and made inevitable by the impact of the new information and communication technologies, equally profound, and equally challenging, is this: 'What is the best way, now, of looking at English? What methodology will do justice to understanding the subject now, in this era?'

Our work rested on the help, the insights, the advice of many people. First and foremost are the teachers who so graciously permitted us to come into their classrooms. Teachers now, more than ever, are under often near-unsustainable pressures, and the presence of a researcher in a class might seem to be simply that straw that will break the camel's back. But we met with great generosity and openness, and without exception we found dedicated professionals whose single aim was to do that which would be best for the young adults in their classrooms. Second must be the students, whose presence speaks everywhere in our discussion. We came to see that in the production of English they too have a significantly agentive role. In a time when their role in society at large is subject to such deep change (the 'disappearance of childhood', their incorporation into the forces of the market), their place in school is anything but easy and straightforward.

We would like to thank the teachers and the students at the three schools who participated in the research project that this book is based on. And then there are the many colleagues who have helped us in essential ways: specifically we would like to thank Courtney Cazden and David Russell for taking the time to look at some of our data with us, to comment on draft papers and be part of an ongoing discussion of the issues we address in this book. Many of the chapters in this book have benefited from comments on earlier versions from a number of colleagues. We would like to thank the following people for their comments, challenges and insights: on working papers, Eve Bearne, Jeff Bezemer, Andrew Burn, Jan Derry, Ian Grosvenor, Kris Gutierrz, Roxy Harris, Ingrid Gogolin, Bethan Marshall, Peter Medway, Gemma Moss, Jon Ogborn, Sigmund Ongstad, Philip Scott, Mary Scott, Brian Street, Jan Sturm and Theo van Leeuwen. In addition, each of us benefited from ongoing conversations with colleagues and students 'in' education, at Keele University, at Southampton University, and at the Institute of Education, University of London. Specifically we would like to mention Tony Burgess, Caroline Daly, Charmian Kenner and Anne Turvey.

To all of them we give our thanks. Such acknowledgements are customary, yet it is the case that in a project such as this there are innumerably many pitfalls, and the chance to avoid at least some of them was a great help.

Lastly, making use of the role of 'director' of the project – a role that otherwise remained only notional – I wish to step back to make a comment on the work of the project team, and the writing of the book. The team, all of whom are the listed authors of the book, worked together over a period of three years and a half. What made our work constantly interesting and challenging was not just the inherent interest of our questions, but the fact that every member of the team brought a quite specific set of experiences, interests and competences as their particular contribution, all of which complemented each other. In the writing of the book the different positions, viewpoints, 'takes' are at times readily discernible. We have attempted to write in such a way as to reflect the fact that we collectively hold to and share the position taken in the book; we have also thought it good to leave the differences in 'voice' or 'tone' that are noticeable at times. There seemed no need to deny that we were seven people with distinct positions, who had come together in joint work on a single project.

Gunther Kress

Introduction

The questions

In the project on which this book is based we posed two questions: one about the school subject English, the other about a way of looking at English in the classroom. The first question, broadly, was this: how is English *made*; what, actually, ✓ is it *like*; and how is it experienced when it appears in this specific classroom, shaped by the mix of governmental curriculum policy, of the school's response to that policy, the variety of departmental traditions in the school and their ethos, the social and geographical environment in which the school operates, the kinds of students who come to the school, and last – but by no means least – the variations in the professional trainings, experiences and backgrounds of the teachers? The second question, the question about methodology, simply put, was this: what is ✓ the best or the most appropriate *way of looking* at English, so that we might actually get a full understanding of its reality, in all ways, in the experience of students and teacher alike, in any one classroom?

The first question may seem odd in that we were not, in any way at all, aiming at a comprehensive, encompassing, representative picture of what English is now, either in one place or in the whole of England. Neither the project nor this book attempts to do that. What we do want to understand is the impact of fifteen years of 'structural' educational reform at the micro-level of the classroom. Further, we want to be able to show what forces are at work to make the subject as it comes to be in a particular place; in what ways these forces act; and whose power, whose agency and what resources are at work, to what effect. We want to understand how, in these contexts, the activities and relations of the classroom are patterned, and how the school subject 'English' is constructed. The answer, we feel, will give us and others a clearer sense of how we might act or respond to the ensemble of factors that are always at work in any one place in educational settings at any one time, so as to make such changes as might seem needed and possible.

But it may be that the second of the two questions seems more odd still: after all, there has been and still is a clear enough sense, a consensus even, that *the way to look at* English is to look at 'talk' in the classroom: talk around the important objects of English, whatever they might be – valued texts, the texts and the experiences brought into the school by students from their different backgrounds, and now, since the early 1990s, increasingly the objects and demands of the national government. But, whatever the objects – the *entities* of the curriculum as we shall call them from now on – it would always have been language as speech or as writing that one would have been looking at, as has been the case in the definitive studies of the subject over the last 30 or 40 years. So against that past context, we want to understand the construction or realization of English in its fullest sense. For us this requires a multimodal approach.

A *multimodal* approach is one where attention is given to all the culturally shaped resources that are available for making meaning: *image*, for instance, or *gesture*, or the *layout* – whether of the wall-display, or the furniture of classrooms – and of course *writing* and *speech* as talk. *Mode* is the name we give to these culturally shaped resources for making meaning. *Multi* refers to the fact that modes never occur by themselves, but always with others in ensembles. Multimodality is characterized therefore by the presence and use of a multiplicity of modes. So usually, in any lesson, several modes are 'in use' at the same time: the layout of the classroom remains – more or less – fixed, as does the display on the walls; teachers take up certain, always meaningful, positions in the space of the classroom, textual objects are present and usually, but not always, all this is enveloped in talk. We see all the modes as resources for making (different kinds of) meaning-as-signs. These signs are of very many different kinds and 'sizes', but they are always inextricably fused conjunctions of meaning and form. Putting it in disciplinary terms, our theoretical approach is a semiotic one, an approach that focuses on meaning in all the ways it is made and read in culture.

This is an approach that cannot be taken off the shelf, as it were, but which must be developed almost from first principles as part of the effort of understanding how English in urban schools comes to be what it is. Lest we be misunderstood, we say at once that this approach does not mean, of course, that we are not any longer interested in speech (as talk) or in writing in its many forms. These are and remain central means of producing that which English is; central means of making the meanings of English material. We might even insist that our emphasis on looking at all the means whereby the meanings of English are materialized entails a more serious look at speech and at writing than hitherto taken. Where before there was a common sense about the capacities of language, which left the potentials of what language can do in many ways implicit and unexamined, now, looking at language in the context of other means of making meaning gives the possibility of a much sharper, more precise, more nuanced understanding both of the (different) potentials of speech and of writing, and of their limitations. A multimodal approach to meaning-making provides a fuller, richer and more accurate sense of what language is, and what it is not.

So our assumptions were and are different to those of past work. We assume that what constitutes English is not to be found in language alone, but exists in many modes, and in many tasks other than talking, reading, writing and listening. It is not possible to restrict our ways of looking at English, our gaze, to English as constituted in language as speech or as writing. The meaning of English may now reside as much in the teacher's 'bearing', how he or she dresses, how the furniture in the room is arranged, what the displays on the wall are, what gestures are used at particular moments in the teacher's practice, and so on, as much as they do in speech as talk, or in writing. Our book provides many examples of this.

A brief interlude: a comparison of 'English' and 'science'

If we wanted to ask, at a deep level, what school subjects are 'about', not focused on contents so much as on deep orientations or dispositions, perhaps even on epistemologies, we might say that some subjects are about the inculcation of skills – dance might be an example, or sport. Others are about specific contents – science or history might be examples here; and yet others might be about meaning and about ways of knowing. English would be an example of the latter – or at least it would have been until quite recently. If there is some point to our assumption that English is about meaning, then everything in the English lesson and in the English classroom that is meaningful contributes to what is taken to be the meaning of English by students in the classroom. This is the basis for the multimodal (semiotic) approach that we have taken in the project and are taking here – rather than the linguistic approach that has dominated so much research on English classrooms since the 1970s.

Meaning is made by individuals, though always acting in social environments, using socially and culturally shaped and available resources. We might say that the meanings made in the English classroom – as indeed meanings made elsewhere – are social meanings, collectively made by different individuals as social agents; or we can see them as individually made meanings, made with others, with socially and culturally produced resources, in conditions of social constraints. Our formulation is meant to capture the constant and real co-presence and tension between social agency and a recognition that there also always exists something that appears to be more like individual agency.

Because the English classroom is about meaning, all meaning in the classroom is (at least potentially always) significant. Everything, whether pedagogic or curricular, is at least potentially likely to be seen as part of the meaning of English. In contrast, we said that science, as an example, has traditionally been about knowledge (Kress *et al.* 2001) – it is only recently that questions of ethics, or of science's problematic social impact, have begun to be raised in the school curriculum. The *entities* of the science curriculum have thus for the most part been known and stable: the agency, or even the personality, of the science teacher is unlikely to make a decisive difference to the appearance of the entity 'magnetic field', for instance, in the classroom, nor of a 'wave-form', of 'blood circulation' or of a 'plant cell'. The manner in which an entity is taught may differ significantly from one classroom to the next, but students coming from different science classrooms would recognize these entities without difficulty.

In the case of English that can not be assumed quite so easily, as our discussion will show. Even though government policy attempts to move the English curriculum in the direction of the established paradigm of science – by making the curricular entities much more explicit, for instance – it remains the case that the form in which a specific entity is produced will vary in significant ways from classroom to classroom: the entity 'character', to take an example that we discuss in detail later. In one classroom 'character' may appear in a form that makes it quite like 'person': a person maybe like you and me, or maybe different, but a person whose characteristics are not remote from our everyday experience of people. In another classroom, the 'same' entity may appear as the vehicle for the development and realization of elevated and complex moral and political attributes: quite remote from – even if still connected and recognizable to – our everyday experience.

The social participants in the construction of entities in the English classroom have an effect on the shape of the entity, a situation that can not readily be imagined in subjects such as mathematics, science, geography, and others. The possibilities of the fusion of (inter-)personal and of ideational meanings is very different in English compared to other subjects, even though there is now a strong move to make English conform in these respects more and more to the model of those other subjects. In some of the schools we visited this was more the case than in others: some teachers had welcomed the move and had begun to incorporate its possibilities into their teaching, in interestingly different ways; others were more resistant. In any case, it is a matter that is very much in process.

Given this difference, there is a further reason for our multimodal 'way of looking'. Even though in science the curricular entities are clearly established, the manner of their materialization is very often now an open one: should it be materialized in the form of image; should it be word; which textual form would seem best? Nevertheless, in science, the distinction of pedagogy and curriculum is clear, and whatever the pedagogic approach taken it has very little if any effect on how the entities eventually emerge in the classroom: a bar magnet, or a magnetic field, remains just that, whatever the pedagogy. In English that is not the case – some entities may never appear explicitly, some may never appear as spoken or written: the question of 'literary sensibility' for instance – not directly a part of the official curriculum, but still very much a part of the unofficial curriculum for many teachers – is never spoken but emerges in actional modes. And the appearance of those entities stipulated by the official curriculum do appear in very different form. The meaning of English can lie as much in curriculum as in pedagogy, and in any case the distinction is often quite unclear or implicit.

The question of what modes might be best for the materialization of different kinds of meanings is a real one in science as in English but differently so: in English, quite often, what cannot be spoken (because it is and needs to remain implicit), might need to be enacted. In science the question of choice of mode never focuses on the need or the facts of implicitness. Where choice of mode becomes an issue in science it is around two different questions: 'What is the apt mode to materialize this entity?' and 'What is the best way to materialize this entity for this audience, this group of students?' – that is, the matter of rhetorical effectiveness. So the question of choice between image and writing might be resolved by asking for any particular group of students 'Is image or is writing better to materialize this entity ("magnetic field", "water-cycle", "solar system", and so on)?' and 'Is image or writing better, in the sense of 'more appealing?'

Of course, in this counterposing of science and English, we posit a re-emergence of a split between a world of 'fact' and a world of 'value', a distinction that is not be completely tenable; our point is rather to draw attention to a tendency, for slightly polemical purposes.

The data

This book is based on the research project 'The Production of School English', funded by the ESRC. The project took place over three years, from November 2000 to October 2003. The project data is primarily in the form of classroom observation and video-recording, together with in-depth interviews with students and teachers from our project schools. It was collected in the spring and summer term of the school year 2000–01. It is important to note here that the project data was therefore collected before the introduction of the (now no longer new) Key Stage 3 Strategy – a strategy that has attempted to unify pedagogy in the same way as the National Curriculum attempts to unify curriculum. Despite this important shift in policy and practice, we feel that our research aims retain their validity and that our results still enable an understanding of how the subject is currently produced and of the forms it can take.

The analysis we set out – which explores the ways in which policy, made at a macro-level, is inflected in the actualization of English in the micro-level of the classroom – has explanatory power beyond the immediate moment on which it focuses.

The schools

Our research focused on urban schools, specifically on three 'state' secondary schools in Inner London. There were several reasons for such a choice, beyond the researchers' familiarity with this kind of social setting. First, we wanted to find out what might be happening in schools where the vision of uniform entitlement embodied in the National Curriculum encountered the 'contexts of disadvantage' of which Inner London schools tend to provide examples. In this encounter, we thought, there was much to learn about the difficulties of the National Curriculum project. Secondly, we thought that the attempts of teachers to actualize English in contexts of social, cultural, ethnic, religious and linguistic difference would produce illuminating data about the variable and negotiated qualities of English. Thirdly – knowing that Inner London had historically been a region where English teachers had developed a rich and heterodox tradition of subject development – we wanted to explore the continuing effects of such a history on present-day classrooms, and therefore to understand 'English' as something created in an area of tension between contending projects and influences.

We have named the three schools Springton, Wayford and Ravenscroft. Each is co-educational, with an English department known (as credible) to the project team – the schools are all part of the initial teacher education partnership scheme with the Institute of Education. The demographics of the student population were also used as a criterion for selection. Each school has a student population that can be described as ethnically diverse (including a settled White working-class population), with a significant refugee population (over 20 per cent), and with many students from low-income families (indicated by the percentage of students receiving free school meals, with 43 per cent being the lowest figure). We selected schools that were similar in that they met these criteria and different in that they represented a wide range in terms of their officially perceived 'success': *improving* (Springton School), *under special measures* (Wayford School), and a *foundation school*, so called (that is, a school judged to be successful: Ravenscroft School). Each of these is described briefly in the next section. We do not wish to characterize the schools other than through our descriptions of the practices as they appear in our data, and instead of offering three thumbnail sketch of the institutions we discuss each school in the context of the analysis of specific aspects of the production of English. In this way we hope that a more nuanced sense of what the schools do and what they are will gradually emerge.

Springton School

Springton is situated in a locality made up of different ethnic communities, and as it has a policy of open entry it has a diverse ethnic population. There are, and have historically been, considerable tensions between the ethnic groups in the community that the school serves, tensions that are realized along racial and ethnic lines, which at times emerge in the form of severe street violence.

The school has a high proportion of minority ethnic students (81 per cent) primarily Bangladeshi and a significant number of BlackAfrican students. A high percentage of students have English as an additional language (80 per cent), and of these students a significant number (14 per cent) are at an early stage of language acquisition. Of these students a significant percentage are refugees (30 per cent), mainly from African countries. Springton also has a high percentage of working-class families (65 per cent of students receive free school meals). Standards in English overall are well below the national average in all forms of assessment at Key Stages 3 and 4. English classes are mixed-ability, and the school itself does not have a policy of selection.

Wayford School

Wayford is a large school serving a number of wards and boroughs that are characterized by significant social deprivation. At the time of the research the school

was placed under 'special measures'. The school's student population is ethnically diverse. It contains a high percentage of students of minority ethnic backgrounds (primarily Black Caribbean, Black African, and Bangladeshi); there is
also a significant White student population including (8 per cent) White UK.
Around a third of the school's students (33 per cent) are from refugee or asylum-
seeker families. Overall the school has a high percentage of students with English
as an additional language (66 per cent) with a significant percentage of these
students at an early stage of language acquisition (29 per cent), with native
speakers of Arabic, Bengali, Portuguese and Farsi. The school has a significant
percentage of students from working-class families (53 per cent of students
receive free school meals). Student levels of attainment when they arrive at the
school are well below the national average and standards in English overall are
well below the national average in all forms of assessment at Key Stages 3 and 4.
English classes are mixed-ability. Like Springton, this school does not operate a
policy of selection.

Ravenscroft School

Ravenscroft is a foundation school – formerly a grant-maintained school – and it
operates with both a policy of selection (25 per cent of the total intake) and
streamed ability classes. It is situated in an area with a significant Black population that is characterized by social deprivation. The school student population is
ethnically diverse with 60 per cent of students from minority ethnic backgrounds
(primarily Black Caribbean, Black African, Indian, Pakistani, Chinese and
Bangladeshi). A significant number of students (27 per cent) have English as an
additional language; many of these are speakers of Cantonese, Bengali, Gujarati
and Urdu. The school has a significant number of students from low-income families, with 43 per cent of students receiving free school meals.

The teachers

We observed the lessons of three English teachers in each of the schools, over the
spring and summer terms in the school year 2000–01. The teachers were identified by the head of department in each school to reflect the range of experience
within the department, although all were teachers who volunteered to participate
in the project. Here, rather than give a 'biography' or 'characterization' of each
teacher that we observed, we will just name and locate them in relation to the three
schools (teachers and students have been given pseudonyms throughout the
book). We have resisted the tradition of characterizing the teachers: our focus is
on the production of English, and for reasons that have to do both with utility and
ethics we do not want to focus unduly or over-emphatically on the roles and
responsibilities of individuals within the very complex setting in which the
subject is actualized. However, we do offer some details about teachers' backgrounds, experiences, roles or philosophies wherever we have thought these to be

appropriate to understanding the production of English.

The teachers we observed at Springton were Julia, Anna and Susan; at Wayford John, Stephen and Lizzy; at Ravenscroft Irene, Diane and Paul.

The lessons

We observed each of the teachers teaching one or two lessons per week over a half-term period (between seven and eight weeks). The selection of which module and sequence of lessons to observe was influenced by the demands of the field-work and the time available. Overall we attempted to observe lessons on the range of topics being taught within the schools. These included Shakespeare, Wider Reading, Media, Twentieth-century Drama, and Poetry. Below we sketch the content of the lessons that we observed in each school.

Springton

- Julia: Shakespeare (*Romeo and Juliet*)
- Anna: Shakespeare (*Macbeth*)
- Susan: Poetry ('Hearts and Partners' NEAB anthology)

Wayford

- John: Wider reading (*Kiss Miss Carol*, and *Superman and Paula Brown's New Snowsuit*)
- Stephen: Media in English (film trailers)
- Lizzy: Media in English (film title sequences)

Ravenscroft

- Irene: Wider reading (*Theresa's Wedding, Three Sisters*)
- Diane: Twentieth-century drama (*The Crucible*)
- Paul: Media in English (comparison of broadsheets and tabloids)

In the classroom observations we did not set out to seek particular activities and we did not ask to see specific aspects of teaching; we aimed instead to observe the 'mundane' flow, the 'everyday' production of English in each of the classrooms.

Data collection

We combined a number of methods of data collection. We observed the teachers and students over the half-term period, and video-recorded a series of lessons. We video-recorded between three and six lessons with each teacher. Lessons were recorded using two small digital cameras, one focused primarily on the students and the other on the teacher and his or her interaction with the students. (Students were asked for consent to be video-recorded and students who did not want to be recorded were not included on video.) The video data was supplemented with observational notes made by the project researcher. Copies were made and details collected of the materials used in the classroom (such as worksheets, books, videos, and so on). Throughout the data-collection phase the project researcher asked teachers for clarification of aspects of the lesson, engaged in informal discussion with teachers and students, and gathered information and comments from students and teachers alike.

Formal in-depth interviews were conducted with each teacher at the end of the observations. These interviews were audio-recorded and transcribed. The interviews were based on a topic guide. This topic guide covered general areas such as the teacher's 'career biography', 'the school and its student population', 'visions of English', and 'the curriculum'. The topic guide also addressed specific points raised by the lessons observed, such as the teacher's use and selection of texts, the history of work units, and the rationale behind specific events that had occurred.

Group interviews were conducted with between four and six students from each class that we observed. The students were selected to reflect the range of students in the class (in terms of ethnicity, gender and 'ability' as determined by the teacher). These interviews were audio-recorded and transcribed. The interviews used a topic guide that covered areas such as what students read outside of school, and focused primarily on 'scenarios' from the lessons that had been observed and were considered to establish what they thought of specific instances of school English.

Policy documents from each school were collected. These included English department policy, such as homework strategies, and school policy, such as behaviour policies. Documents were also collected in relation to nationally driven policies and activities, as manifested in Ofsted reports, National Curriculum documents and so on.

The question of theory

One problem that we have faced in the project and in the book is that the world we investigated consists of many agents, actors, institutions, practices and traditions. Hence in our data-set we deal with quite disparate kinds of things, different kinds of data, which are not easily or at all accommodated within one theoretical framework. For instance, how can one deal with government policy on curriculum and at the same time connect that with the matter of layout of a classroom? Or set out a theory that claims to bring together wall-displays with forms of pedagogy? Or how do we group, in one coherent framework, a notion of (say, the literary) text with an approach that sees classroom layout also as text-like – how, in what ways are both these objects text-like? How can these very different elements to brought into meaningful conjunction?

Our solution has been to adopt as our overarching framework a semiotic theory. We explain in Chapter 4 how the layout of a classroom, for instance, as much as the wall display is an indication – *a sign* – of a teacher's sense of English, and how both layout and wall display are therefore full of meaning in relation to English. The semiotic notion of the *sign* allows us to show how meaning and form are inextricably intertwined: layout (and its use in classroom practice) provides a *form* through which the *meaning* of pedagogy is strongly realized; form and meaning jointly making a *sign* that realizes the meaning at issue. The semiotic approach allows us to provide coherence across all the different kinds of data in our description and analysis.

However, our presentation of the theory is written with the interests of practitioners in mind. Any reader who would like to follow the lines of our theory further can do so by following up some of the books referenced (such as Jewitt forthcoming; Jewitt and Kress 2003b; Kenner 2000; Kress and van Leeuwen 1996, 2001; Kress *et al.* 2001; Pahl 1999; van Leeuwen 1999; van Leeuwen and Jewitt 2001).

There is one further point to make here. We have not focused on talk, and have given some of our reasons for doing so already. Yet we did collect data by interviewing teachers and students: we conducted 'focus groups', all of which have produced much talk. This raises the question of the mode of transcription that we have used. Transcription is translation, and all translations are partial; the partiality in the case of research derives from the theoretical perspective of the research. Transcriptions are never value free; they are theory laden. Some of our readers will find our transcriptions of talk – whether of the teachers or the students – pretty rough and ready, which they are. Anyone who has transcribed speech will have found that what sounds entirely articulate when spoken looks ragged and often inarticulate when transcribed. As our collective sense of what constitutes 'proper' English is shaped by the written form, the consequence of transcription is that the speech transcribed seems to 'fall far short' of the seeming standards of the written norm. The speaker of the transcribed speech seems inarticulate. The plain fact of the matter is that the structures even of formal speech are quite unlike those of formal writing, which provides, inappropriately, the standards of comparison. The textual and syntactic structures of informal and even of formal speech are, quite simply, different from those of writing – and for very good reasons. In the face of this problem, our choice was either to 'prettify', to edit the speech of teachers and students – a falsification of the data, for bad reasons – or to draw attention to the fact that speech is different in its syntax and texture to writing, and that 'speaking like a book' is not necessarily something we ought to attempt in all aspects of our lives. The teachers and the students whose speech is represented in this book were fully articulate; and we did not wish to engage in cosmetic work of some kind in order to continue to support deep misconceptions about speech.

The organization of this book

Chapters 2 and 3 sketch the essential broad theoretical framework of our study. Most of Chapter 2 is devoted to questions of history and social and political context. Chapter 3 offers an outline of the theoretical framework of multimodal semiotics – it is the descriptive core of our theory, as well as being the least-known component of our approach. We deal lightly with theory – here and in other parts – but to avoid all technicality is actually to sell readers short in important ways and so we provide such theoretical background as is essential for understanding our argument. At the same time we have provided what we hope is a persuasive, concrete and useful account of the actualization of English, available to theorists, policy-makers and practitioners alike.

From Chapter 2 and 3's theoretical framing of our work we move, in Chapter 4, to the description and analysis of classroom layout and wall displays, suggesting that they have a quite specific role in shaping and defining what English is in that classroom. In Chapter 5 we move from this microanalysis of *space* to an account of the *time* practices of the classroom, and their relationship to the ways in which policy (though teachers as well) seeks to organize educational time.

In Chapter 6 the focus moves to a quite other organizational principle. Here we explore how teachers' understanding of 'ability' – an understanding expressed at times in the formal organization of the school, and sometimes in the more informal but nonetheless deliberate groupings of the classroom – has profound effects on the interaction of teachers and students, and on the actualization of English, for both parties.

In Chapter 7 our focus shifts overtly to the curriculum. We want to show how curriculum entities appear in quite different ways in different classrooms. To do so we focus on one central *entity*, namely that of *character*. Our aim is to show how specific, concrete decisions taken by a school or by a curriculum authority, by a teacher or by her or his department, interact with the students' own interests to bring forth quite different conceptions or versions of what 'character' might mean. To put it another way, the chapter seeks to show that even in conditions of strong prescription, a degree of freedom of movement exists and can be utilized by the teacher in line with her or his sense of English *for that class.*

In Chapter 8, one teacher is in focus. Here we wish to illustrate on the one hand how so much that goes on in the classroom is dependent on modes other than spoken or written language, and on the other to show that in a school that has made the decision to select a significant proportion of its students, and to use streaming in addition to that, English comes to have a quite specific appearance that we think can be traced back to these decisions, in large part at least. It is not that the aims and demands of the National Curriculum disappear here, but that they are not immediately in the foreground. What is foregrounded for this teacher, in this class, is what English might offer to these young people as a means of making sense of salient problems in their lives. One feels this teacher's sense is that the demands of the curriculum can be met better if the students' needs have priority over those of the subject as such. The 'subject's needs' are by no means forgotten by this teacher, but they are approached and met via attention to the needs of the students.

In Chapter 9 we focus on a common practice in the English classroom, namely that of annotation of texts. Here too we are interested in demonstrating how the wider set of conditions of the school's environment, and the school's and the teachers' response to these, crucially shapes what English comes to be. With that chapter we want to begin to show that there is a consistent, insistent pressure from all these many factors on all areas of the curriculum: the factors shape the layout and use of the layout of the classroom; they shape notions of ability; they shape the curriculum, and what is considered a 'text' in English. In Chapter 10, our last data-based chapter, we look at how texts are chosen for the English classroom; here we want to round off our discussion by showing how the selection, and use, of texts illustrates the 'fit' of all the social factors that constitute the environment of English, and come to shape its appearance.

Chapter 2

A social and political framework for thinking about English

Introduction

This book is about the construction of the secondary school subject English in multi-ethnic urban settings. It is thus in some respects a case study, but in method-ological, theoretical and substantive aspects it aims to be something wider. It brings together two aspirations. The first has to do with a history of the educa-tional present. Since 1988, education in England has been remade at every level from national systems of governance to classroom pedagogies. The roles and identities of education's social actors have also been transformed, in ways that have profoundly affected parents, teachers and students. In the research project on which this book is based, we wanted to explore one particular facet of this remaking, in ways that could illuminate the wider process and contribute to an understanding both of curricular and pedagogic change, and of the way such change has been lived by those involved in it. The focus we chose was the school subject English – a choice that arose both from our professional and academic formations and from a sense that English remains, in many ways, key to under-standing aspects of change that had barely been grasped by other researchers. We make the case for such a focus in the pages that follow.

Our second aspiration is methodological and theoretical. This, too, is elaborated below. Here it is enough to state our belief that English – like other school subjects, of course – is not an entity that can be understood solely through the analysis of formal curricula, or even through extensive interviews with those who teach it. English is 'actualized': however powerful the regulatory frameworks that scaffold it may be, they do not determine its nature – for this is not pre-established, but real-ized in practice. This is an insight shared by many pedagogical theorists (such as Menck 1995 and Englund 1997), but to operationalize the insight is a problematic matter. Traditionally, researchers have explored actualization through an analysis of classroom language (for example Mercer 2000; Sinclair and Coulthard 1975), but such a focus can produce only very partial data. As we have already insisted, classrooms are places where communication extends far beyond the modes of spoken and written language: they are multimodal sites, sites where meanings are made through many differing means, and where resources such as gesture, gaze, posture, and the deployment of visual objects are crucially important to meaning-making. Our research aimed to explore these dimensions of communication and in doing so to present a more complete account of English as an actualized subject. In other words, to understand English in its full dimensions, and to understand the ways in which it creates new kinds of identity for students and teachers, we regarded a multimodal approach as essential.

The two aspirations provide combined rather than separate perspectives. The forms taken by multimodal communication are shaped through social agency – the agency of teachers and students, of the immediate environment of a school, and of 'remoter' but nonetheless potent forces, such as those which contribute to policy-making or the definition of curricula. To explain why and how school English assumes the shapes that it does entails attention not only to the contexts provided by educational policy but also to a microanalysis of communicative forms. That latter is the focus of Chapter 3; here, in this chapter, it is policy and social issues that are the subject of our attention.

Re-agenting the school

We spoke in our opening paragraph of a deep remaking of educational practice. In the section that follows we offer an account of the main features of this transform-ation. But we need first of all to note that not all that is significant in the class-rooms we observe is new. The teacher's situation has always been linked to the cultural, moral and occupationally allocative roles of the school. These roles have varied according to the relative distance of the populations of the school from the positional social good constituted by 'education'. As Bourdieu (1974) insists, school is a site of an encounter between formal, organized prescriptions relating to knowledge and behaviour and the value orientations and cultural capacities and experiences of students – an encounter that is marked by difference and inequality. We claim, along with Bourdieu, that the interpersonal and ideational transactions of education are shaped by social relationships of this kind and that the classroom is in important ways a site of conflicts, to which the teacher's rhetorical activity (about which we say more below) is a response. It is in this context that we should note the consistency over time of the forms taken by such aspects of material culture as the architecture of schools and the design of class-rooms, as well as by the classroom regulation of such activities as speaking, silence and movement (Hamilton 1989; Walkerdine 1990).

Our focus, though, is more on the conjunctural than on the enduring; the perspective that we seek to develop is one from which can emerge a consistent pattern of change in the social relations and communicative forms of contempor-ary schooling. Especially significant in this context is the tendency to which we give the name 're-agenting' (Jones 2003a). Re-agenting involves a redistribution of the capacity to shape the work of the school, so that the power of some kinds of agent is increased, while that of others diminishes, or is re-directed to other levels of the system – from curriculum design, for instance, to curriculum 'delivery'. We can trace such a process across several fields of post-1988 educational reform, and in relation to varied types of educational actor.

Most evident, of course, are the regulatory frameworks that government has designed for curricula and now, increasingly, for pedagogy. These include the National Curriculum, examination syllabuses, and the National Literacy Framework, which was extended from primary to secondary schools after the period of our research. These function so as to increase the extent of central direction of teachers' work – a direction that at the same time reduces teachers' autonomy. Regulatory frameworks are accompanied by enforcement strategies, which include Ofsted inspection, national systems of testing, and the stipulation of targets for student attainment that schools are expected to achieve or else face various kinds of additional supervision and penalty. Targets are monitored by school management whose role has become, since 1988, an increasingly active one, and who are equipped (as Hextall and Mahony (2000) have shown) with a varied armoury of devices with which to stipulate, measure and assess teacher performance. Teachers themselves have developed several new kinds of expertise, especially in relation to organizing higher levels of student achievement measured against externally determined performance criteria.

We can discern similar changes among students and among parents. In the 1970s, the success rate in GCE English Language amounted to no more than around 30 per cent and most students were untouched by high-stakes public examination. Since 1985, when GCSE examinations were introduced (to be followed at the end of the decade by the National Curriculum), there has been a steady rise in measured attainment, with more than 50 per cent of students obtaining an A–C grade in GCSE English. More and more students have been drawn into the certification process; success or failure in public examinations has become a central experience of the careers of most secondary school students. This we take to be a cultural change of some importance, one that has reshaped values and behaviour.

If many students have been drawn into a process of what some have termed 'responsibilization' (Gewirtz 1998; Rose 1990) through which they are incited to involve themselves in the performance culture of the school, the same process extends to parents. There is much research that demonstrates the role of middle-class parents as active pursuers of the opportunities presented by parental choice in a 'marketized' system of schooling (Gewirtz et al. 1995). Likewise, researchers have studied the level of parents' investment of time and money in home learning as a preparation for success at school (Buckingham and Scanlon 2003; Reay 1998). But what also needs to be recognized is something akin to a regulation of parenting by a school system based on cultures of academic performance and orientated also towards a version of social inclusion. Miriam David (2002) has pointed out the importance of the 1998 School Standards and Framework Act in this respect – it legislated for 'a whole range of home–school relations through statutory home–school agreements and homework policies, including study support and home-work centres, literacy and numeracy strategies and … various forms of parenting education'. Many parents, among them some of the authors of this book, have found themselves being (re)positioned by such processes, in ways that give an added edge to academic discussions of schooling and cultural change: what teachers and students experience is not that remote either from the working lives of researchers, or from their involvement as parents in a performance-orientated system.

To write of *re*-agenting is to evoke change, a movement from one condition to another. We've suggested above something of the condition to which policy-driven re-agenting aspires. But we also need to understand the condition from which it seeks to depart, not least because the understanding of policy-makers is that they are involved in a process of conflictual transformation, in which one of the main targets of policy is an educational past understood in extremely critical terms. New Labour is less inclined to celebrate previous reforming projects as an earlier part of an ongoing process of incremental change than to present them in a critical light, as flawed and failed. Comprehensive reform, and local and professional autonomy are from this perspective blighted by their low expectations of students, and by their preference for 'egalitarianism' above 'standards' (DfEE 2001).

From the discontent of policy-makers developed an intention to reshape the attitudes, values and behaviour of all groups involved in schooling – students and parents as well as teachers. But teachers, especially, have been regarded as the necessary object of a strategy of modernization (Luke and Luke 2001), and as various writers have suggested (Hextall and Mahony 2001; Moore 2001) much government policy has been directed towards such an end. English has been strongly involved in the resultant conflicts.

English has a past that has worried recent designers of policy. Its former lack of a defined subject content meant that especially between 1960 and the late 1980s, the period of what Grace (1987) has called 'licensed teacher autonomy', it was a subject more autonomous than most, and as such came later to be a particular target of government reform. But the peculiarities of English have extended beyond questions of autonomy. Particularly in urban schools, English has at points connected to wider projects. Its vision of learning has always been informed by cultural purposes of various kinds – as the influence of Leavis early in the period demonstrates. Increasingly in the 1970s and 1980s, such projects were developed in ways that were attuned to issues of cultural diversity among students. Grace suggests that the core of this development was adherence to a principle of radical dialogue that 'dignified the student and the status of his or her language, theorising and culture' and that hoped to see the school become 'an arena for the representation of a rich variety of cultural patterns, forms of communication and levels of consciousness' (Grace 1995: 219).

To put it another way, there developed in pockets of the state system a radical educational culture that questioned the values, traditions and allegiances of the school, and worked on alternative practices that were to some extent sympathetic to the experiences and cultural meanings of subordinate social groups (Jones 2003a).

Such practices have been the focus of a governmental strategy of attrition, carried on explicitly in the period of Conservatism, where school English faced both ideological criticism and curricular reshaping; and also pursued with less of an ideological 'edge' but arguably to more potent practical effect under New Labour. To write an account of the construction of English as a moment in the history of the present thus involves seeking to identify the impact of a number of forceful social agents on an already established field. It involves attention to questions of conflict, replacement and rupture, and looks for their traces in the practices it examines.

But of course, the construction of English in urban schools cannot be reduced to a collision between two kinds of movement, one professionally based, the other governmental. The space of classroom English is much more disparate than this – there are many discourses, many communicative practices at play, and we need to work an understanding of these into the overall framework of analysis if it is capture the complexities of 'realization'. To do so will have the effect of qualifying some of the deterministic connotations of the term 'reagenting': government may have deeply rearranged the working practices and life worlds of teachers, but there remain nevertheless school spaces of varying 'sizes'. Within these spaces, the (always social) histories of individual teachers, the evolved working practices of departments, the character of relationships with students, and the organization and culture of the school all contribute to the realization of English, demonstrating that agency is not a capacity possessed only by government. Certainly we think that the impact of government-driven redesign, and the re-agenting that goes with it, can be registered in all of the data that we assemble in this book. But it does not represent – as it were – the only discourse and legitimated practice in town. Schools remain spaces of multiple discourse and practice. National norms and regulatory frameworks have without doubt worked themselves into the 'capillaries' of the school. But they are inflected and modified by other positions, which stem from local situations as well as the associational cultures of teachers. The balance of power between national framework and classroom practice has been altered, but not to the extent where the influence of the local and the associational has been entirely eradicated.

English as combination – English as construction

We move now from considerations of agency more directly to those of realization. In 1995, Gunther Kress wrote:

> English is a number of curricula, around which the English teacher has to construct some plausible principles of coherence. It is, first, a curriculum of communication, at the moment largely via its teaching around English language … It is, second, a curriculum of notions of sociality and of culture: what England is, what it is to be English. This is carried through a plethora of means: how the language English is presented and talked about, especially in

multi-lingual classrooms; what texts appear and how they are dealt with; what theories of text and language underlie pedagogies, and so on. English is also a curriculum of values, of taste and of aesthetics. Here the study of canonical texts is crucial, in particular their valuation in relation to texts of popular culture ... And ... English is the subject in which ethics, questions of social, public morality are constantly at issue ... in terms of giving children the means of dealing with ethical, moral issues ... and absorbing the ethos developed in the classroom.

(Kress 1995: 5–6)

Curriculum and pedagogic change since 1995 has perhaps simplified some of these issues, but without attenuating Kress's central point: the ensemble of classroom English is complex – a bricolage of methods, a plurality of purposes and objectives. Moreover, it is one that is constructed, and reconstructed, day after day, in the work of teachers, teaching in contexts over which they never have full control, which are subject to the influence of policy, institution, department and students, and shaped also by a wider politics of education.

We want to understand this process of construction. We differ here from others who have asked the question 'What is English?', and who have sought their answers on terrain defined by the ideas of teachers, elicited through interviews, or the codified and inevitably over-coherent representations of the subject to be found in policy documents or canonical statements (Ball *et al.* 1990; Davies 1996; Doyle 1989; Marshall 2000). Such work is invaluable in mapping terms of debate, and in identifying textual evidence of paradigm shifts. But as a means of exploring the more tacit understandings and enactments of the subject English that come to the fore in teachers' classroom practice it is less useful.

By contrast, we are interested in studying the moment of the subject's actualization in the practice of the teacher. As Peter Menck puts it, the teacher is a key social actor who must 'interpret a multi-levelled contextual situation and in doing so actualize his/her subject' (Menck 1995). Likewise, for Tomas Englund, the teacher has different possibilities in relation to the creation and construction of meaning, and these possibilities become 'concretized in different ways in different classrooms' (1997: 277). The analytic work of subject description, for Englund, entails identifying the ways in which teachers draw from the academic disciplines that stand behind the school subject; it involves sketching the ways in which they position their teaching against the various paradigms of the subject that exist in educational practice. Importantly, this positioning has a social as well as a knowledge-focused element. Subjects, actualized in particular classrooms, can be inflected in radically different ways, from patriarchal to democratic.

Up to a point, these are productive approaches, which go beyond the methodological simplifications of some paradigms of subject-based research. In particular, they shift the grounds of discussion away from the abstract essentialism implied by the question 'What is English?', to the more productive question 'What happens when the subject called English is taught and learned?'. But for our purposes, they are in several ways incomplete. First, they do not analyse non-linguistic forms of communication. Second, in their over-emphatic concentration on the teacher, they tend not to see the subject's relationship to the school as a social organization, and to the system of resources and constraints that is embedded there. Third, they lack a strong historical or conjectural dimension; unlike the work of, say, Ball and his colleagues, they're relatively uninterested in describing and explaining shifts from one type of curriculum and pedagogy to another.

In these respects, our work moves beyond the 'actualization' paradigm. We share with it a focus on the work of the teacher, which we see as central to the production of English, but our understanding of the teacher's role is more strongly textual – in its attention to the modes of meaning-making in classrooms – and at the same time more strongly social, in its attempts to explore forces that shape these classroom processes of semiosis. Thus we are interested in the ways in which teachers structure their communication with students, and organize the events that occur in the single space of the classroom. We argue that in their communicational practice teachers create texts – multimodal combinations of communicatively orientated utterances and actions. We seek to understand these texts socially. To explain this ambition requires a brief résumé of the theories of communication and meaning-making on which we depend.

We see language and by extension other modes of communication as resources constituted by sets of semiotic alternatives, which have taken on their particular forms because of the social functions they have evolved to serve. These resources form the meaning potential of a culture. We see individuals as social agents who in organizing their communication make choices from among these resources. Such choices are motivated – that is, signs relate to the social interests of the sign-maker and represent the sign-maker's decisions about the expression of the meaning that he or she wishes to make in a given context. These decisions are not, of course, fully explicit or conscious. Moreover, they are not the creation of a single maker. They are, as Volosinov (1973) argued, multi-accentual. Whomever they are made by, they are always also a response to, and an anticipation of, other signs. They need to be understood relationally, and to understand them thus is also to understand them as an enactment of *social* relations. In addition, signs have regularities of use. The more work a culture has put into a semiotic resource, and the more it has been used in social life, the more fully and finely articulated and 'regularized' it will have become. These regularities are what have traditionally been called 'grammars', and an aspect of which more recent communicational theory has addressed as 'genres'.

Teachers are engaged in particular kinds of sign-making, which very often take the form of public communication. The analysis of such communication has a history that goes back to ancient Athens, in the form of rhetorical, Aristotelian theory. In such theory, rhetoric is 'speech designed to persuade', to affect an audience and to effect particular actions. To do so, the rhetor must discover among a pre-existing repertoire of communicational resources some available means of persuasion, and must link them to strategies appropriate to situation and purpose.

To this extent, the rhetor is an improviser (albeit an improviser whose performance is based on an existing repertoire of communicational devices) so that improvisation does not imply an absolute freedom of choice. On the contrary, the rhetor's strategies are subject to the constraints imposed by situation and audience. Contemporary reworkings of rhetorical theory (Freedman and Medway 1994) identify the patterning of the rhetor's utilization of resources and responses to constraint. In doing so, they produce a social typology of rhetoric – that is to say, they link particular formal characteristics of language and communication to particular social situations, in order to argue that particular kinds of situation tend to elicit particular communicational forms. In this way, it becomes possible to provide a relatively full explanation of the choices that a rhetor makes.

This is our ambition too. We aim to identify, analyse and explain typical curricular and pedagogic forms of secondary-school English, as they are actualized by teachers. Following Halliday (1985) we understand these forms in relation to a dual function: they attempt to convey ideas, in the broadest sense of the term, and they seek to manage interpersonal communication. We aim to explain how in terms of both these functions, these forms are shaped and generated by the social relations of the classroom and by the wider institutional pattern of resource and constraint within which English teachers work. We thus hope to produce an account of English written neither in terms of relatively abstract 'paradigms' nor in terms of relatively context-free 'practice', but attentive, rather, to the regularities of the subject's realization. We see our task in this book as one of achieving the 'thickest' possible explication both of the teacher's communicational work, and of its 'determined' character – that is of the social agencies that go into its making. This is a complex task, to say the least, whose intricacies are explored in the chapters that follow.

Chapter 3

A new approach to understanding school English

Multimodal semiotics

Introduction

In the first chapter we sketched the broader social and policy framework in which we set our attempt to understand English. In this chapter we provide a sketch of the theory and methodology we used to look at and describe English as it was being produced. This answers, we hope, the question of how our means of understanding and describing meaning-making differs from that of others who have written on English, and, in particular, how it goes beyond accounts that have been based on speech or writing alone. We have already mentioned the term multimodality several times, as a means of seeing meaning in visual displays, in classroom layout, in the voice-quality of the teacher, in diagrams and wall displays, in students' posture, just as much as in what is said, written and read.

Multimodality is based on the assumption that meaning is made through the many means (we call these modes) that a culture has shaped for that purpose; and we think that these are used to fashion the meanings of English curriculum and pedagogy no less than elsewhere, even if this is achieved differently. However, we are clear that we need to set such descriptions and analyses within theories of social explanation in the way begun in the previous chapter.

We think it is most useful to start straightaway with a demonstration of our methodology; on the one hand it shows what our approach is like, and on the other hand it begins to indicate what our methodology does reveal. Our aim is to understand how English comes to be 'produced' in the interaction of a multiplicity of (social) factors at work in the classroom. To do so, we need to connect issues of policy and social context, the characteristics and policies of urban multicultural schools, teacher formation and tradition, the ethos of English departments, and the political and institutional changes of the past decade with the issues of micro-level classroom interaction. All shape what English becomes in a specific site, and how it impacts on students' experiences of English and of learning English. However, the task of establishing a connection between this range of factors, and their actualization in multimodal form – the linking of macro-level social and policy factors and micro-level features, such as classroom practices of all kinds – is not at all straightforward.

A specific example of the kinds of question we have in mind here might be: 'How does a change, say, in policies around "selection" reflect itself, how does it "show up", in aspects of the English curriculum or in its pedagogy?' To establish the possibility of such a link we draw on semiotic theory and in particular on a social theory of 'sign'. Semiotics is the discipline that concerns itself with meaning of all kinds, in all forms, everywhere. Sign is the central concept of semiotics; it is an entity in which meaning and form have been brought together in a single unit – of signified and signifier, to use the technical terms – seen, always, as reflecting the meanings of those who make the sign. This relationship between social environment, signs, and the agency of those who make signs in the production of English are explored in all of the chapters that follow.

Policy is articulated in discourses of various kinds – of targets and attainment, of ability and achievement, of economic utility and cultural value. But it is only in their articulation as signs that discourses become 'visible' and effective. Signs are always multimodal and each modality brings the possibility of expressing and shaping meanings. A poster, part of a display on a wall for example, is a complex of signs: it may be a student's handwritten text, left with spelling and grammatical slips, rather than the word-processed writing of an official document, carefully edited, mounted on board rather than pinned up, laminated maybe, displayed in a prominent position or perhaps somewhere barely noticeable. When we look at such a poster-sign, the many meanings made as signs in the various modes are there in the one complex multimodal sign. The question is then how such complexes of meaning realize different aspects of the social life of the school, and that is discussed in many of the chapters following. In the example just given (a real instance from our data) each of the modal choices makes meaning and realizes a specific discourse among the many that are active in schools. For instance, how students' work is valued is lodged in a specific discourse around what it means to be a student; whether spontaneity counts more than careful work invested in editing is lodged in an educational discourse around learning, creativity, innovation, itself maybe part of a discourse around notions of human subjectivity. And the prominence given to student work may point to discursive contestation over the 'weight' to be given to students' agency relative to the demands of performativity, and so on.

Taking a multimodal look

The data from our research project (together with our experience of the subject as teachers, teacher educators and researchers) suggests that English, in contrast to other core subjects in the curriculum (such as science and mathematics), is unusually diverse in its appearance from one classroom to another. Yet despite the many differences between the lessons that we observed, each lesson remains clearly identifiable as an English lesson. This raises two questions, one which we do not set out to answer ('So what is English?') and one that is the focus of this book, which here we can formulate in this way: 'What is the cause of such differences in the appearance of English?' After all, at the time of writing in 2004 there has been a National Curriculum for some ten years, which has specified quite closely what the curriculum of English is. Our answer circles around the question 'What are the conditions in which English gets actualized, realized, "produced", in all the variability that one encounters across classrooms, and how can we account for these differences?'

Here we start by describing two brief instances of an English lesson. In both we focus less on curriculum than on pedagogy, which we see as the enactment of social relations in the (already and always anticipated) service of mediating specific curriculum knowledge. Curriculum, by contrast, we take to be the social organization of knowledge for a specific audience – school children – always with the purposes of the school in mind; what Bernstein (1990) called the re-contextualization of knowledge.

We use a number of descriptive tools. Here we start with the 'look' of the English classroom, its layout and furniture, and how English happens in that. For us, the look of the classroom is as significant – in principle at least – as are the teacher's and the students' uses of gesture, the images displayed on the walls, or indeed talk and writing for that matter, even if always differently so. Everything that happens in and shapes classrooms is for us a realization of the meanings of English. From the micro-level of specific instances of classroom interaction we 'look out' to the macro-level of government policy, for instance, and refocus our analytical lens to provide social explanations to understand why English is realized as it is in this specific classroom.

Pedagogies of English: two examples multimodally described

We start our account with a description of parts of two lessons in classrooms in two different schools. We give a fairly sparse account of these segments of the lesson, and we provide a gloss on these as we go along, providing our sense of what meanings may be at issue. In our description here we focus on showing how pedagogy is made, actualized through different modes, in the two classrooms. So in the account below we deal with several modes in turn, with the intention of showing our methodology, our way of looking, in action.

Wayford School: John

The layout of the classroom

Before a teacher has even begun to speak, one foundational aspect of the meaning of English is already present for students and teacher alike, namely the layout of the classroom. The manner in which tables, chairs and desks are arranged distributes students and teacher into particular places, and into a frame of social relations with each other. The teacher can arrange the furniture in various ways (in this school there is no departmental policy on classroom layout or wall displays), and so in this case the room layout can be seen as an expression of the teacher's preferred spatial and social relations with the students. This spatial relation is a sign made by the teacher to express his (in this case) sense of the social relation, of the pedagogic relationship with the students, as well as his sense of how the students might work with each other and with him. What is particularly significant here is that this aspect of the pedagogic frame for English is already present and realized in a classroom when the students come into the room, each day, and in the experience of the students (as of the teacher), it becomes so 'normal' as to become unnoticed. It comes to be the way English – as social or pedagogic relation – is experienced, 'naturally'.

In each of the classrooms that we visited the furniture was arranged differently, and each of these arrangements placed teacher and students in different spatial, and therefore social, relationships to each other. As we will show, this spatially realized pedagogic arrangement contributes to the shaping of English curriculum, in this as in all classrooms, even if never straightforwardly so. While these spatial arrangements never fully determine all aspects of the social/pedagogic relationships in the classroom, they are one part of their production.

As the lesson is about to start, and the students begin to arrive and take their seats, the teacher, John, a man in his mid-fifties, is already in the room. The everyday, absolutely commonplace and prosaic 'journey' of the students into their usual 'places' in the room, is the starting point for our look at English.

This classroom is a rectangular space with the teacher's desk at the front-centre of the room, and six pairs of tables arranged in two 'rows' (see Figure 4.5 in the next chapter, which focuses on classroom arrangements in detail). Four students are seated at each table; the grouping at the tables is suggestive of a 'participatory' pedagogy, a sign of a 'constructivist' approach. However, this sign of a 'discourse of participation' is set within an arrangement of the tables in two rows, which, starting close together at the teacher's desk, are angled away from his desk to realize a perfect panopticon. That structure superimposes a different meaning: a sign of a 'discourse of surveillance' overlaid onto a sign of a 'discourse of participation'.

The position of the teacher's desk in relation to the panoptic arrangement of the rows of desks is suggestive of a specific teacher–class relation – that of the teacher who occupies a central position in the classroom and who teaches from the front, able to survey all that happens. This combination of three discourses, the 'participatory discourse' of a pedagogy suggested by the table-grouping, the 'discourse of authority' of a pedagogy suggested by the desk at the front, matched with the 'surveillance discourse' realized by the panoptically arranged rows, makes a complex pedagogic sign. The former actualizes a meaning of mutual construction; the two latter actualize different meanings of control. However, what actually takes place in the classroom is different yet again. For most of the lesson the teacher makes no use of this quite complex spatial/pedagogic sign, either in his actual positioning or in his movement in the room as he teaches. During the lessons that we observed, he rarely sat at his desk, or stood at the front-central position in the classroom.

Instead, he paced in an arc that started from his desk and went to somewhat to the left of the door along the wall on the right side of the classroom. The arc traced by his pacing movement in effect reconfigured the classroom space yet again, creating a boundary and barrier across the door of the classroom to the corridor (see Figure 4.6) – a boundary that in effect he 'patrolled' by his pacing.

This movement transformed the classroom into a pedagogic space different to the one indicated by the arrangement of the furniture. Neither his positioning nor his movement made any use of the existing potential for surveillance of the students; from any point on the arc the teacher could only see the faces of those students seated on one side of either 'row'. But it did require great bodily effort from those students who were not seated facing him but who wanted to see the teacher. They had to contort their bodies, twisting around in their seats in order to face him. The students had to do the work and make the effort of maintaining 'contact', which the teacher's movement and use of space demanded. The teacher's movement and his positioning both served to maintain his authority and reinforced the separation of teacher and student space in the classroom. For instance, the teacher never walked around in the space of the class, entering the space between the 'rows' and tables. The teacher was only made 'fully available' to the students if they actively worked at making it so – the students had to re-position their bodies uncomfortably to engage with him.

If we treat space, disposition and movement in space as means for making meaning, then we have here a complex and multiply contradictory sign of pedagogy, which is constantly re-enacted and imposed; and which requires real – and uncomfortable – work from the students. The tables with the four students seated around each table suggest a democratic, participatory pedagogy, and a constructivist approach to curricular knowledge: it suggests that knowledge can be produced by the students in the work of talk and discussion, out of their own resources, augmented by the teacher. The panoptic arrangement of the rows speaks of the teacher's wish to 'know' fully, of his need for surveillance, a need to control. The positioning of the desk at the front speaks of a transmission pedagogy, with the teacher as authority. This complex and inherently contradictory structure lays down one possible ground-plan for a pedagogy of English. Overlaid on this is the structure produced by the teacher's pacing; this could be seen as the classical Stoic perambulation, with his pupils, of the philosopher (who, with a mind deep in thought, produces and shares profound insights for those willing and able to attend and comprehend as he paces up and down). Yet the fact that this stroll happens in front of the (always open) door makes it at the same time into the patrol of a guard who can expel and readmit – as we will show.

If we treat layout of the classroom as a text, we could, as with written genres, try to invent a label to name the multiply ambivalent pedagogic relation produced by the arrangement and layout of furniture, and the use and apportioning of space in this class. Yet the label is less important than the recognition of the complexity of pedagogic forms produced here and the realization that this complexity is constantly enacted through the spatial disposition of teacher and students in the classroom.

The example shows the significance of the mode of spatial arrangement, and supports our contention that it has a shaping effect not only on the pedagogy of English, but on how English is experienced by students in the classroom. We will now show how a multimodal approach shows (aspects of) this complex pedagogy realized in other modes as well, in talk, gesture, gaze, writing, in visual displays (on the walls of the room), and in body posture.

Movement of the teacher in the classroom

Movement has meaning. In the space of the classroom the meaning is produced in the interaction of three factors: the teacher's movement itself, the meaning of the space in which the teacher moves (at the front, in between the desks), and whether, how and where the students may move. For instance, in some of the classrooms we observed, the room was arranged in such a way that there was no clear 'front' or 'back'; rather there was a space that all, teacher and students alike, inhabit – even if not necessarily equally – and in which all can and do move. There the space is, in some ways, everyone's space; and that in itself serves to realize yet another form of pedagogy. In other classrooms, space and its use is much more strictly controlled. In each case meaning is produced.

Here, in our first example, only the teacher moves, except for some students who are temporarily expelled from the class and then readmitted. The teacher moves slowly, deliberately; occasionally he comes to rest – when he is 'invigilating' rather than teaching – from his desk. The path of his movement describes an arc, between his desk and somewhat to (his) left of the door (which is always open). It is the reason why we call his movement a 'patrol': it reconfigures or transforms the space into 'teacher's space' and 'pupils' space'. In this classroom there are several overlapping definitions of pedagogic space, indicated by the placement of the teacher's desk in relation to the rows of tables; and produced by the transforming action of the teacher in his pacing. The underlying configuration positions the students in one way; the transformation of that configuration forces (some of) the students into the contortion of their bodies to make it possible for them to conform to the transformed configuration. In short, the pedagogy realized spatially and in the teacher's movement is multiply ambivalent, and contradictory.

Visual display

Broadly the same complex pedagogic discourse is realized in the visual displays on the walls of John's classroom. The contradictions appear through the manner and the form of display, as well as through the choice of materials displayed. Discursively it is again a mixture of 'participation' – realized through materials that (might) link to the cultural world of the students – and of authority through the simultaneous presence of materials from an elite culture. The visual display can be understood as a sign of the teacher's sense of what the domain of English is: to account for the phenomena of the cultural world as defined here. Hence the visual display might seem to be more a statement about the curriculum than about the pedagogy of English. Yet the display has a pedagogic force in the sense that the content also gives expression to the social relations of teacher to students.

The display in this room includes a range of texts, from a wide range of sources. There are 'official' texts such as policy documents, curriculum resources, examination questions, school homework clubs, and the school timetable. Alongside these, 'unofficial texts' are displayed – photographs of students reading, a handwritten poster on how to analyse a poem, and a few student poems. The visual display also includes posters from London art galleries, film posters, posters of poetry publications and several articles from magazines and broadsheet newspapers. That is the world which defines what English is and which English must explain.

The texts that come directly from the world of the teacher are displayed on the walls behind the arc traced by his movement. These are texts of 'high-culture' – English art and canonical English poetry. The texts made by the students are displayed on the wall at the back of the room. The texts that bridge these two spaces consist of 'official' texts: National Curriculum policy and resources; for example, a photocopy of the National Curriculum grade system for all areas of English (literature, reading, and so on) is displayed in full, detailing the grading criteria and the marking code. Displaying this text can be read both as a display of the (source of the) authority of the teacher – legitimating his marking for instance – and as a move towards transparency by making this information openly available to his students, in a desire for democratic participation. There is no attempt by the teacher to mediate these official – densely printed and photocopied – policy documents for the students. We think that this realizes the contradiction at the base of his 'participative-authoritarian pedagogy'. The information is present, there, on the wall, and yet it may well remain inaccessible to the majority of students, unless they are able and willing to work hard at making sense of it.

The (National) Curriculum itself is not foregrounded; it exists in the space between the display of the teacher's valued texts and those of the students. The teacher and the official National Curriculum speak with different voices – they remain distinct, and, as far as the display indicates, the teacher's voice is dominant. For instance, his casual, spontaneously handwritten sheet on how to analyse poems is pinned over the top of the document setting out the National Curriculum criteria for writing. The official text is effectively obliterated by his 'poster'. And yet the contrast between the hard, shiny permanence of the laminated official curriculum text, and the dull yellow of the sugar paper of the teacher's text, serves to create a tension between the two, which brings both into play. The work of the teacher is overlaid on the official curriculum text, whose edges, visible below it, form a frame for the method advocated by his poster. So, spatially and visually, the work of the teacher is located in the context of the official curriculum, it 'rests on' its authority, and yet, literally, in the manner and mode of this display, it places itself above it, as a challenge to it.

Speech

In our theoretical approach speech is the name of the mode, the meaning-resource, and talk indicates a particular social use of that resource.

The teacher's talk embodies the contradictions that we have described; it too realizes the same 'authoritative/participatory' pedagogic discourse, with its constant structure of affirmation of one kind of relation that is simultaneously negated/contradicted by its opposite. A somewhat superficial and commonsense description of the characteristics of John's talk would be this: his voice is soft, low, friendly, at times bordering on the 'familiar'. The grammar and syntax are those of 'indirection'; that is, commands are 'disguised', not given using the direct, usually imperative form. For example: 'I would like everyone to be reading silently for about five/ten minutes, please' (syntactically a declarative; semantically a state-ment; but pragmatically, in its illocutionary force, a command) rather than '[Please, everyone now] read for five minutes'. Similarly, rather than saying 'read with a pencil [for annotation] in your hand, please' John said 'if you're reading with a pencil in your hand that's pretty sensible', and 'people who are looking at Superman, you might be thinking about this' (rather than 'read with a pencil in your hand' syntactically an imperative, and semantically/pragmatically a command), and so on. Indirection of this kind is a sign of power, namely the power to force those who are addressed to do the work of interpreting the message correctly.

The teacher operates a reward scheme in the class, in whose operation 'indirec-tion' and 'implicit criteria' are entirely merged: neither the principles for the award of points (nor the quantity awarded) are usually made overt. So we have 'Prince, could you have five points please?' (syntactically an interrogative, semantically a question, but pragmatically a command: 'Prince, take five points!'), 'Lawrence, you can have five points' said without any explanation, and to another child 'that's very interesting, that's very clever, that's five points'.

The authority, the source of knowledge and the point of reference, are generally the 'I' of the teacher: 'I'm not at all pleased', 'I would like everyone to be reading', but it is not an 'I' that reveals the principled grounds of its authority, or of its knowledge. The principles are portrayed as though they might not even be avail-able to the teacher himself: 'I'm thinking maybe … is it that…?' as if he, and maybe he and the students together, are producing these insights into English in difficult, inspired labour, here and now.

That is, the pedagogy embodied in the form of John's talk, in the quality of the voice as much as in the syntax and texture of his speech, shows the same complexity and contradictions as we have shown in the layout of the room and in his movement. It is simultaneously a disguise of power and its assertion; an implic-itness of statement and an expectation of understanding what is at issue. In other words, what the form of talk suggests is a world in which directness is not the normal mode of operating; rather it suggests that there is a cultivated, cultured sensibility that makes such (indirect, implicit) understanding and knowledge self-evidently available, accessible to those who are 'a proper part' of this community. Such understanding cannot be made available through direct, explicit, overt teaching; it can only be modelled, in the allusive manner in which it is here made available. That, it seems to us, is the significant aspect of English pedagogy here; it is at the same time a potent content and meaning of English itself.

Gaze, gesture and embodiment

Through most of the lesson (and certainly in this segment) the teacher does not really look at the students. Even when he addresses a student directly through talk he does not often look at her or him. The exception to this is when a student is admonished or about to be punished: teacher, hands on hips, looking at Kamala (who is putting on make-up): 'I'm not at all pleased; you had break-time to do that kind of stuff'. The more usual disconnection between the person who is addressed and direction of his gaze is another realization of the 'split' pedagogy. The students are addressed via talk (in contrast to some other teachers in our data-set, who use gaze as a means of address). For this teacher the task of management of the classroom is done via talk; it is something to be accomplished in order to let the teaching happen. He would, literally, rather not look at it. The real task is handled by his gaze, which ranges 'over' the class and beyond it: it is in gaze that we see the development, unfolding and communicating of the curriculum of sensibility. That is a task which is 'above' the plane of classroom management; and perhaps it is not even meant for real people actually there as members of the class, but a task somehow 'above' all of them. When he awards the five points to Lawrence, for instance, his hand touches the student's shoulder lightly as he says 'Lawrence you can have five points'; his gaze, however, is directed away from the student.

A typical gesture (and accompanying facial expression) used by this teacher is that embodying the attitude of the now puzzled, now anguished intellectual. He holds his right hand to his mouth or chin (with the elbow cradled in the left hand), in a thinking pose, while one of the students says 'cos she's normally ... cos I think she sees the world as fiction, like'. He responds 'That's very interesting, that's very clever, that's five points'. He moves to a new gesture where he holds his right hand up, forefinger touching thumb: 'That's very clever: she's seeing the world like a fairy tale', and he continues to hold this gesture, as though carefully holding a small, valuable and fragile object.

In general John uses gesture (when it does not represent and communicate his puzzled or anguished attitude) to handle those aspects of his interaction with the students which he does not do with his gaze, and which are not fully done with his talk. These gestures indicate 'receiving of information', 'astonishment at the information', and are used as a kind of 'conducting' of the interaction, often achieved by means of the duration and 'holding' of a gesture.

All this provides the effect of embodiment: that is, the meanings made in the mode of gesture are, as it were, meanings in the body of the teacher, just as the effects of his positioning, movement and use of gaze have the same force. In this manner, English and its meaning seem to be held in, displayed by, actualized through the body of the teacher: English is the teacher; the teacher is English. This is an effect that we think is not characteristic of other subjects in the school curriculum.

Voice quality

In and through voice quality (van Leeuwen 1999), the teacher performs and realizes sensibility and sensitivity. This, too, has pedagogic significance: the meaning of a social relation in which explicitness is inappropriate, in which directness would be too 'heavy' for the gossamer lightness of what has to be communicated, where to be explicit would be gross and mundane.

If pedagogy is an effect of and the actualization of social relations, then this is a pedagogy communicating that in English direct expression or explicitness – whether it is about content or about the means of communication – is simply inadequate to achieving such fragile aims. In this, too, voice quality represents, realizes and communicates the form of pedagogy that we have described so far.

So far we have tried to avoid direct comments on curriculum, though that has, at times, proved impossible. As we will say at different points throughout the book, English remains, for a number of reasons and despite the attempts of policy, a subject with a weakly explicit curriculum. In its implicitness, much of what English is and does is precisely about forms of social interaction and 'social being'; it is and remains still the domain of subjectivity and of identity of a certain kind, although it is by no means the case that this is equally so in all of the nine classrooms that we visited. Yet pedagogy and curriculum are very often too close to disentangle, in ways that are not so in other subjects. In science the two are distinct: here is the curriculum (in a way that would vary little from classroom to classroom), and here is the pedagogy as the means I use to communicate it (which can vary from classroom to classroom). By contrast we can say that in several of the English classrooms, pedagogy as social relations was realized, at least in part, through aspects of curriculum.

This situation poses real difficulties for students in a multicultural, multi-ethnic classroom and society. It becomes very much a question about access and equity when curriculum is, or is made available as, pedagogy as social relations. Inevitably some forms of pedagogy are 'closer to' the forms of social relation of the cultures of some members of the classroom than of others.

Ravenscroft School: Irene

In the first example we looked at the beginning of a lesson; now we show an extract some little way into (a series of lessons and) one particular lesson. We demonstrate the same multimodal methodology at work in the discussion of the 'core' of a lesson rather than in its initial framing. Although curriculum is here more an issue, we still want to continue with our focus on pedagogy. Although this example involves a different set of issues, we continue to focus on the same modes; nevertheless here our methodology brings different issues into focus. We hope that the contrast gives a better sense of our way of looking – which is our aim in using these two contrasting examples.

To make comparison and contrast easier, we use the same headings as in the first example, and we depart from them only where the material itself suggests that we should. So here, for instance, it becomes necessary to speak about the students' posture as significant and meaningful; and this allows us to reflect on the first example to see whether posture might have been significant there.

The layout of the classroom

This classroom is arranged in what is now called a traditional form: the teacher's desk is at the front, the students sit at desks that are arranged in rows, by and large all facing the teacher, Irene (see Figure 4.12). In the disposition of chairs and tables there is no suggestion of pedagogy of 'democratic participation', nor of 'constructivism' in relation to the curriculum. This classroom layout signals 'transmission pedagogy': the teacher is positioned as authority, and the students as the recipients of knowledge, explicitly provided, by the teacher. From the layout it seems that there is none of the complexity, contradiction and confusion of the classroom in the first example.

The teacher's desk is at the front, and beside it, on the wall behind her, is a whiteboard that she uses throughout the lesson. The arrangement of the room provides and realizes a pedagogy: this is a pedagogy in which authority relations are clear; power lies with the teacher, and students are recipients of knowledge. We might call it a 'pedagogy of authority'.

Movement of the teacher in the classroom

Given how the classroom is arranged, this teacher's scope for movement is circumscribed compared to our first example. It is she who has arranged the class-room in this manner and, clearly, movement in the way that it appears necessary for the first teacher is not what she wants. She has a different sense of the class-room space and of its pedagogic potentials, and her classroom is arranged to allow her to realize her sense of the pedagogic relations.

This is not to say that this teacher does not move. At times she sits at or behind her desk (a table like the other tables in the room, with a chair like the others behind it). At times she stands up, slightly behind and to the side of the chair, at times she moves slightly to her left in order to write or draw on the whiteboard, or to gesture at it. The most significant movement is when she moves quite some way, maybe three steps to the right of her desk, so that now her relation to the (centre) of the class is no longer directly 'front on', but somewhat 'side on'. If the meaning of being at the centre-front is that of 'direct involvement' (with a group a person or an object), then the move to the side suggest a less direct involvement, maybe a certain detachment (see Kress and van Leeuwen 1996). At that point she also, at times, half-sits on the edge of a table that is there.

Her movements in the classroom space are much less pronounced than John's, in terms both of the distance that she moves and of the pace, frequency and regularity of her moving – she definitely does not 'pace' up and down. Her movement doesn't transform the classroom in a radical way, even though her movement to the side does change the authority relation somewhat. What does happen is that the 'genre' of the interaction changes. So when she half-squats on the edge of the table, she assumes the role of chat-show hostess, not directly involved yet not marginal to the action either. This produces a meaning of an active audience debating an issue of concern to them. That change in genre was not an effect of the teacher's movement in the first classroom. But here it can produce a switch in formality, even though what is teacher's space and students' space is clear and remains stable.

Yet, pedagogically speaking, while there can be change in the pedagogic relations in this classroom, in the genre of classroom interaction, there is no sense of contradiction, of tension, or of the overlaying of fundamentally incompatible pedagogic forms.

Visual displays

The form, and the clarity, of the pedagogic relations is also signalled by the form of the visual display in the classroom. The 'visual layout' of the display is careful: it is precisely aligned and linear or rectangular. The displayed elements are all carefully produced, rectangular, framed and laminated. Its content is student writing, word-processed and neatly framed on a background of cardboard, and there are book covers of 'good-quality' literature read by the students. What is displayed is either that produced in the classroom – poems, book reviews, essays – or as the result of work done previously in the classroom. What is shown as valued in this classroom is on the one hand the students' own work, treated seriously, and valued texts as entities in the curriculum. Both in the choice of texts that are displayed, and by the value with which they are endowed or imbued through the preparation and care of display, the teacher's social and pedagogic relation to the students is clearly realized: students and their work are valued; the teacher bestows the valuation.

The conception of English here is clear, at least in one sense: English is that which happens in this classroom; it is 'good writing', whether that of the students or that of valued literature; it is demonstrated by the achievements of the students themselves. There is consequently a much greater uniformity and clarity on this matter.

Speech

Syntactically and grammatically this teacher's talk in the classroom is direct: questions appear in the form of interrogatives, which is the direct, 'unmarked', syntactic form for a question. So, for instance, when discussing a text she said: 'What is the major revelation in this story?'; 'What's the thing that we discover?'; 'What happens towards the end, when the wedding celebrations are coming to an end?', and so on.

Similarly, commands are given in the form of imperatives, also the unmarked form: 'Put your hands up'; 'Somebody else read out'; 'Keep your hands up, keep your hands up'. Statements (in the syntactic form of declaratives) are used by this teacher to state things – things that she judges significant: 'And then we have this revelation'. In other words, the use of syntax in talk is as straightforward, as direct as her use of other modes. 'What you see and what you hear is what you get' we might say.

This linguistic disposition extends to a somewhat more abstract issue, one which in this series of lessons straddles pedagogy and curriculum, namely the switch between 'this is a literary text, to be discussed as "literary text"' and 'this is a text that is about life, and needs to be related by me and you to your lives'. So for instance: 'Mmm, it's like women and men. Men can feel free to talk about your … their conquests'. Here the switch in pronoun indicates that difference. At this point in the lesson, the teacher still wants to keep this text as the literary text, not yet as the text of life, which is where she intends to go with it; it is that which motivates her recasting, the switch from 'your' to 'their'.

Gesture, gaze and embodiment

Throughout the lesson, the teacher holds her body in an upright posture, whether sitting or standing; it is a posture that conveys an attitude of authority, confidence, stability, 'settledness'. This strongly suggests one form of the pedagogic relation that she has with the class: she is there as a source of knowledge and authority. This is a constant throughout the lesson, and mediates her relation to the whole class. Gesture is used pedagogically, in selecting students, in subduing others, in reinforcing what is being said, and in keeping 'the floor' free for a particular argument – whether for herself or for the students she chooses to act as her spokespersons. And as we will discuss in another chapter, the teacher uses gesture for curricular purposes.

This teacher, Irene, uses gaze in what we shall frequently refer to as orchestration. She uses gaze where the teacher, John, in our first example used talk – as a means of (classroom) management – except that here management is much more than what is usually understood by that term. She selects those students with whom or through whom she wishes to advance the argument of the lesson through gaze; equally, those who are asked to remain silent for the time being are discouraged by not receiving her gaze, or by being 'held at bay' through a gesture.

Unlike John, the teacher in our first example, Irene uses gaze very much to engage with the class and individuals within it. Again, there is no contradiction: no verbal address or nomination of one student while the teacher's gaze goes somewhere else entirely. In this respect the clarity of the social–pedagogic relation is also reinforced and realized in the use of gaze. This is in tune with Irene's use of syntax that we commented on just above. Gaze is used as a means of social interaction, of control, but in an unambiguous manner.

What is embodied in these lessons is a sense of how English is to be handled in a frame of specific clear social relations, where the teacher is a point of stability, of authority, and the students are valued in their rights through what they do and say. What is embodied here is English pedagogy as pedagogy; what is embodied in our first example is English pedagogy as the content of English, as curriculum.

Voice quality

The teacher speaks quite slowly throughout, she speaks very clearly and audibly, strongly and deliberately: what she has to say is given weight by all aspects of the quality and her use of her voice. Her voice is a clear sign of her authority. She has something to say that she regards as significant, and her voice signals that; she is the person in authority, and her voice signals that also.

Students' posture

We made no overt comment on the students' posture in the discussion of the first classroom, other than where the contortions of some of the students' bodies seemed an effect of the teacher's actions; it did not seem to be a resource made available for meaning-choice by the students. In our first example, the teacher commented frequently on the students' posture, in order to 'correct' it. In this second example the students' posture appears as a meaningful action. The students sit at tables arranged broadly in (three) rows; each student sits at one table. This arrangement of the tables creates a particular relation of student to student – each student 'has' her or his 'own' table, and this provides a different structure of potential interaction between them: not co-construction of knowledge, but equality in being members of an audience that receives knowledge from the teacher. The relation of each student to the teacher's table or desk is also clear and constant.

The classroom layout does not speak of 'participation' in the construction of knowledge, nor is there any sense of equality between teacher and students. However, what is immediately noticeable is that the students feel free to 'lounge' or 'sprawl' across 'their' tables. In other words, here there is a contradiction: it lies in tension between the authority relation suggested by the strict order of the layout of the classroom, and the freedom permitted to the students as to how to comport their bodies individually. In the first classroom there was a constant censuring effort by the teacher to control the students' posture with a variety of reasons given (for example, the teacher frequently comments on the need to sit up straight to avoid 'cutting off the supply of oxygen to the brain'). In the classroom discussed in the second example, students are free to express their sense of participation or distance in their bodily postures.

Whereas in John's classroom contradictions seemed to arise in all the meanings or signs made by the teacher, in Irene's classroom the contradictions lie between the sign of a clear structure established by the teacher, and the freedom that she grants to the students to transform that meaning by making their signs through posture. In John's classroom the students do not have that freedom; they are forced to conform to the contradictory structures of the teacher, and are subject to his disciplining of their posture. In Irene's classroom there are clear structures of authority, and the ceding to the students of the freedom to express their meanings through posture. The contradictions of the first classroom are those produced by the teacher, who expects the students to conform to them, somehow; here the contradictions and tensions arise from the fact that there are differences between teacher/authority and student/agency, and these differences are recognized and allowed to be given expression.

A provisional summary

Our examples show how the teacher in each classroom has orchestrated a range of modes to construct a set of social relations, a pedagogy in each classroom. In both classrooms we argue that the effects of policy, of the social composition of the school, of the professional formation of the teacher, can all be 'seen'. In other words, both the effects of external and internal constraint, and the effects of real agency in making the meanings of English (pedagogy) are present.

The person of the teacher plays a role: Irene comes from a former background of social work with young people, while John comes from a traditional English degree. Although the social composition of each school, and of their immediate environment, seems at one level quite similar, they have clearly constructed a different relation with their environment: for instance, and among other things, through selection in the one case and its absence in the other (though this would need to be stated and explored in much greater specificity than we do here). Of course, both schools operate under the requirements of the National Curriculum.

What we notice, and it is something that will be a cautionary fact in our interpretation, is that the appearance and form of a single sign does not tell the whole story. Take the sign of classroom layout: John's classroom starts with a structure that promises participation, but, in a variety of ways and through a variety of modes, realizes one where close control and disciplining of all forms of students' action is the rule. The second classroom, Irene's, starts with a clear structure of authority, but allows the teacher to shift from interactional genre to genre, including genres of real audience participation; it makes important concessions to the students, giving them the freedom to make their meanings.

The meaning of any event or of any structure does not lie in the meaning of one sign, but has to be seen in the complex meanings of a set of signs all read together. Here, in Irene's classroom, we can notice that there is a broad homology among the signs made in the various modes: the meanings made in one tend to recur in the meanings made in another. For the students it is of course absolutely crucial what signs are made, what signs are there to be read, transformed, and remade by them, and, above all, how they are positioned in relation to these complex signs, given their own specific and, as a group, diverse backgrounds.

Chapter 4

The English classroom as a multimodal sign

Introduction

In the preceding two chapters we have looked at the broader environment of schools, and of English, and we have provided a brief sketch illustrating our mode of looking, our methodology. We turn now, in the following chapters, to explorations in greater detail of specific issues in order to build up a rich picture of the complexity of the work that constitutes the production of school English.

School English is changing, and our research suggests that under the impact of policy the English classroom itself is also changing, though not in a uniform direction. Each of the classrooms we discuss in this chapter was organized by the teacher whom we observed in the course of our research, and the significance of the classroom space to the teachers we watched and interviewed was always evident. The design and displays of the English classrooms that we visited during the research project, and the many more that some members of our team visit in their role as PGCE tutors, varied considerably. These displays can be seen as one material sign of the diversity of English. In this chapter we discuss this diversity by looking at four classrooms, across the three schools. Our four examples allow us to offer a social explanation of both historical change and current diversity, with a particular focus on the changing role of government educational policy and regulation, and on the other kinds of agency that contribute to shaping the classroom setting. We aim to show that the classrooms in which teachers and students work play a key role in the shaping of pedagogy: the spatial organization and visual displays of the classroom are central elements in the production of school English and its social relations. We see the material aspects of classrooms as signs of the pedagogy of English that a teacher has produced, and of the social and political forces that stand behind its production.

A classroom of my own

Many urban schools suffer from a shortage of useable teaching space, and this creates particular pressures on teaching there. One of the teachers at Wayford School, Stephen, did not have a classroom of his own. His problems were exacerbated by the allocation of classrooms: he taught the Year 10 class we observed on the seventh floor on Mondays, and on the second floor on Thursdays; on Fridays he taught them on the fourth floor. This constant moving between floors frequently resulted in his lessons starting late and in the students' confusion over which room they were supposed to be in. The practical inconvenience was a problem, but the teacher faced a still more complex problem – how to teach English without a sense of 'place'. Two of the classrooms he taught in were organized by other teachers to actualize versions of English that focused on media studies, a focus not shared by this teacher. The third 'classroom' in which he taught was the school's break-time canteen and snack area. In each of these spaces the desks were arranged differently. In one, they were laid out in a horseshoe shape; in another, 'cabaret-style' (with groups of tables each seating five or six students); and in the third, desks were organized singly into three long rows. Each of these arrangements placed teacher and students in a different pedagogical relationship to one another. Hence the relationships between Stephen and his students were constantly being reconfigured, and they had to work to produce a space for 'their' English, often in opposition to the place in which they were located. They were involved in attempting continually to 'rewrite' the pedagogical practices encoded in the layout of classrooms, and in doing so they had to take into account the socializing systems that were already established there (Larsen 2001). A significant part of each lesson involved establishing a frame for what was to happen, for what English was to be for a class that lacked a settled experience and a material history of 'being together'.

Pedagogy and the classroom

Lawn (1999) comments that many teachers, himself included, do not recognize the impact of the classroom as a material environment on teaching. The classroom – like any other physical, constructed site – is designed with built-in values and purposes that contribute to shaping the work and behaviour of the teachers and students who occupy it. Seaborne argues, in his history of the British school (Seaborne 1977), that a building literally 'makes' the teaching method. Fiske (1995) develops the argument further, suggesting that school architecture is deeply rooted in nineteenth-century values and that the successful reform of the educational system requires rethinking the design of schools and the overall learning environment. For us, too, 'the pedagogical order of the classroom is mediated in its spaces' (Grosvenor et al. 1999: XX), though our data suggests a less emphatic approach than Seabourne's: the classroom is a spatial resource that constrains and enables different kinds of pedagogy rather than a force that exercises a completely determining influence; as we pointed out in Chapter 3, space is constantly transformed by those who use it. So our focus is not on the designing of the school or classroom by government, local authority or – since 2000 – by private-sector company. Such design is influential, but not definitive. Instead we explore the ways in which teachers, working in these already designed spaces, shape and transform English: in one of the cases we discuss below, a class-room initially designed to abet a strongly didactic model of teaching, with pupils arranged in neat rows of desks, is reshaped by the teacher to realize a radical teaching environment in which students can challenge the authority of tradition.

Multimodality – the perspective that forms such an important part of our meth-odology – extends beyond questions of classroom layout. Most classrooms contain one form or another of visual display. Display is often discussed in terms of the ways in which it might create an attractive environment for learning – an environ-ment that reflects student interests, communicates ideas, provides materials for teaching, creates a sense of place, rewards or recognizes pupil work and contrib-utes to a work ethos (Williams 1989). From another more critical perspective, display can be charged with naturalizing the classroom environment and with making opaque the exercising of power (Foucault 1991). Our starting point is different, in a way that we hope avoids either too great an emphasis on a celebra-tion of display as worthwhile pedagogy, or too immediate an assumption that the visual elements of the classroom can be linked to issues of authority and power. For us, spatial organization and display are aspects of a design for English, devel-oped within a specific set of social relations. They are the products of living labour, doubly made by their originator (pupil, artist, printer, and so on) and by the teacher or teachers who produced their current spatial arrangement and textual environ-ment in which the initial text is relocated. As the product of the work of teachers, classrooms display outcomes of labour that has been performed out of hours. But the displays and arrangements of the classroom do not remain as an 'inert', 'pre-created' background to the work of a class: they are activated, or reactivated, by classroom pedagogy. In this respect, the teacher's role is central: the teacher medi-ates what is displayed and what is enacted in the classroom; it is the teacher who connects the spatial material display of English to other aspects of the subject's realization. In this sense, classroom arrangement and display provide pedagogic resources; they are part of the technology of teaching and serve to transmit to students the pedagogic practices and 'fundamental regulatory principles' that govern a school (Daniels 2001: 169). Displays, activated by the teacher, relay the regulatory framework of the curriculum, and the criteria that are taken to signify appropriate learning within a school, and they socialize students through their activity into the expected competencies of a classroom and the teacher's desired models of good practice. Visual displays and the arrangement of the classroom are thus a 'pedagogic tool', a medium to communicate the qualities and expectations of the teacher or school in a language that is to be lived as an identity-building and identity-confirming experience (Kress and van Leeuwen 2001). So teachers' work of display, and their reactivation of display through pedagogy, both legitimates the work of students and draws them into pre-established systems for classifying knowledge and skills. In some of the classrooms we observed, this was an explicit aim of pedagogy: the classroom was understood and designed as an attempt to broaden the knowledge base of the students – to increase their cultural capital. In the course of this activity, there was revealed a tendency to replace, as a safeguard against examination failure, the uncertain labour of the students with the authorita-tive labour of the teacher. In what follows, we aim to explore in some detail the workings of this process.

The changing English classroom

In order to be able to identify what is specific and new about the present 'moment' of English teaching, we start with a brief discussion of the classroom of the past, turning first of all to the visual record.

There have of course been major changes in educational design, particularly since 1944, which have impacted on the spatial arrangement of the classrooms and the organization of their furniture (Maclure 1984): the classrooms of schools built from the 1960s onwards are smaller; they have lower ceilings and more windows, and therefore more light and a stronger (intended) connection with the community outside the school. These changes can also be seen in classrooms built in a more distant past, and later transformed through the addition of false ceilings and new windows. The strictly ordered rows of single desks have been replaced in many classrooms, although not all, with desks arranged into 'dining-room layouts' – desks joined to seat small groups of students, and 'cabaret-style' arrangements in which students are grouped around tables all facing the front (Waterhouse 2001). The arrangements of tables into groups is a marker of a theoretical shift in concep-tions of learning, in which student-centred ideologies have played a major part, and in which the teacher has been redefined as a facilitator. Following Hamilton (1989) we might see enacted here a shift from the values of mass production and social efficiency to an agenda formed by a more diverse set of purposes. Certainly, the spatial arrangements serve to change the relationships between teacher and students, and among students themselves.

Visual display has also been transformed. Photographs of elementary- and primary-school classroom walls in books documenting education in the early part of the twentieth century (Bourne and Mac Arthur 1970; Grosvenor 1999) depict a classroom world of dense visual display, including landscapes and portraits, scien-tific images and posters about language. It is difficult to reconstruct the purposes of such display, but one might suggest that it was related in part to a project of 'bringing the world into the classroom', combined with a more directly pedagogic project, related, for instance, to communicating the rules of spelling and parts of speech. So far as we can tell, the walls of postwar secondary education were somewhat barer. In the English classrooms that some of us attended as grammar-school students, and in which some of us taught in the comprehensives of the 1970s, English was modelled as the product of an interaction of teacher, students and text, with visual display not taking a significant pedagogic part. The most common practice was for the walls to be used to display students' 'best work'. In some classrooms there would be some teacher-supplied posters – gleaned for instance from the Royal Shakespeare Company – or postcards from the world's art galleries. Athena's poster shops had been established in the late 1960s, and the kinds of display found on the walls of a student flat were carried over into the classroom. The anti-racist and feminist moments of the 1970s and 1980s also found their way into English classroom display – providing images related to 'self-esteem' and sometimes exemplifying non-traditional Englishes. In addition, there were often examples of students' work-in-progress on display: teachers used the walls of the classroom as a working tool, a visual space in which students and teacher could co-produce texts, stories and narratives as a reflexive tool for thinking and discussion.

The paragraphs above describe a history that has in some respects now taken a new turn. Visually, the English classroom appears to be a denser environment. Increasingly, it provides a resource for a new kind of pedagogy, at the same time as it reflects the impact on schools of new forms of governance and accountability. Pedagogically, visual display emphasizes to what is, historically, an unusual extent the influence of official policies for the teaching of the subject – hence the presence of extracts from exam syllabuses, guidance on grammar, exemplary work, and commercially produced designs incorporating newly canonical poems. This material is part of an effort to make curriculum and assessment procedures explicit – not so much in respect of an 'inner logic' of the subject, as in terms of a performance-driven, exam-centred agenda.

Changes in forms of visual display have been accompanied by a different approach to the layout of the classroom. The Key Stage 3 strategy's pedagogic recommendations of the horseshoe arrangement of classrooms can be seen as an attempt by central government to exercise a more direct authority over the classroom. The horseshoe classroom embodies a pedagogy – teaching from the front with a large element of whole-class work – that in its panoptical dimension relates as much to the management of behaviour as to intervention in learning.

We must be careful, though, not to overestimate the extent of current change: it is not as if each historical period breaks completely from those that preceded it. Classroom arrangements and displays often appear heterogeneous, in that the physical sediments of earlier practices coexist with the results of newer work. But this heterogeneity is not accidental: the material environment of the English classroom offers insights into the relation between 'old' and 'new' and thus, also, into the tensions and relations between educational policy and pedagogical practice. Certainly, there is thus no single set of signs that convey an authoritative and widely agreed meaning of English, and the English we encounter in these classrooms is a divided and complex practice.

Turning a multimodal lens on the English classroom

In order to explore the English classroom as a sign of English and a pedagogical tool or technology we turn to social semiotics (see Chapter 1, and Hodge and Kress 1988; Jewitt and Oyama 2001; Kress and van Leeuwen 1996, 2001). Through our analysis we address three central questions. First, we examine the texts, objects and furniture in the classroom and ask which domains of knowledge the classroom displays represent to the students (and others) as a part of English.

Is literature included, and if so what kinds of literature? What resources are the students offered for their learning, and how are they positioned, physically and conceptually, in relation to this knowledge? Second, we ask which representational and communicational modes are used to represent English, which modes are used to explore aspects of English, which modes are foregrounded, and by what means. Third, we focus on the arrangements and connections made between these elements in the classroom to ask what is given importance or made central through the resources of visual display and spatial arrangement. In short, then, we approach the classroom as a complex multimodal sign of English. We draw on our observations of lessons and in-depth interviews with teachers and students to attempt to provide social explanations of these features.

While our analysis of these signs is, we think, plausible, we recognize that all analysis is interpretation and our interpretation is informed by our social positions as researchers. Signs are made in outward production – such as the layout of a classroom, and also in inward production – as in the activity loosely called 'reading'. In all signs people as sign-makers realize their own histories and interests. Hence readings always differ, as we all bring our interests to the making of signs. The teachers and students who inhabit the classrooms discussed in this chapter brought their experiences, interests and interpretations to their classrooms, hence their interpretation will, necessarily, differ from ours. In light of this we present our analysis not as fact but as a hypothesis focused on the exploration of the multimodal production of school English.

Springton School, Susan's classroom: English as competence in language communication

Susan's classroom is typical of the other English classrooms in this school, in its arrangement of desks, overall use of space and visual display. The uniformity of the classrooms is a multimodal marker of a well-organized English department, and of its ethos of sharing and co-ordinating the teaching and learning of English. As Susan said when interviewed:

> We have a very strong vision of how we want it [the English Department] to be and it is the same, or very similar. We are trying to put that in place really. ...
>   I think it is very, what I was saying, focused on English teaching. I think you have to work as a team and that is quite a strong way of how I want things to run.

The school population, as described elsewhere, has a high proportion of students with English as an additional language, a significant percentage of whom are at an early stage of their language development in English, and a sizeable number of students are refugees. English is taught to mixed-ability classes and teachers differentiate within the class. Within the English department there is a strong emphasis on group learning and the layout of each class reflects this. In each classroom the desks are arranged to seat groups of three to six students (see Figure 4.1).

The effective use of group work in the English department was singled out for praise in a recent Ofsted report.

In this classroom, as in several others, the teacher does not have a desk and does not occupy a fixed space in the room. The students' seats are not arranged to position them in relation to the teacher's gaze. While the concept of the classroom as a cellular space positions the teacher as the authority (Peim 2001), the layout of the furniture here does not emphasize this. In the lessons we observed the teacher at different times taught from 'the front' of the classroom, sat amongst the students and read from the board and overhead projector, and spent a significant amount of time moving around the class to work with groups of students.

On walking into the classroom it was striking that there were few images among the classroom displays; in the main, display material is written or typed, and focused on concerns with language. The majority of the texts on display originate from or relate to official texts, usually policy in the form of the English National Curriculum. These official texts are given more importance than the other texts on display through their prominent positioning on the walls. They include the teacher's mediated versions of the curriculum as instructions on how to write, genres of writing, deadlines, examinations, and the criteria that must be met to attain particular grades. A series of texts explains key words used in the Key Stage 4 examination papers I and II (Figure 4.2).

Through these texts the teacher has selected, adapted and transformed the National Curriculum into a series of instructional materials for the students, focused on the genre of examination. Resource cupboards, containing dictionaries and thesauruses, run along one wall of the classroom. The texts displayed on the doors of these cupboards (Figure 4.3) are resources for writing within the frame of the curriculum: how to present a written text, phrases to use in the construction of a written argument, starting a sentence, points on how to write for examination. These texts act as an 'extension' of the cupboard's contents.

There is one visual reference (Figure 4.4) to popular culture, in the form of stills from Luhrmann's film *Romeo and Juliet* (starring Leonardo di Caprio) provided by the teacher to display the theme of masculinity in *Romeo and Juliet* and *West Side Story*.

The work of students is displayed as work from across the year groups. This display consists of terms from 'media language' – *mis-en-scène* and so on, alongside images from Luhrmann's film. The display foregrounds the National Curriculum's and the Literacy Strategy's terminology for English, focusing on that which is not known or rather that which is to be learnt; that which is beyond the everyday. It acts as an exemplar and presents the teacher's (now hidden)work through the work of the students, as idealized student work. The still images are a visual annotation of the English/media studies entities.The use of these images in an otherwise written environment serves to make this text stand out, to make it salient.

The position of the displays of student work on the 'back' wall, that is, away from the activity of the teacher and the general gaze of the students, gives these texts the least prominence in the room.

Figure 4.1 Springton School: Susan's classroom layout

Persuade
Inform
Describe

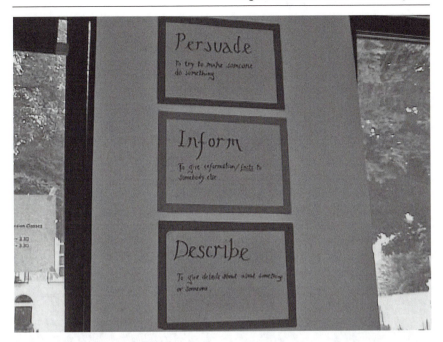

Figure 4.2 Posters from Susan's classroom that use key words from examination papers

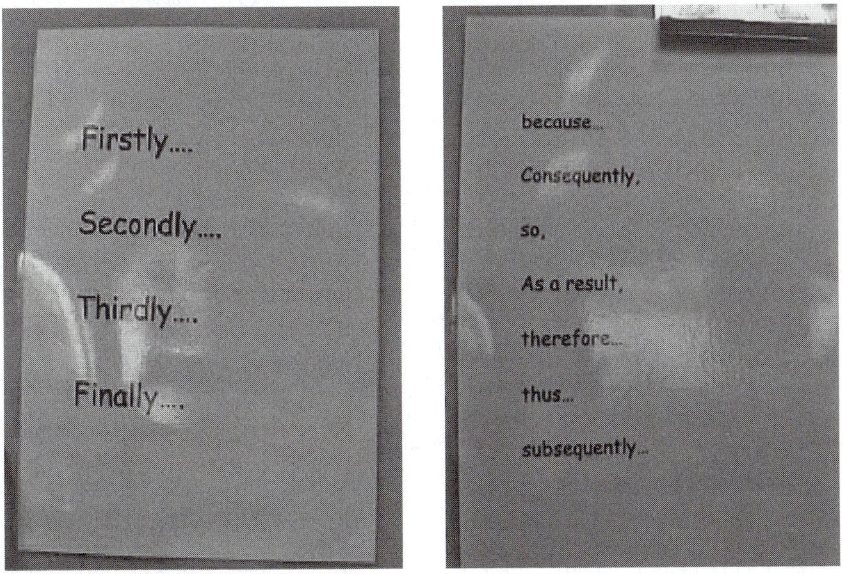

Firstly....
Secondly....
Thirdly....
Finally....
because...
Consequently,
so,
As a result,
therefore...
thus...
subsequently...

Figure 4.3 Examples of the posters on the resource cupboard doors in Susan's classroom

Figure 4.4 Teacher-made text on 'Masculinity in *Romeo and Juliet*' displayed in Susan's classroom.

All of the texts on display in Susan's classroom are neatly framed, as discrete elements one from another, each text arranged in a strict vertical orientation; no texts overlap. However, the texts are framed to different degrees. Those that relate directly to the curriculum in the classroom are most strongly framed, through the use of double mounting and colour. The use of mounting and colour makes connections of 'sameness' or 'of a sort' between the texts that relate to the curriculum and to 'instructions' concerning how to write. The use of mounting, of double mounting, and of colour is a visual actualization of the classification of activities within the modular curriculum.

In addition to the framing for display, some texts are also framed *by* display. These texts are arranged on the walls in positions that are further framed by the furniture, or by spaces of the classroom such as cupboard doors, pillars, windows or the whiteboard. This framing by display imbues the texts with different qualities and relationships to the activities of the classroom. For instance, the whiteboard, which is used by the teacher in each lesson and cleaned at the end of each, is the place of current and changing information. By displaying texts on the frame of the whiteboard the teacher positions them in the 'here and now' of the classroom: they are literally framed within the activity of the lesson. The texts that relate to Key Stage 4 examination questions are arranged as a series on a pillar between two windows (Figure 4.2). They are framed both by the pillar and by the windows. This vertical compositional arrangement presents them as a list – in the genre of 'to do'. The lack of framing of the texts on the resource cupboards can be seen as a visual connection between the texts and the contents of the cupboards (Figure 4.3). The teacher, Susan, said of these texts that they are '…the things I used to forget'.

The use of colour serves to connect and disconnect texts in the room: curriculum is in a range of blues, and instructions are in red. The red frame around the entire collection of student texts indicates that they are a set. The use of red to frame the work of the students and the teacher's instructions on writing in the classroom that are displayed above the whiteboard serve to connect the ongoing activity of the classroom. Colour and physical location are signs that position the displayed work of students in a particular relation to the English curriculum.

The teacher's combination of colour, framing, size, materiality and position serves to make the teacher-produced texts more prominent than those made by the students. The size, double-framing and colour collocation of the teacher-texts and their salient position in the classroom give importance to the 'official' curriculum in the classroom (Figure 4.4).

Discussion

The Springton School English department (of which this classroom is a typical teaching room) is preoccupied, and not without reason, in getting students, mainly from ethnic minorities, to perform well in GCSE exams. It thus assumes that it has to privilege a particular version of 'official knowledge'. In the process it conveys to students that they are the sort of people who need a basic level of assistance to cope with assessment demands. It provides in this sense an example of a strategy for distributing what is 'cultural capital' in what are seen – in both economic and cultural terms – as impoverished places. Distribution, in this context, involves rationing. This is clear in Susan's comments:

> Well it [the student population] is diverse; a lot of students don't read very much at home. That is one of the major things and I think they need quite a lot of support and you couldn't just say 'do this' with any task. Every task has to be broken down – you do lots of tasks to build up what you want to do – maybe in a different type of school I think you would approach – you might get to the text more quickly or something like that.
>
> I suppose at Key Stage 4, unfortunately, it is quite exam orientated. I mean I am, that is what those lessons are about really and I want them to know and understand the poems that they are studying and to be able to kind of also know what they need to do in an exam. I don't really like that but I think I have to do that – that's what my role is.

Susan's use of visual resources and her arrangement of these in the displays of the classroom combine to produce English as a coherent, 'boundaried' and univocal space filled with language. The dominant mode in this classroom is writing: the images of di Caprio, derived from popular culture, are in a very literal sense cut down and tightly framed (Figure 4.4), so that the very thing that appears to have engaged many young people in Luhrmann's filmic reshaping of Shakespeare's play – the display of masculinity (through the use of rap, dress, and imagery of gang fighting) – is the subject of the teacher's critique, and occupies a minor position in a classroom that is a strongly 'boundaried' place – clear, sparse and uncluttered, like the version of English that is produced there.

In this classroom 'What English is' is constituted as a completely explicit entity. The curriculum is displayed, the language of examination is literally written on the walls, the deadlines are clear. The politics of the English curriculum as articulated in this classroom are 'access to language': language is, literally, made available as a resource. English is about competence in written language. The pedagogy is about the politics of equality of access. There is no wavering towards the pleasure of the text, or the place of English in the world. In this classroom what English is and how to teach it are certain. The dominant producer is the teacher. The dominant source is the National Curriculum. The content might change, from poetry to popular culture, but the pedagogic frame will not. The desire for explicitness has in this sense made the text an irrelevance.

The visual display of the classroom fits into an instructional genre. Policy in the form of the National Curriculum is selected, condensed and strongly framed. Everything else has vanished. The curriculum is so pervasive that it is difficult to overlay it with anything. This genre of instruction positions the teacher and student in a particular relation to the production of English, beyond the obvious power relation that they are in. The teacher represents English as a series of competencies that the students are to learn – the classroom display reminds them why they are there and why they must work: they are to aim for the teacher's idealized student text.

Wayford School classrooms

Whereas Susan's classroom is typical of all the English classrooms in Springton School, there is no 'typical classroom' in Wayford School and for this reason we discuss separately the classrooms of John and Lizzy (Stephen, as we discussed in the introduction, did not have his own classroom). In the Wayford classrooms, the arrangement of the furniture, the furniture itself, the visual displays, are all quite different. The school has analogous organizational features: Lizzy, John and Stephen all commented that there was no regular meeting of staff, and little sharing of ideas, strategies and teaching plans within the department. When Lizzy was asked about the ethos of the department she commented:

> I think that is the problem: there isn't a coherent ethos … There is a shared ethos, which is about caring for the kids in a very kind of general way, but in terms about an ongoing debate about learning and learning within English and the best way to be planning for that and the strategies to use, it has become

very much each person does their own thing and there is very little coherent discourse. There is not a departmental discourse about that.

The diversity of these classrooms is a material sign of the lack of a departmental ethos in the school. In this context the classrooms are much more clearly the products of the individual teachers than is the case in our previous example. They also serve as a material expression of teacher autonomy and power – a fact negatively highlighted by the case of the classroomless Stephen, whose nomadic situation was a factor in his eventual departure from the school.

John's classroom: English as 'embodied sensibility'

We introduced and discussed John's classroom in Chapter 2, where we were interested in the contradictions and tensions created by the arrangement of the furniture and the teacher's movement in this space. Here we return briefly to these issues before discussing the classroom displays in more detail.

The room is arranged, as shown in Figure 4.5, in two angled rows of grouped tables, each table seating four to five students. The teacher's desk is positioned at the front of these two 'rows' to make a panoptical arrangement.

The arrangement serves to position the teacher as an authoritative figure, able to survey the students. However, the teacher does not teach from this position.

Figure 4.5 Wayford School: Photograph of John's classroom layout (map in Figure 4.6)

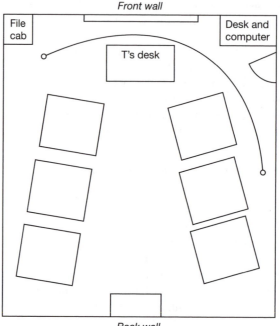

Figure 4.6 John's 'arc of movement' in his classroom

Instead, he repeatedly walks from the left of the door around his desk and to the right in a curve, shown in Figure 4.6, and teaches mainly from a position near to the classroom door.

In doing so he gives up the potential to make direct eye contact with all of the students in the class, half of whom are seated with their backs to him. Unless they turn to face him, which most do not, he has no eye contact with them. Through his movement the teacher 'divides' the classroom space into two kinds of space: the space of the teacher and the space of the students.

The walls of the classroom that correspond with this 'arc' (at the front and beside the door of the classroom) are full of posters of films, art exhibitions, and texts that mark the activity and interest of the teacher. These walls appear over time to have come to 'belong to' the teacher, like a personal pantheon. The display of curriculum and student-made texts occupy other walls in the room. There is no merging of student with teacher texts; they remain distinct much in the same way as they do in Susan's classroom.

A number of art gallery posters, posters of English poetry, an ICT poster, a newspaper article ('paradise in the garden?') and a map of the world are displayed in the space used by the teacher during his teaching. These texts are all made salient by being positioned around the blackboard and in the space of the teacher's activity. In this way importance is given to the sensibility of the teacher, and to 'high' cultural forms. The position of the art gallery and poetry-on-the-tube posters high on the front wall (above the blackboard and the door) frame them as distinct elements – quite literally out of the reach of the students.

Texts related to the official curriculum outnumber other kinds of text displayed in this classroom; however, here these texts relay the curriculum differently from those displayed in the classrooms of Springton School. While in Susan's classroom the curriculum is neatly framed and re-presented to the students as 'things to do', in this classroom, the teacher has not mediated those texts concerned with the National Curriculum for the students. Official government texts include a photocopy of the National Curriculum grade system for all areas of English (literature, reading, and so on). These are displayed in full, detailing the grading criteria and marking code. Texts from official curriculum resources are also displayed, including a Teachers' Resource sheet relating to the analysis of a text, and a page from an official anthology for students about 'explaining the text'. In addition to these photocopied texts two handwritten examination questions are pinned to the board. Teacher-made texts include a series of photographs of students reading – arranged around the pages of the National Curriculum dealing with reading, and a handwritten poster on how to analyse a poem, stuck over the 'criteria for literacy' (Figure 4.7). On other walls there are a few student-made texts, all of them poems. There are several film posters (of mainstream Hollywood and Bollywood) and alongside these there are several articles from magazines and broadsheet newspapers.

While the texts of the official curriculum outnumber the other kinds of text in the classroom, they are made less prominent through their position in the classroom than the texts dealing with art and poetry selected by the teacher. Several kinds of 'official' texts are displayed on the right and back walls of the classroom, placing them in 'the space of the students'. The curriculum is not foregrounded in the way that it is by Susan (in the previous example). In the previous example the teacher is 'fused' with the curriculum – she speaks it, gives voice to it, through all her practices; she herself is backgrounded. In this classroom, the teacher and the official curriculum have different voices; they remain distinct and the teacher's voice remains the most dominant. Having said this, there are only two teacher-made texts: a handwritten A2 sheet on how to analyse a poem, written on sugar paper and *pinned* to the wall, and a series of colour photographs of students working in the classroom. These feature on the right wall (as seen from the door) of the classroom. This is a point in the classroom that serves as a meeting-point between the space of the teacher and the space of the students.

The teacher-made texts are made salient through their size and the use of colour. The sheet on how to analyse poems is placed over the National Curriculum criteria for writing. In effect, the official curriculum is obliterated by this 'poster', and yet the contrast between the shiny permanence of the laminated official curriculum and the dull yellow of the sugar paper serve to create a tension between the two texts that brings both into play. The work of the teacher is displayed as overlaying the curriculum itself. The edges of the curriculum frame this analysis: the curriculum of the teacher, present as his work, is clearly located within the context of the official curriculum, and yet by its positioning it is a challenge to it. A series of photographs of students reading newspapers (Figure 4.7) – leaning over the texts but acknowledging the presence of the photographer – are displayed. These images of students reading in the classroom frame the side and bottom edges of the (EN2) curriculum document on reading. In other words, the images made by the teacher are displayed in such a way that they are seen as being connected to the National Curriculum – almost a realization of it.

The texts produced by the students have least prominence in the whole display. They are few in number, positioned on the right and back wall, they are smaller in size than all others, and show no or little use of colour. They sit quietly amongst the noisy mesh of the texts that are, in one way or another, the teacher's. The students' texts have no teacher commentary. Their location – alongside the photographs of students reading and of the official curriculum on reading – suggests that they are there as a kind of visual evidence of students' reading of such texts. Three student poems are displayed in the classroom (see Figure 4.8). These focus on the issue of identity (two focus on the loss of identity through language, and one on the author's bad behaviour at school). The teacher's selection of these poems makes a link between the student texts and the teacher's selection of articles from broadsheet newspapers displayed. These focus on issues of identity (an article on refugees; 'I wanted her dead', an article on family relations; 'When the lying had to stop', an article on (family) relationships; and 'The men who make home hell', an article on domestic violence. The theme of identity is echoed in the film posters among this display, which juxtapose posters for mainstream Hollywood and Bollywood films. These posters do not relate to film adaptations of texts studied in the curriculum (as was the case in the previously discussed classroom): they connect with the world outside the official English curriculum.

The teacher's framing of the texts in the display creates a physical and visual web of connections between the (official and the teacher's) curriculum and the teacher, between the two curricula and the students, between the teacher and the students, and between the students and popular cultural representation of identities. In this web of texts, the teacher's framing of the three student poems stands out. They are the only texts in the display that are framed by the use of backing-paper rather than by location alone. In other words, they are the only texts that have been framed *for* display rather than *by* display. These framed poems make a 'just visible' link between the order of the front wall and the web of connections on the right and the back wall – maybe suggesting that there is hope after all of realizing the teacher's version of English. Their framing as texts-for-display indicates their status as the products of English in this classroom, indicating their relation to English 'over time' as they become covered and connected in the web of experiences of English here: they are a visual trace of the teacher's idealized process of realizing English.

Just like Susan, in Springton School, John uses the possibilities of spatial arrangement as one means to mediate his sense of English in the classroom. He

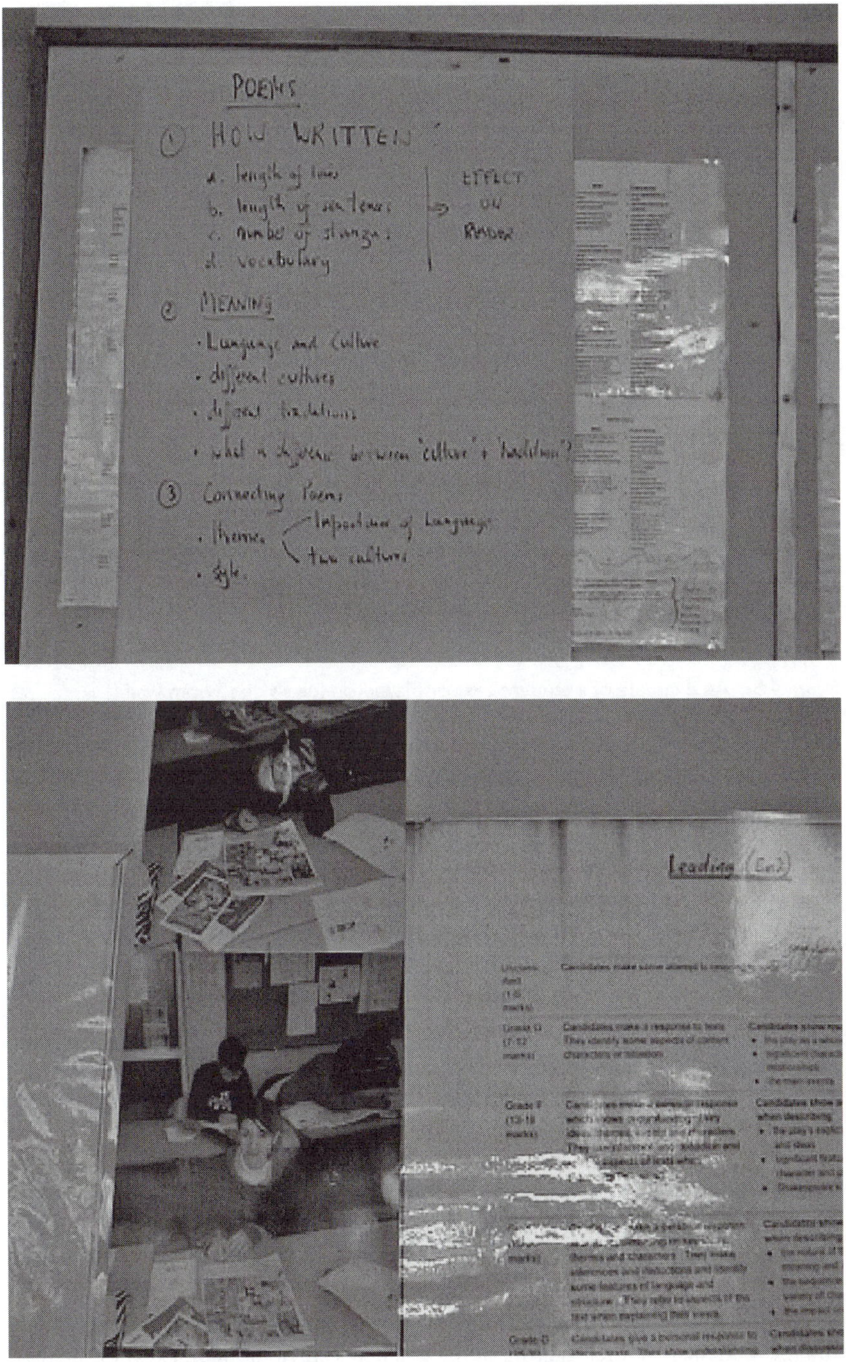

Figure 4.7 Images of the curriculum on John's classroom wall

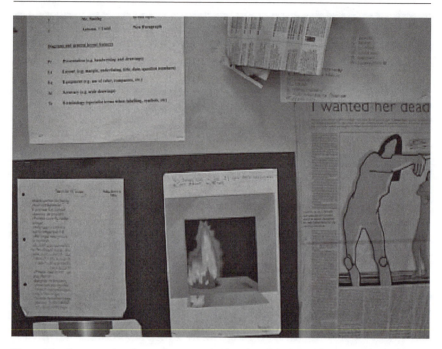

Figure 4.8 An example of a student text displayed on John's classroom wall

does so less through his selection of texts than through the prominence that he accords to his favoured texts, and through the subtle valuations expressed through the connections between the texts. Where in Susan's classroom there is an entire sense of coherence around curriculum (though as we will show in later chapters, this coherence is at times interrupted by some students) in John's classroom there is a loosely established sense of connection, differential valuation, and loose integration. It is English as and through 'bricolage'.

John's signs of English

The visual display and arrangement of John's classroom realizes a different sign of English to that of teachers in Springton School, particularly so in the role of the National Curriculum. Whereas Susan clearly mediated the official discourses of English this is not the case in John's classroom. The fact that all the curriculum criteria are displayed on the classroom walls suggests that this teacher is not interested in selecting, adapting or transforming in some other way the official curriculum: it is, simply, copied, and stands unmediated. The only form of mediation occurs through its location among the other texts, which creates implicit and ambivalent connections between the curriculum and the activity of the teacher and the students. Neither the role of the teacher's curriculum, nor that of the official curriculum is made explicit; both are, quite literally, 'just there', though modally very differently there. Official policy is present in the classroom but not prominently; it is overlaid with the teacher's sense of English, and the shape of his vision of the conflicts of the students' lived identities with the requirements and the value of schooling, which he expresses when he says: 'English is the only thing at the moment [in the National Curriculum] that really focuses on the nature of how to get anywhere in society – it isn't a question of just getting a grade.'

The texts displayed on the different walls of John's classroom realize two signs of English. The two signs of English are located in different spaces in the classroom. The first sign, English as high culture, is located on the front wall and round to the side of the door (on the right wall). Our observations, and our analysis of the video data, show that this area of the classroom is the 'primary space' for the teacher in this classroom. The second sign, English as a web of references to identity and curriculum, is located on the right and back walls – the walls that 'surround' the students. There is a sense that the students are positioned as engaging with texts but not as producing them. The work of English is engagement primarily with written texts, all texts. This fits well with John's comment on the role of English: 'The main thing we deal with through the stories is to do with the relationship between parent and children or adults and children and there is another theme that goes through the other stories to do with becoming an adult, realizing what the world is like, kind of thing.'

There are several posters on the windows along the left side of the classroom; they are curriculum related (Shakespeare, for example) and appear to act as potential mediators between the two signs of English. The two signs together form a complex third sign: 'English as a perspective on life; English as a position in life'. The display on the walls of the classroom can be read as the means for a transformative journey toward English culture. This journey starts with a newspaper article about the experience of refugees; it links that to the English curriculum via student engagement with questions of identity through reading and writing, through an understanding of film, and the analysis of all texts. This journey leads to Shakespeare and to higher education, to travel in the world (the map of the world), engagement with English poetry and art. English is life and therefore school English is about the students developing an understanding of what parts of life should be attended to.

Wayford had a low rate of achievement in examinations, together with a high truancy rate and severe behaviour-management problems. It had a high percentage of students on free school meals – a crude indicator of income – and a higher percentage of students who had English as another language. In the classes that we observed there was a lot of truancy. These problems greatly concerned John, and shaped his idea of the purposes of English:

I have done the hippy bit. I have done waiting six months for the child to be ready to write ... this was in Australia in the 70s with 100 per cent employment and they could afford to waste their time and there was no national curriculum so we did 'wonderful things' ... [Now] I want children coming in to work, to do their best, to have sense of what their best is. To listen to me when I speak. To listen to each other. To show respect to each other, to me, to the subject. To understand what the assessment is, how you learn to ultimately become independent learners who don't need me. To kind of know how education and learning works and then where it fits in to the scheme of life ... that language is power and knowledge is power – [being] able to use language will get you power of the broadest possible sense – it will get you what you want when you go to a meeting or see somebody – being able to go to a library and use it; being able to speak in the right way at the right time to get your jobs. It comes down to that. Power is the main thing. That is what I teach. How to get power.

Alongside this backdrop of the potential of English to empower students, John's pedagogic strategy is one of high authority and control as we have seen; they are present in his comments on his pedagogic style:

I use a combination of being very very hard and very very nice. I use charm a lot. I also use raw naked power ... I have order in the classroom. Everything is clear. There is no discussion, argument, whatever. This is how it is and if you don't do it that way you are out. You are on time, you sit where I tell you to sit and take your coats off ... The weight of a school is always greater than any child.

I have just started doing points and the thing is it is essentially based on reward but it is also based on gamble because it is not consistent and so it is even more evil than just giving them a reward because they don't know after a while when they are going to get the points and after a while they don't care anyway.

Alongside this focus on authority and behaviour John comments on the need to maintain a 'sense of excellence' and to identify and foster the 'talent' of students:

If they are dropping out a lot I don't want them there and I make it difficult so that they either come regularly or they don't come. I know that is not the solution for them but it might be the solution for the others. I would prefer to have 18 or 20 students being as successful as they can be than 15 being successful because I am spending too much time with the people who aren't coming ... It's kind of recognising, really recognising, talent when you see it and that is something you actually have to go out and look for a bit because it is easy not to see.

Stepping outside the immediate frame of our project, we might see in this teacher's practices the response to the deep contradictions that mark contemporary society, so well described in the writings of commentators on contemporary social life (such as Beck 1992): the wish for order and authority, for clear ethical and aesthetic frames, matched with a recognition of the ever-increasing individuation of humans brought by the harshly insistent demands of the new forms of the economy, of the market in its present form. We have no doubt that this teacher wishes to do what is best for the students in his class, as in her very different way does the teacher in our first classroom. Both are faced with irreconcilable tensions, conflicts, contradictions beyond the school; each attempts to do what each sees as professionally and ethically possible and necessary. In this classroom two strong discourses are present as a resource for dealing with these momentous problems. One is the older discourse of stable ethics and a settled aesthetics, of the development of an individual with a certain 'sensibility'. The other discourse is the new, the more recent governmental discourse of English as a powerful tool in the shaping of new subjectivities fit for the new economy, marketed as the road to authority, power and participation.

Lizzy's classroom: English and the life worlds of students

In terms of visual display and spatial arrangement, Lizzy's classroom differs significantly from John's room, from other classrooms we saw in Wayford School and, in fact, from all of the classrooms in our study. Nonetheless, her room (Figure 4.9) was clearly recognizable as an English classroom to the research team and doubtless to others.

Lizzy's classroom literally 'stands apart' from the others in the school. Physically it is positioned at the end of the playground, reached by leaving the main school building and walking about 100 metres across the playground, through a wire-fenced 'basketball' area, to a stand-alone building, which houses both a sports area and this classroom. On the outside walls of the building the teacher has set up a graffiti wall, which the students have painted on. Lizzy told us that she had deliberately chosen the location of her classroom: 'I grabbed that west wing when nobody else wanted it.'

The majority of texts on display in the classroom are posters from the domain of popular culture – music, film and television, in particular cable television. Posters of musicians are taken from across a youth music spectrum, including rap (for example Tupac, Eminem) and rock (Kurt Cobain) alongside the ubiquitous boy-band (Blue). The film posters are of horror films, kung-fu, action films and comedies, several of which have an 18 certificate and could therefore not legally be seen by the students in the class. There are many posters of characters from the television series *Buffy the Vampire Slayer*, the spin-off *Angel*, and classic series such as *Friends* and *The Simpsons*. These posters are representations of the (teacher's sense of) the 'world' of the students outside of the classroom. They create a highly visual environment, in full colour, large and 'loud', with references that go outside the traditional range of texts of English. In Lizzy's classroom these posters are salient through their number, their size and their placement.

Students' texts are also on display; the two texts described below are typical. In the first, the students have imported images of actors, singers, and fashion models from magazines to represent the different characters from *Macbeth* (Figure 4.10).

Figure 4.9 Wayford School: Lizzy's classroom layout

Figure 4.10   Student texts displayed in Lizzy's classroom

The images are arranged on the page to classify them in relation to one another. Each image has a written label with the name of the character it represents in a gothic font. In the second text an image of Eminem is placed next to the written question, 'Would the bad boy Eminem make a good boyfriend?'. The student has then labelled the elements of the question 'verb', 'object' and 'subject'.

Texts such as these are displayed all around the classroom. Through these texts English is displayed as produced by the students at the point where English interacts with (engages with) their life worlds. For example, in the work on classic

English texts (for example *Macbeth*, *View from a Bridge* and *Son's Veto*) the students engage with the characters via images of pop stars, supermodels, and TV stars from popular culture. In these texts English is not an annotation of popular culture, in order to foreground the curriculum (as we argued was the case in Susan's classroom). In Lizzy's classroom popular culture survives the engagement with school English, and is a part of its realization: English is about people, about relations, and about the social.

There are a few curriculum texts on display: a model examination script, and the criteria for grades. The teacher's transformation of the curriculum is realized through her repositioning of curriculum texts among a web of student and popular culture texts (as in the case of John's classroom). However, the web of texts that Lizzy creates as 'English' is very different from John's. There is no one wall for the display of students' texts, nor is one wall given over for the display of teacher texts. This use of framing realizes a visual 'equality' between the texts. The curriculum is not framed as being of more value or more connected to what English is than, for example, a poster showing Eminem or the poster for the film *The Spy Who Shagged Me*. The teacher does not use framing as a semiotic device to demand or realize connections between the texts on display. Instead she presents the texts as belonging to English through their location in the English classroom. The work of making the connections, selections and relations between texts is left open to the students.

The meshing of different kinds of texts in this classroom is reflected in Lizzy's arrangement of furniture in the classroom. The furniture is arranged to create a fluid space that is not marked into areas of teacher and student activity. The teacher has bought soft furnishings into her classroom: a carpet, several soft swivel chairs, a soft armchair, and a sofa – creating a home-like space in her classroom. She regularly reorganized the furniture and desks in the room, and the arrangements were always non-symmetrical. She used open areas, semi-open classrooms, 'flexible' furniture, and multiple spaces for learning.

Lizzy's classroom as a sign of English

The furniture and spatial arrangement of the classroom can, we want to suggest, be seen as an example of the organization of the 'progressive primary school' finding its way into secondary-school English and redefining the place to learn and the future of the school (Stuebing 1995). Lizzy commented on the need for students to have ownership of the classroom space, the need for opportunities both to 'feel safe' and 'feel challenged' and the need for students to have some control of the process of grouping: 'If it is all just teacher-dominated grouping I am not quite sure what the educational value is for students who actually have to learn how to manage relationships in later life without someone telling them how to do it.'

Lizzy's 'design' of her classroom can also be seen as a rejection of formal secondary-school arrangements and an attempt to create a learning environment in which the curriculum is, as she commented, 'only a small part of what is actually going on within the whole learning experience':

The curriculum of the whole learning experience is much more to do with being the child whatever age you are and the potential adult that you are and the kind of human being that you are and what you have therefore brought to the classroom ... the process of being a learner and how you then bring that to what you are being offered in an English classroom ... you are responding and being sensitive to what is going on actually over two years ... most of my students I work with over a two-year period, then the results in the end are infinitely better than if you have that immediate what looks like a very positive response but actually is quite limited and the students may then never achieve what they are capable of and some students may never achieve really at all.

The home furnishings of Lizzy's classroom – the sofa, carpet, and pop posters – and the location of the classroom all serve to distance it from the school as an institution. This serves to construct the classroom (and by implication 'school English') as a 'pseudoliminal' space that is neither school nor 'out of school', bordering on the style of a 'teenager's room'.

Lizzy's choice of students' texts for display serves to reconstruct the relationship between writing and text within the domain of school English. In contrast to Susan's use of popular culture as a visual annotation of aspects of the English curriculum, Lizzy has reframed English as popular culture (and in doing so she has reframed popular culture as English). In short her visual display serves to position English and popular culture as interconnected forms of 'knowledge'. The meanings of popular culture are foregrounded and the position of English in this is backgrounded. The display shapes the relationship of popular culture (media) and English as a more traditional set of texts and work on language into a new form that reflects Lizzy's current notion of school English and literacies:

I think it [school English] is very much about literacies and that is it is about ... different ways of reading the world and reading the text ... I would define that [literacies] in a very kind of broad way and that is quite a neat one because you can use that to apply to so many different situations ... I suppose the core it is about using, studying and learning how to use language to make meaning and ways of using language to make meaning.

Her focus on popular culture and image also relates to Lizzy's sense and knowledge of her students. She commented on 'the mess of learning' and the need to appeal to the 'different learning styles' of students, including those who are more confident in visual than linguistic representation, especially in the context of what she describes as a very mixed-ability class:

It is mixed ability in terms of experience of English, if you like, or experience of being in school and ability, of being able to manage the expectation of being in the classroom. On that level it is very mixed ability. It is mixed ability in terms of language, linguistic ability, certainly mixed ability in terms of what kind of product they can come out with. It is also very mixed in terms of ability to negotiate relationships with me, with each other and then also in terms of preferred learning styles.

The sign – or complex of signs – realized via the visual display of Lizzy's classroom is one of English as a space in which to collect the life worlds of students – not to mention that of the teacher, present in the form of kung-fu posters. Here the world of popular culture is pervasive, and the curriculum is laid over it – gently, offering the students a filter of 'school English' for viewing this everyday world in another way. The mesh of references on display is not placed in any hierarchical order through their position in the classroom, nor through the use of colour, size, framing devices, or lamination. There is no narrative journey mapped through them as we suggest is the case in John's classroom. Instead there is a dynamic between the texts and the frame of 'English classroom'. The question 'what is English?' is raised and the role suggested to students is one of determining how to explore such a question in relation to the artefacts of their worlds. For Lizzy, English is about communication in a 'whole range of literacies' and the process of learning that underpins this process:

> I think part of learning is that learning about your learning and being able to … evaluate and take risks and to plan for the next step and to consolidate what you have learnt and to link it with other things you have learnt, all those aspects – and also to start to grasp conceptually ideas to do with literature, to do with poetry or whatever aspect of the syllabus it is but it is not just about learning mechanical skills. It is clearly an intellectual conceptual development and so it is all those aspects of learning which I have talked about in the context of the English classroom … That is where you need to build up this reflective and consciousness aspect of the learning.

Irene's classroom in Ravenscroft School: English as the means for 'having your say in the world'

At Ravenscroft School, as at Springton, the English classrooms adhere to a similar model and we therefore focus on the description of one classroom, Irene's, which is typical of the school's classrooms. We argue that the coherent character of the English department in Ravenscroft School stands behind the similarity of the classrooms. Departmental meetings are regular and most of the English department have worked together as a team for over ten years. In interviews, teachers advanced very similar conceptions of their work.

In Irene's classroom (introduced in Chapter 2) as in the other classrooms in Ravenscroft School, single desks are arranged in three neat rows, with the teacher's desk at the front-centre of the classroom (Figure 4.11).

The texts on display in the classroom originate from a number of sources and they include the students' work, posters publicizing fiction, poetry, and a reading campaign.

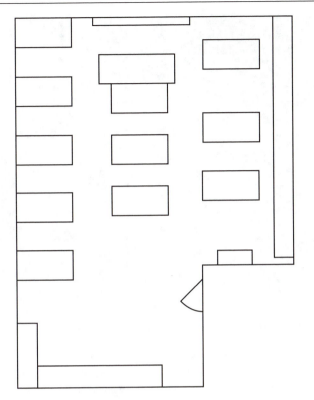

Figure 4.11 Ravenscroft School: Irene's classroom layout

Unlike the displays discussed in the classrooms of Springton and Wayford, no official National Curriculum documents are displayed (such as copies of the grade criteria that appear in each of the other classrooms). The National Curriculum is not displayed directly in the classroom; nonetheless it is present in the teacher's organization of the displays. In these displays, made by Irene, there are two large titles that are arranged in the centre: 'wide reading' and 'NEAB English and English literature' (Figure 4.12); these titles mediate the National Curriculum. The selection of poems on display (Stevie Smith, John Agard, and so on) relate to the anthology for English and the National Curriculum. As in Lizzy's classroom, the teacher-made texts are few; it is Irene's arrangement, creation of titles and framing of the texts on display that is the main evidence of the teacher's activity in relation to the classroom displays.

Most of the displays in Irene's classroom include visual references – in the form of posters – to contemporary fiction. These include novels by Steven King *The Girl who Loved Tom Gordon* and *Hearts in Atlantis*, Fiona Walker's *Kiss Chase* and *French Relations*, John Nicol's *Stinger*, and Maya Angelou *I Know Why the Caged Bird Sings* (Figure 4.13). The books selected for display are books that in Irene's

Figure 4.12 The curriculum as displayed in Irene's classroom

opinion relate to the students' interests and are also central to her and more broadly the department's view of the role of reading and literature. Each of the posters is surrounded by texts written by the students in response to the themes of the novel.

The salient displays are those of students' texts framed by the curriculum headings (Figure 4.12). These are the largest displays, and use a strong yellow background with red and black frames. All of the student texts are strongly framed for display and arranged in a firmly rectangular manner. The careful framing of every text on display presents each one as a 'thing in and of itself' – a product of student labour. On one of these boards the positioning of the student word-processed texts in a downward diagonal line creates a strong sense of dynamic movement, which connects these texts to a published poem. In two displays the student texts are framed by a heading drawn from the National Curriculum, positioned at the centre-top of the board. The headings themselves are framed by the teacher's use of borders and the texts on display. The yellow background of the display board connects the collection of texts as a group – a device for providing coherence. The strong framing serves to echo in this classroom the English curriculum classification of *literature* and *reading* as discrete modules.

Irene's classroom as a sign of English

The classroom arrangement and furniture in Irene's classroom is 'traditional' – a tradition that is most typically associated with transmission pedagogy, high teacher authority and low student participation. However, while Irene maintains her

Figure 4.13 Literature displays on the wall of Irene's classroom

pedagogic authority within the class she encourages the students to participate in debate very actively and encourages them to challenge her. In doing so, the students often 'slouch', lying across their desks. In a sense – as we discussed in Chapter 3 – through their body posture they challenge this sign of a pedagogic tradition that the teacher has established in the classroom. We think that the creation of an environment in which 'tradition' can be challenged and 'authority' questioned is the pedagogic strategy of this teacher; it is part of her pedagogy of English.

Irene's framing of the students' texts by the headings drawn from the National Curriculum can be read as a sign of the organizing influence of the official curriculum within the classroom. Yet while the curriculum is present in the work of the teacher, it is not foregrounded by her, either in her teaching or in the display, as Irene comments in interview:

> What it [the National Curriculum] does is to make it more explicit – you do these things anyway but it is not ... put in this formalised way ... in terms of mapping the curriculum, it is a better approach in my opinion. Initially we felt, because a lot of people were panicking at the time, that this was something new and it really wasn't until later on as we implemented [it] that we realised that this wasn't new, it is what we had been doing.

The displays, in particular the posters on display (Figure 4.14), provide a connection to the popular culture of the students, but it is more restrained, and with clearer boundaries than those surrounding the use of the images of popular culture in Lizzy's classroom. By contrast, here popular culture is clearly framed in the context of English, in a manner that maintains both the centrality of writing and reading, and the focus on 'valued literature'.

A key priority of this English department is to improve the students' writing skills – to 'develop writers'. The orientation of the displays in Irene's classroom is towards 'production'. Through the visual displays the students in this classroom are positioned as 'emergent authors' with the potential to publish. From this perspective, English is about learning to write for expression, *and* for future publication. The arrangement of novels and students' texts in the displays reinforces both the priority given to writing in the English department, and the curricular focus on the production of a personal response to a text. Both of these were key themes in the lessons we observed and were highlighted by Irene as central to what English is:

> They [the students] too must have a kind of viewpoint. It doesn't matter what, Shakespeare, it is not the be all and end all, if everybody has a view, so a personal response. In a sense really you have given them, ultimately you have given them, it is literature, it is in a sense a window through which they view that world. You see because they are not able and they are of a young age to participate in the things they are reading about, it gives them some insight. It is personal development and intellectual development as well. It is the world really, they are looking [through] the window because they are young and therefore we are trying to prepare them, something for that world, something that they possibly might encounter later in life.

The importance of writing in Ravenscroft School is not linked to the (official) curriculum alone; Irene links it also to the social situation of the students, who come from a variety of social backgrounds and experiences.

For all the students writing is a key issue. No matter how engaged they are in the activities you see in the classroom, the writing is that which they are examined through, and so we embrace all those wonderful things, but we feel that we have to work in their favour and that is what society expects of the students and we must prepare them – because they are citizens and we are turning out a whole rather than pieces, we have to look at when they leave here, what they leave with. So for a child to be seen as able, [it] is the writing that is taken into consideration so that is going to be and has been for a number of years our main priority. How do we make these students writers? It is important because we are talking about a subtly class divided society where our children in the past... Take a school like this one, they would not have been able to structure a letter in the way it should because people were, so to speak, only concerned with their creativity and it was nice to read an imaginative story – but could a child punctuate? Could a child spell? ... All those are possible political issues but at the end of the day we have to look at it from a child's, student's point of view, parents, and prepare them for that wider world.

The connection between student texts and published works is prominent in each aspect of display in Irene's classroom. The students' texts are displayed alongside published material (publicity posters, book covers, and poems), and at the same time, their work frames each of the published works of fiction or poetry. In the other classrooms that we have discussed in this chapter there is not that same meshing of published works and student texts that we see in this school. English as it is displayed here is essentially about the students' work in *reading*, reflected in their *writing*, in *responding* to the written model texts. As Irene commented:

For any child to learn, to pick up a story and you want them to read this story – why do I want them to read a story? Why should they read this story anyway? So you have to therefore make it relevant to these children's experience. What is the purpose? Either I want them to model their own writing. If they write a story you can look at the particular writing that they have read, model their writing. Have this sense of achievement because there is a story I've written, it, it is imaginative, it is engaging. For them in terms of sense of purpose it is a sense of achievement, so that is one aspect. The other is, as I said, for them to be able to use it as a tool. It is a tool in today's world. They have to be able to understand how things are put together and see inside. If you take that into it rather than around something because they are authors themselves. It's a craft. So what you are trying to get them to do is create something. Not just eyeing other people's creation but to say 'they have put a short story like this together; how do you put a short story together?' I think that is where I am with English but when I see it is a tool creating something, if you are giving a viewpoint and you are making an audience, this is your tool.

As we have said, the classroom displays in Ravenscroft School are oriented towards 'production'. Through the visual displays the students are positioned as emergent authors who have the potential to publish. English is about learning to write for expression and for future publication. English is the means for having 'a say' in the world.

Conclusion

We have shown how the visual displays and spatial arrangements of the English classroom can be understood as multimodal signs of English. In particular we have attempted to show how these signs of English are socially shaped by and intimately connected to a range of factors. These factors include the teacher's view of learning and of English, their perception of the students, social forces, histories and demands that operate on the school and the English department, and their relationship to governmental policy (for example in the form of the National Curriculum). The displays and arrangements of the classroom feature in the production of English in different ways, and we will return to this in other chapters. The displays and arrangements, like any other resource made available, constitute constraints and possibilities for meaning-making, and, like all resources, how they are taken up and used varies with teachers, students, and instances of teaching.

We think that the multimodal way of looking enables us to see some of the spaces in which 'school English' resides that other approaches might not. Our approach more widely is to show how these resources serve to position students to curriculum, to school knowledge and to one another in particular ways, to show the link between policy and practices in English. We want our insights to have practical effects, and so we hope that this way of looking helps teachers to think about how they construct or might be able to transform their own classroom as a learning environment. Our examples show that there are many ways to construct the relationship between the formal curriculum and student cultures, that despite the heavy pressure of regularization of English the potential for alternative positions and commitments remains.

Chapter 5

The organization of time in the English classroom

A brief history of (school) time

The organization of time is a central aspect of the work of the school, as it is of other social institutions. But its centrality does not imply homogeneity: the processes of schooling do not all follow an identical tempo. On the contrary it is possible to devise a typology of educational time that is highly variegated, from the relatively long timescales of child and learner development, to the short-term objectives of lessons. Moreover, time is contested, at many levels; and different social interests propose and implement different strategies and practices for its use. The contests and overlaps that result from such differences feature constantly in the organization of classrooms. The production of English, like that of any other school subject, involves a particular combination of imperatives and resistances, resources and constraints, regulation and agency that cluster around the use of time. In this chapter we explore the relationship between policy time, teacher time, and students' time. In the process, we try to show how the systems of time-organization established by policy have a substantial effect on the time-practices of English lessons. But we also suggest that the relationship between teacher time and policy time is not simply one of conflict.

We can begin with the time of policy – a time that is strongly influenced and shaped by policy-makers' responses to the rhythms of economic activity. In *The Condition of Postmodernity*, David Harvey discusses – as many others have done – the acceleration of economic and social life characteristic of the late twentieth century, where 'capitalism ... has been characterised by continuous efforts to shorten turnover times, thereby speeding up social processes while reducing the time horizons of meaningful decision-making' (1989: 229). Harvey also points out that this tendency towards acceleration has encountered many obstacles – from the costs of replacing fixed investments in plant and machinery, to the resistance of workers and consumers to changes in established patterns of life. In response to such problems, writes Harvey, 'there is a whole history of technical and organiza-tional innovation ... everything from assembly-line production ... to electronic banking' (1989: 229). But close to the heart of any programme of acceleration are attempts – as we suggested in the previous chapter – to enhance the 'adaptability and flexibility' of workers through the destruction of old skills and the inculcation of new ones. Such attempts are particularly intense in periods when there is a crisis of profitability, of the sort that Harvey argues has been in place for much of the post-1976 period.

Extrapolating from Harvey, we might identify three consequences of accelerated economic rhythms for education systems. First, these systems are pulled towards the centre of economic life. In fast-changing times, where profitability is a constant problem, employers cannot themselves train an 'employable' workforce, whose skills are generic and transferable rather than unique to one sector or workplace; nor do they wish to bear the costs of prolonged training. Instead, the function of ever more prolonged and in some respects more complex forms of education and training is shifted to schools and colleges, and at the same time the performance of education in raising some kinds of skill level becomes a focus of policy-making and of political debate. Second, the time horizons of educational change are compressed. Rapid and continuous change becomes the norm. Policy objectives need to be realized quickly; 'innovation' follows hectically upon 'innovation'. The third consequence is that the work of teachers is transformed. Harvey writes evocatively of a 'process of "creative destruction" which rests on the forced devaluation or destruction of past assets in order to make way for the new' (1989: XXX), and his insight could be transferred from the analysis of balance-sheets to the study of schools.

There are several elements to this process of transformation in the area of teaching and learning, and in most of them questions of time are important. Here we deal with four. First, school managements have been enabled – through legislation and training – to win new powers over the use of teachers' time. The 1987 Pay and Conditions Act, which defined the extent of teachers' working hours, and enforced their attendance at times required by management, was the starting-point of such change. Second, in the 1990s, a stipulative National Curriculum, and a comprehensive system of testing and league tables, transformed the work of teachers, so that the relationship between the 'events' of the lesson, the formal objectives of the curriculum and the certificated outcomes of schooling became closer. At the same time the effects of the teacher's work have become measurable. Third, the same causes have produced an intensification of teachers' work – not just a lengthening of the working day, but the creation of an instititutionalized consciousness of the need to maximize the 'efficient' use of time. The seminal *Fifteen Thousand Hours* (Rutter *et al.* 1979), inspiration of the school effectiveness movement, was significant for its alertness in this respect. The modularization of the school curriculum – influenced by the Hargreaves report (*Improving Secondary Schools*, ILEA 1984) and generalized through the National Curriculum after 1988, was a further incitement to teachers to focus on the productivity of specific units of time. In the 1990s, Campbell and Neill's concept of 'evaporated time' (1990) – lesson time lost through routine non-pedagogic activity – was another indicator of the anxieties that surrounded time-use. The National Literacy Strategy (1998) in primary schools – and the Literacy Framework, which was just edging its way into secondary schools at the time our research was finishing –

carried the specification of time-use by national policy to a new level of detail.

Fourth and finally, we should note the ways in which the teacher's time outside the classroom – the time of preparation, assessment and administration – came, in the 1990s, to be strongly and directly shaped by policy. Preparing lessons, marking work, recording progress – all were carried out in relation to national criteria, and in this sense extra-classroom time was as much subject to guidance and regulation as time spent with pupils. The effects of this change on ideas and practices of professionalism, and on the traditional notion of autonomous professional space, need noting.

These processes have reshaped the 'time-organization' of schooling. By 'time-organization', we refer to the ways in which policy at national and institutional level establishes a template for the use of time by schools. But as we have argued elsewhere in the book, we cannot assume that policy is in any easy sense directly and immediately reflected in schools. Schools are, as it were, deeply 'located' places. They are sites of fixed investment, for instance, whose architecture imposes constraints on any sudden reorganization of time and space. More importantly for our argument, they are social places, where particular habits, cultures, values and traditions have developed to the point where they exercise, for better or worse, a considerable inertial force and are not susceptible to sudden change. Most obviously, many of the governmentally generated processes described above have provoked resistance, which took its most spectacular form in the testing boycott of 1993/94. There has also been a continuous conflict over workload, pursued through union resolutions and occasional local action.

There is much material here to support Harvey's claim that the acceleration of economic processes intensifies 'struggles … over the use of time and the intensity of labour' (1989: 234). But one should also note less visible responses. For instance, the high rate of resignation among teachers could also be understood as a form of critical response to pressures of time and restrictions on autonomy. In addition, as we discuss at several points below, teachers respond to the time-demands of policy in many ways, most of which entail some kind of adaptation, resistive or otherwise, of templates of time-organization to local circumstance and history. In discussing the classroom-level production of English we need therefore to use a term capable of registering these multiple perspectives and conflicts – hence our employment below of 'time-practices' rather than the more unilateral 'time-organization' to describe time-related events in the realization of the subject.

David Harvey's discussion, like ours, owes much to the argument of E.P. Thompson's classic study 'Time, work-discipline and industrial capitalism' (1991 [1965]), with its dense exploration of the relationship between new systems of time-measurement, and the subjective, 'lived' experience of time by factory workers and managers. Thompson is insistent that the 'new time' of the factory was created through struggle and active discipline, rather than through some form of consensual arrangement. He writes not only of the formation of new labour habits but of the 'imposition' of a new time-discipline among workers. It would be tempting to apply the terms of his argument to contemporary schooling, and to speak of the new time-organization being imposed on teachers and students. Certainly, this is what other researchers have argued. Linda Evans and her colleagues, writing of the early impact of the 1988 reforms on the work of infant teachers, identify a felt 'loss of control over time', and an experience of 'forced redirection' and 'reduced autonomy' (Evans *et al*. 1994: 131). But such a claim, though insightful, does not fully capture the complexity of current developments. There is certainly much evidence that teachers respond to the new time-order with disquiet, even as they accommodate themselves to its rhythms. But we should not overlook a range of much more positive responses – responses that become apparent when we consider the ways in which teachers understand and *narrativize* recent educational history. We take narrativization to be a 'second-level' form of time-organization. If the first level consists of the material systems of resources and constraints that organize life-courses and create schedules and rhythms of work, then narrativization consists of the ways in which social actors make sense of these systems, and place themselves within them. This 'second level' process feeds back, of course, to the first level: the ways in which people understand their location in time – in everyday terms, and in terms of career and history – have an effect on the time-practices they develop.

In narrativizing their work, teachers draw from a potent repertoire of public discourse. New Labour has created its own way of periodizing historical time. For much of its existence the Labour Party, like the wider labour movement, has celebrated its distinguished forebears ('our martyred dead' and so on), and tended to trace back a line from the reforming present to its antecedents in previous decades. In this kind of narrative, continuity is the central feature. But since the mid-1990s, through work such as that of Michael Barber (1996), a much more sceptical attitude to past achievements has developed, and with it a narrative that emphasizes breaks and contrasts more than continuities. Ken Jones, discussing the 2001 Green Paper *Schools Building on Success*, summarizes Labour's new understanding of educational history: '[According to Labour] the governments of Attlee and Wilson – like the Tory regimes sandwiched in between – presided over a largely "unskilled" working population which had possessed "jobs for life" in local industries ... An undynamic economy produced a school system in its own image. In the supposedly static society of 1944–76 there was no strong demand for certification and there was a "general acceptance that only a minority would reach the age of 16 with formal skills and qualifications"' (Jones 2003a).

Comprehensive reform had not done enough to challenge this acceptance and by setting 'social' as opposed to 'economic' goals – emphasising egalitarianism at the expense of standards – it had contributed to stasis. Over-reacting to the failings of the eleven-plus exam, and dominated by the 'ideology of unstreamed teaching' (Blair 1996: 175), it had failed to differentiate among students and to 'link different provision to individual attitudes and abilities' (Jones 2001: 5). One of the results was mass illiteracy; another, relatively slow rates of economic growth.

New Labour places these ills on the far side of the historical chasm that separates it from the past. On the near side are those objectives that Blair's government works towards, and the new kinds of social agency that will achieve them. Thus, 'standards' supplants egalitarianism, 'differentiation' drives out 'mixed-ability teaching' – and new, purposeful and managerially determined school cultures replace the fragmented landscapes created by professional autonomy. It is on the basis of such a narrative of past and present that New Labour can describe its own project as one of modernization, and describe the cultures of teaching that developed in the decades after 1944 as 'forces of conservatism' (Blair 1999).

For many teachers, this omnipresent narrative of progress creates a sense of having been by-passed by the current development of policy – and devalued too. Yet it is undeniable that there are others who accept New Labour's account, and see the changes of the 1990s as providing new kinds of skill, support and collegiality, in contrast with a past practice understood as uninformed, undirected and based more on individual preference than on collective approaches. Returning to Harvey's motif of 'creative destruction', we can therefore speak not just of the dismantling of previous forms of work-community, but of the sponsored growth of new ones. Certainly, in the schools we researched, there was strong evidence for the existence of a commitment to the new, and of an approval of modernization, with the capacity to cope with its intensity and pressure understood as a source of self-worth. Teachers thus tended in some sense to endorse New Labour's periodization and narrativization, to accept the basic features of its system of time-organization and to develop different forms of time-practice in their own classrooms – akin to the 'new labour habits' and the 'new time discipline' of which Thompson speaks – and we will explore the nuances of this below.

Time and the production of English

In this area of our research we pursue two sets of questions, both intended to explore further the social shaping of classroom English. The first set consists of questions such as 'How is the organization of time materialized in the production of English?', 'How is the relationship between policy time, teacher time and student time configured?', 'What time-practices thus result?' At the same time as we explore these questions, we attempt to address others that relate to the explanation of such time-practices in social terms.

As with all our explorations, the conclusions we arrive at are framed in plural terms: there is no single form of time-organization, and no single category of agent, that exercises a determining influence on the time-practices of the classroom. Nevertheless, we can speak of more and less powerful shaping factors, even though the balance between them alters from school to school, and their presence – as motivator, as 'bad object' – varies from department to department.

In several senses, teachers to whom we spoke in Wayford School expressed a sense of time that was at odds with the time-organization preferred by policy. The central difference concerned understandings of the relationship between time and learning. Teaching, for instance, was evoked by one teacher as a process of learning – developing or shifting over time – in response to personal inquiry and engagement rather than to a policy agenda: 'every year I have a different idea; that is what is so fascinating about it … I think I do just keep on changing' (Stephen). At the same time, teachers were keenly and contrastingly aware of the ways in which their work related to historical shifts in the management of teaching by government. At one important level, these were perceived as shifts for the worse:

> I should be able to do what I want with them as long as – I think I do have a responsibility for them with exams and with getting qualifications. That is obviously part of it. But within that I think I have – a part of that responsibility is that the Authority and the parents should have faith in me in me that I can do all that, juggle all that and obviously what the National Curriculum attempts to do I think is to take away that faith a little bit and say 'Well, people need to be accountable, we need to prove this person is doing this and this', whereas I would say that a system in which teachers are given all sorts of training and resources and help in order to have that freedom is a far better thing than where all that time, energy, money whatever goes into telling us what to do.
>
> (Stephen, Wayford School)

Likewise, another teacher at the school, Lizzy, whose classroom was very different from any other we entered, talked about the different time-orientation of her preferred ways of teaching, contrasting them implicitly but unfavourably with the module-based approach that organizes the work of many departments:

> Q: You see it as sort of building up a sort of learning environment?
> A: Definitely, and I think the way I work is not short term. The short-term results often look quite chaotic and quite negative sometimes, because I think learning is really messy. I think good learning often looks really messy … and you have to have to have the confidence and trust that if you keep on giving the reassurance and support, and also assessing what is going on, and where necessary putting in more structure if that it what is needed … then the results in the end are infinitely better than if you have that immediate what looks like a very positive response but actually is quite limited, and the students may then never achieve what they are capable of and some students may never achieve really at all. (Lizzy)

In this perspective, the organization of the classroom must relate to the long-term developmental needs of the child: learning time is necessarily elongated. Historically, of course, this is a well-established position, a significant element in progressive educational philosophy, with its emphasis on 'devising the right environment for children' so that they could 'be themselves and develop at the pace appropriate to them' (DES 1967: 187). But it is precisely this position which has become the central focus of attack from anti-progressives (see Jones 1989), and to align oneself with it is to take sides in a historical controversy, to present a particular, heterodox narrative of educational change, to refuse to position oneself unequivocally within the 'modernization' project and to inhabit in terms of one's practice a zone whose reference points are not those of current policy debates.

From such a position, classroom time must be responsive to needs that go beyond the academic – hence Lizzy's use of circle time. Students sit in a large irregular circle, on a mixture of chairs and desks. Some are almost reclining, some sit on chairs that face backwards. Some students comb each other's hair while they sit, such that students arrange themselves at disparate heights. Some choose not to join the circle. Once the circle is more or less constructed the teacher, Lizzy, says she has two reasons for the circle time. The first has to do with reflectiveness – looking backwards in order to go forwards: 'I want you to be thinking back over the lessons last half-term in order to gain the best amount that you can; we need to stop and think from time to time about what we've been doing, why we've been doing it and what we can learn from that to help us with the next bit of work that we do.' The second reason, the teacher is careful to state, arises from examination requirements: 'That's one of the reasons why we're doing this and of course another reason is that as you know all the time I am assessing you and your speaking and listening and this is another brilliant opportunity for assessing those skills ...'

The discussion proceeds. To order the process, the teacher passes round a small Tigger key-ring: students have to hold the key-ring to be able to speak. If they don't want to talk, they can say 'pass'. The overall effect is one of intimacy, of a coming together outside the constraints to which exam-related courses often give rise. As the teacher explains:

> The circle time work that I do with them [in English lessons] is specifically working on the group dynamic, working on relationships and communication and thinking about what kind of choices they might be making and why they are making those choices ... [This has to do with] my understanding of what the learning process is about and it being a mixture of cognitive and emotional, social and individual and that actually if you are not doing that, addressing that, I am not sure how you are planning for learning.
>
> (Lizzy)

What is suggested here, then, is a way of organizing classroom time (and space) that is based less on the requirements of modular stages of curriculum organization than on a long-term creation of what the teacher hopes will be a group of self-motivated – albeit exam-conscious – learners. Transcripts of the lessons show a teaching style related to the paces of individual learning; different students inhabited, as it were, different zones of time and space, working at different speeds and in different parts of the classroom. There was no strong attempt explicitly to organize lessons around examination requirements. Boundaries between teacher-shaped and student-shaped time were weak: students had a considerable role in determining, through choice or 'resistance', when a task had reached its end. So, although the teacher did introduce these requirements she was rather dismissive of them and distanced herself from them, making in some sort a mockery of the forms.

But this apparent defiance of the timescales of the National Curriculum and of examination syllabuses was more complex than an explanation in terms of rejection might suggest. Although the teachers may be sceptical about the official shaping of English, they are at the same time critical of the almost anomic character of their own working situation:

Q: Is there an ethos of the English Department here?
A: I think that is the problem, there isn't a coherent ethos. It is very difficult for me because the thing I spent four years building up I have seen disintegrate ... There is a shared ethos about caring for the kids in a general sort of way but in terms of an ongoing debate about learning, and learning within English ... it has become very much each person does their own thing.

(Lizzy, Wayford School)

And:

There is very little sense of your being in a department and that you are working with colleagues although on a personal level obviously everyone is friendly ... In a way that was very nice because it makes it very easy because you are just left to get on with it on your own and what help and support [there was] was all very informal.

(Stephen, Wayford School)

The department does not, from this perspective, offer an alternative set of resources to those of official policy, and the absence of such collective support contributes to a sense of isolation and decline:

[There is] precious little debate at all. I think there is a lot of feeling that we are under pressure and it is a question of keeping your head down and hanging on and doing what you have to do to survive ... I think that is the problem of working through Ofsted inspections, because we no longer have what we used to have, the teams of advisory teachers maybe building up relationships with schools. It means you are neglected for a long time and then get a big slap and that is not helpful for a school's development.

(Lizzy, Wayford School)

In this situation, what remains for the individual teacher is to 'negotiate' with National Curriculum requirements in personalized ways:

I am not saying I haven't got reservations about the National Curriculum and certainly in the early days I actually resisted and was very critical ... but I think [now] it is a bit more informed ... I actually think it is an excuse – people blame the National Curriculum for not being able to think about the right way to organise learning because I don't actually think that does stop it.

(Lizzy)

When I hear people talking about the constrictions of the National Curriculum I think, 'Well that is rubbish because you are in this room and you can do what you want.'

(Stephen)

To summarize: we encounter in Wayford School critical orientations towards current forms of time-organization. Teachers do not regard themselves as being in step with current policy, and locate themselves in terms of the pedagogies of an earlier period. But at the same time there is no strong point of reference, in terms of a culture of teaching, that they feel might inform their work. In this context, the time-practices evident in lessons are based – as a result both of teachers' intentions and pupil attitudes – on weak time-frames, with a preference for continuity and implicitness of objectives, rather than explicit, exam-related, time-limited units of work. In all of these senses, Wayford School stands out as different.

Springton School

By contrast, the English department in Springton was working to develop a homogenous form of time-practice, to which all teachers could adhere. They were very clear about the ways in which external constraints guided them towards such a reshaping, but they believed at the same time that such re-development was in the interests of the students they taught, and that from the point of view of issues of access and achivement, it was a necessity. To this extent, they were engaged in a government-driven rhetoric of teaching not so much in spite of their own commitments, but because of them. 'The English department is very committed to inclusive education', said one teacher (Anna). This meant that nearly all students were entered for two GCSEs – English and English Literature. But the GCSE literature course was 'just vast' and the teachers found it very difficult to cover it all; what the students were expected to do was 'amazing', and difficult. Teachers talked in great detail about the ways in which they planned time so as to ensure that the whole range of tasks was covered – with each piece of coursework, for instance, taking one half-term. They thought that the students needed prolonged and close assistance to complete these requirements: 'to actually get them to do those pieces of work you have to spend a lot of time with them and then they have all these huge three exams and everything. It is quite vast' (Anna).

The teachers' consciousness of the difficulties that the exam presented for their students, and their adherence to principles of access and inclusivity defined in rela- tionship to the prevailing requirements of the curriculum and assessment system, meant that they developed measured and synchronized forms of time-practice in the department, with teachers sharing a common approach. In this approach we can distinguish two major elements, which together distinguish the time-practices of English in the school.

First, and overall, there is the extent of teacher control over the use of time. At Wayford, time boundaries tended to be 'fuzzy'. The timings of lessons – their beginnings and ends – were conditional upon the levels of consent offered by students. Within quite broad limits, students could choose on what activities their lesson time could be spent; teachers' work involved, to an important extent, an intervention in students' activity, which took as its starting-point the tempo of learning established by the student. In Springton, by contrast, teachers established the common tasks of the lesson at an early point. Characteristically, they went on to subdivide tasks into several discrete activities, the time allocated to which had been pre-measured. The time-boundaries of the activities were clearly stated and monitored. In much of what we observed, student activity (writing, discussion) was preceded by a long period of teacher input: as we note in a later chapter, students tended not to get their hands on texts until beyond the halfway point in the lesson. In such circumstances, students experienced classroom time as directed time, whose organization was shaped primarily by the teacher.

In Springton, in Julia's half-term module, the focus of study was *Macbeth*. Over a series of twelve lessons the students focused exclusively, in terms of text, on the study of Act 1, Scene i – 'When shall we three meet again?' – ten lines in total. This extreme selectivity and textual fragmentation were material realizations of the teacher's perception of the difficulty that the students would have in coping in their examination with a complex text. The perception was further realized in the teacher's decision to divide each of the twelve lessons into a series of small tasks. In one lesson, for example, the teacher repeatedly showed the students a short two-minute video representation of the scene, directing the students to focus on partic-ular aspects of the production – the use of music, the visual representation of the witches, and so on. She gave the students a specific amount of time to respond to and discuss each successive aspect, and a specific amount of time for them to write down the points to be made before she repeated the viewing of the scene and moved on to focus on the next aspect of the scene for discussion. The teacher's strictly bounded use and control of time created a patterned rhythm of engagement with the text, and with one another. Such time-practice was an actualization of the expectation that she held of students and of their lack of potential for sustained concentration and work. *Macbeth*, as a consequence, had to become bite-sized. (This series of lessons is discussed in detail in Chapter 9.)

We observed similar sorts of textual fragmentation and strict organization of time across each of the three teachers' lessons in Springton. When Anna worked with the students on the realization of character in *Romeo and Juliet*, she set clear objectives for each task, broke each task down into a series of instructions, and spent consider-able time in each lesson talking through these instructions. As with the lessons on *Macbeth*, the students worked on one scene of *Romeo and Juliet* – Act 1, Scene v, the Capulets' 'old-accustomed feast' where Romeo and Juliet first meet and fall in love. They were not given the whole play to read and the scene was further fragmented during the lessons – the students were given one or two lines to read and to focus on the realization of their character through voice and gesture; the students' realization of character was related directly to the National Curriculum assessment criteria for speaking and listening. (This series of lessons is discussed in Chapter 7.)

Likewise, these same processes – relating to the teacher's control of the organization and regulation of time, linked to perceptions of their students' 'ability' and the demands of examination – were apparent in Sally's lessons. We observed her teaching Marvell's poem 'To His Coy Mistress' (from the 'Hearts and Partners' section of the NEAB anthology). One long lesson began with 46 minutes of teacher talk and of collective reading of the poem before the students were given a copy of *a part* of the poem to discuss and annotate. The high level of teacher input indicates the extent to which the teachers in Springton felt students needed assistance and guidance.

So far, we have emphasized the extent of teacher control as a central element of time-practice in Springton School. The second distinguishing element of such practice is a prevailing sense that, as Anna suggests above, time is pressured. Certainly the clattering of Marvell's 'time's winged chariot hurrying near' was very audible to the teachers. In relation to the vastness of the tasks involved, they knew that time was in short supply. It had to be measured, synchronized, constantly monitored and accounted for; there was no other way of getting the students through the examination. The examination itself was constantly drawn to students' attention – through spoken reminders, through handouts and through wall displays. In this sense we can speak of a *proleptic* organization of time: the tasks of the lesson were described to students as anticipations of examination requirements; the final goal had a constant presence in the moment-to-moment activity of the lesson.

To us it appeared that in Springton time was treated as more homogenous than the time of the other schools. Teachers had adapted to national requirements in a co-ordinated way, in which many of the 'traditional' characteristics of English teaching had been replaced by practices that centred on the need to achieve access for working-class and ethnic-minority students to a fixed, explicit curriculum, which was seen offering few possibilities for modification or creative inflection: the process noted by Harvey of destruction and reconstruction was in full swing.

Around the project of access, there was thus a convergence of teacher practice. But this did not mean that students experienced time in an homogenous way. In a school where general opinion was moving in the opposite direction, this department was committed to inclusive education and un-streamed teaching. Nevertheless, as we suggest in Chapter 6, 'ability' remained a prominent factor in Springton's English classes, and no more so than in relation to students' experiences of time. For 'able' students parts of the lesson were dense with conversation, in which teachers participated. For the 'less able', the situation was different: there were frequent occasions when they seemed to experience time as 'empty' – in which the tasks they were set did not serve to stimulate activity, and in which the purposeful regime of the classrooms was such that they could not easily move 'off task'. In these circumstances, time was spent in silence, or in halting conversation. These contrasts at the level of 'ability' were also a feature of Ravenscroft School.

Ravenscroft School

There were few regrets for the past at Ravenscroft. Since the introduction of the National Curriculum, explained the head of department, there had been 'more equality of opportunity'. The changes since 1988 had not weakened teachers' capacities. On the contrary, they were now 'more aware of where a child is at, which again comes back to the heart of everything'. In the head of department's account, they were supported in this awareness not by the child-centred philosophies of progressive days – where 'people were so to speak only concerned with creativity' – but by the insistence of the new system on assessment, record-keeping and breadth of provision:

> How do I know that this child hasn't learned A, B and C? What do I need to empower this child? ... It is good, record-keeping helps – and assessment – to cater for the needs of the individual student rather than assuming you have taught something ... It has made teaching more effective I think.

Like the teachers at Springton, those in Ravenscroft worked with an understanding that success in public examinations was the key to students' successful future. 'The reality is', according to the head of department, 'that the exam, it is going to influence their future'. The consequence for the school was that 'exams have in a sense overtaken a lot of things that we just teach', or, to put it another way, classroom activities in Years 10 and 11 occur under the sign of the examination – the sign in which the students will conquer. One of the lessons, taught by Irene and summarized here in our field-notes, showed very clearly this proleptic process at work, and the ways in which it connected to the assertion of a very strong time-discipline:

2.38 p.m.   The teacher walks to the front of the classroom. She tells the students that they should be looking over their first drafts of their coursework:
When I count to three I want you to be ready ...
The students are silent, engaged, looking at the teacher or getting out their pens and diaries on their desks. The teacher walks around the classroom then walks to the front desk and sits.
2.39 p.m.   She starts to count to three:
Okay, one ...
She sits on her table, her arms folded, looking around the class.
Let's stop, listen. Structure your response for *A View from the Bridge* [Miller's play, which provides a coursework text] – you really get the instructions?
Count the number of words, excluding quotations. 'First draft' means you can go back, amend ... You need to work to deadlines. Every half-term we have a new topic.
She stands, hands on hips.
We do not want any overlapping – I'm not going to be dealing with the *View*

from the Bridge now. We're using a new half-term unit. First draft in Friday – get your organizers out and make a note. The one thing I will not tolerate is 'I've done it and it's at home'. You can write that in your organizers.

Three measures of time-discipline are immediately evident in this brief phase of the lesson. The first relates to students' instantly applying themselves to set tasks, and the second to note-taking that will allow the continuation of lesson work in the near future, at home. The third measure connects to the longer-term processes – the completion of separate pieces of coursework, to which specific units of time are assigned. It is at this level that the examination becomes the central reference point: the paths of learning lead to the GCSE.

Beyond these measures of time, however, is a fourth element, which makes the classrooms of Ravenscroft School generally more complex in temporal terms than those of Springton. The teacher reminds her students that they will be working on a 'first draft', a piece to which they will return to amend and revise. In saying this, she repeats a tactic characteristic of her department: frequently in lessons, teachers will remind students of what they have studied earlier, of topics and ideas that have come to serve as reference points for the course, and around which clusters of meaning can be elaborated. Time-practice in Ravenscroft frequently involves such recursivity – a recursivity that stems from the department's ambition for its able students. It wants them to 'progressively develop their skills to enable them to gain access to a deeper meaning'. This process in turn involves the development of a student's capacity to 'play back' – as one teacher put it – in their formal writing what they have said, and been encouraged to record in writing, during their lessons. Recursivity thus forms a counterbalance to the inexorable movement towards GCSE.

While the prospect of the exam pulls the students on, and provides the motivation and purpose for much of their studies, the students are at the same time incited to turn back, towards the network of meanings that has been established in the working history of the group, and towards their own previous individual learning achievements. In this sense, knowledge enacted at a particular point in local settings is not self-contained, or confined with the moment, but points instead both forward and back, creating strong developmental trajectories. To this extent, Ravenscroft supplies forms of time-organization that are sufficiently strong to sustain time-practices that are not wholly dominated by examination requirements – even though, as we have discussed elsewhere, this level of resistance is enabled in part by a process of academic selection, which has created the student groupings with whom time-practices of this sort can work.

Conclusion

In this chapter we have aimed to explore the relationship between policy time, teacher time, and students' time. In the process, we have tried to show how the systems of time-organization established by policy have a substantial effect on the time-practices of English lessons. But we have also suggested that the relationship between teacher time and policy time is not simply one of conflict. Harvey, borrowing from Marshall Berman (1983), uses the term 'creative destruction' to describe the continuing, accelerating process of social change to which the dynamism of economic life under capitalism gives rise. The term is intended to suggest remaking, as well as demolition, and it is certainly a process of remaking that we have encountered at several points in our research. Quite definitely, many teachers have constituted themselves as collectives devoted to ensuring that their students have the best possible chance of success under the new system of curricular regulation, and in the process they have embraced the 'new', if one may still use that term of a system that has been taking shape since 1988, with an enthusiasm that is far more than tactical. Teachers have – in their accounts – worked with as well as against the National Curriculum. They have developed forms of time-organization – collective, synchronized approaches to lesson and unit planning – that sustain a practice they feel confident in justifying. To this extent, they feel that the time-practice of lessons is under their control, and is working in the interests of students.

Yet there remain doubting voices. Few teachers are entirely happy with the priorities and time pressures of the National Curriculum and examination system. Some are strongly critical, in the name of ideas of learner development that work with very different timelines. And beyond such explicit articulations, there are other tensions. The conflict between different sorts of time-organization is embedded in practice, not simply voiced by means of interview. Perhaps the greatest tensions occur where the demands of institutional time-organization encounter the mass of the student population. It is at these points that time hangs heaviest – and emptiest – and that students, by their attempts to worry at the time-boundaries of lessons and by their reluctance to fill with recognizably meaningful activity the empty time allocated to them by teacher-set tasks, become prominent actors in the classroom realization of educational time.

Chapter 6

The pedagogic construction of 'ability' in school English

Introduction

The teacher's work involves the continuous 'structured improvisation' of English both as a matter of curriculum content (an ideational construct), and as a matter of the social relations in the classroom (a pedagogic, interpersonal one). That is, the teacher always and simultaneously creates both a content for English, and a way of positioning students *differentially* in relation to that content. Here we focus on this differential positioning of students, and on the role played in this by the near commonsense notion of (differential) 'ability'. We argue that 'student ability' is at least partly constructed in social interaction, and may not be stable beyond the context in which it is 'produced'. Out of this understanding comes a means for seeing how the teacher's perception of students in relation to 'ability' gives shape to very different constructions of what English is or comes to be for different groups of students.

One of the most striking features of the three schools and nine classrooms that we researched was the ways in which what happened within them – groupings, tasks, communication (whether in action, gesture, position, speech) – was dependent on the classification of the students by 'ability'. In our study one of the schools we worked in, Ravenscroft, 'streamed' students according to their attainment on entry at 11 years. However, even in the 'mixed-ability' classrooms of Springton School and Wayford School, teachers described their classes in terms of a 'top-ability group', one or two 'middle groups' and a 'low-ability group'. In this chapter we argue that, whether in the streamed school or in the 'mixed-ability' classes, 'low-ability groups' participated in and experienced a very different version of English to that produced for their 'more able' peers.

Teachers described different levels of expectation for the different groups. For example: 'I think only two or three will get a Grade C at GCSE ... So consequently I do very, very basic things with them ... what I do with them is very much, putting it crudely, simplifying stuff in order for them to just finish and complete it really' (Stephen, Wayford School). In contrast, a teacher working with a 'top' group explained: 'I want them to be reaching the highest grades ... I always try and pitch really high with them and deliberately make loads of assumptions so that if they don't understand or if they don't know, they can ask. But if they start up there, they can see where I am wanting to come in at' (Diane, Ravenscroft School).

Although we see 'ability' as produced by teachers and students in the context of their interaction, that context is, of course, made up of the products of other forms of agency. These include a discourse which produces dominant 'commonsense' understandings of differential levels of intelligence: school and departmental 'traditions'; student cultures; the institutions established by national, government policy; and the discourses associated with each of them.

The concept of differential 'ability' is very much a product of the establishment of mass schooling, and of restricted access to its higher levels. In many respects, the role of state schooling in urban areas has taken an enduring form. Schools have always worked to socialize and control students around particular sets of values and forms of knowledge, and at the same time schools have always distributed knowledge differentially, often in relation to social group membership. For example, in the 1944 Education Act, 'intelligence' testing provided what was seen as a technically neutral tool for allocating and targeting limited resources to a selected group of students. Tests were claimed to assess students' suitability for different programmes in different types of school.

'Ability' was challenged in several ways from the 1960s onwards – through the abolition of the eleven-plus examination especially, the rise of unstreamed ('mixed-ability') grouping, and the development of forms of evaluation that sought to be responsive to student interest and experience rather than heavily emphasizing fixed, 'objective' criteria. Nevertheless, the assumption of fixed and differential innate levels of ability has lingered on. This can be seen in the dominant rhetoric in schools of 'meeting each child's needs according to his or her ability', but also in formal and informal teacher assessments that lead to grouping arrangements based on teacher perceptions of 'ability' within 'mixed-ability' classrooms from the earliest years. Once allocated to a group, students have tended to be given differential tasks with expectations of different levels of outcome. Students tend not to be shifted from group to group, so once they are allocated to a 'bottom' or 'top' group, receiving different tasks and different levels of feedback, the gap between top and bottom group widens and widens, creating a self-fulfilling prophecy (Bourne 1994).

What appears to be overlooked in such organizational strategies are the cultural resources that students bring into the classroom with them, and their match with the demands of the school curriculum. This was not always so, and especially not in relation to the teaching of English. The publication from the 1950s onwards of English texts and the dissemination of methods of teaching English that aimed to bring 'working-class experience' into the classroom were manifestations of a recognition of the importance of cultural capital by those who worked in education. This was extended in the 1970s and 1980s by the emergence of the classroom politics of race and gender. Secondary-school English was one of the sites where such work was most strongly advanced.

However, since 1988, in a social context marked by rising levels of poverty, growing inequality and (for some) great precariousness in matters of employment security and quality of life, educational policy has taken a new turn, which has, in some respects, transformed power relations and systems of meaning and value in the school. For our purposes we need to emphasize four such transformations.

First, there are changes in the position of teachers. Compared with the period 1944–88, teachers experience greatly reduced autonomy around questions of curriculum content (Furlong *et al.* 2000). Their performance is more closely audited and managed. Second, there is the development of nationally planned curricula, and of regular forms of testing. These affect all students and all teachers. Third, under these two pressures, forms of pedagogy have changed. Grace noted the presence in urban schools from the 1960s onwards of a 'principle of rapport', which 'celebrated the importance of friendliness and good interpersonal relations, of understanding … "youth culture" and of sympathising with social and economic disadvantages' (1995: 216). Grace noted also that increasingly, in the same period, liberal rapport was challenged by a different principle, which he names 'radical dialogue', that had 'dignified the student and the status of his or her language, theorising and culture' and that had hoped to see the school become the 'arena for the representation of a rich variety of cultural patterns, forms of communication and levels of consciousness' (1995: 219).

Under the impact of the National Curriculum and increasingly frequent testing, the decline of teacher autonomy, and the attenuation of links between aspects of the work of the school and the activity of social and cultural movements, neither of these principles acts any longer as a reference-point for classroom practice. What has replaced them is a curriculum based on the idea of 'entitlement' and 'access'. In England now, under the new educational order, these terms signify the predominance in the curriculum of a single type of authorized knowledge. The role of the school is to ensure that students can successfully access this authorized form. In practice, however, achieving access is difficult, especially among 'disadvantaged' groups. Since curriculum experiment and 'dialogue' around the validity of different forms of knowledge are no longer options, teachers' work is channelled along other routes. They need to devise pedagogic strategies that can maximize success in terms that are pre-given.

Finally, and importantly, there is the renewed prominence of 'ability' as an operational, institutionalized aspect of schooling. Since 1988 – and especially since the election of the New Labour government in 1997 – 'ability' has re-emerged as a central, government-endorsed principle of educational organization (Edwards and Tomlinson 2002). Tests and examinations are 'tiered', so that entry to higher levels is restricted on ability grounds; streaming and setting of classes is encouraged; entry to particular types of (nominally comprehensive) school is connected to student success in national assessments or in entry examinations. In addition, because a school's public recognition and funding levels are strongly affected by its examination results, there is strong pressure for schools to identify 'able' students and to maximize their attainment, often at the expense of others (Gillborn and Youdell 2000).

The role of 'ability' as an organizing concept in a 'streamed' school

In Ravenscroft School students were streamed on entry into three classes, according to their primary school assessment 'bands'. By the time students reached Year 10, the year that we studied, those in the 'top' class, those who had been seen at age 11 as high achievers, were not thought to have problems with confidence. Their English teacher said:

> I think they are quite aware of each other and their voices are very different and their way of expressing themselves is very different and their confidence levels are very different and their expectations are very different and that comes out now where you talk to the students in Year 10 about whether or not they are going to go to university or what they want to study ... They are very aware of each other's strengths and weaknesses ... I think they could rate each other for everything, who is better at reading, who is better at reading poetry, so they are very aware of how they run up and down the pecking order.
>
> (Ravenscroft, Diane)

However, the gains in student confidence were not passed on to those students allocated to the 'bottom' stream. As their English teacher volunteered in interview: 'I think you can't escape from the notion of sheep and goats ... As soon as you start setting, you end up with this bottom-set syndrome' (Ravenscroft, Paul).

In observing the 'bottom' stream English class, we were aware that it included a small number of students still at an early stage of learning English, together with some students with 'special needs' requiring extra 'support' assistance. In fact, two other adults apart from the English teacher himself were present in the room during the lessons, sitting next to their own 'allocated' students and helping them complete individual work.

How is 'ability' realized in this 'bottom set'? In one lesson observed, the teacher's objective was to teach students to make comparisons between broadsheet and tabloid newspapers by comparing the use of 'emotive words'. He began the lesson by reading out two headlines from a list in his hand, asking students to iden-tify which contained the 'most interesting' or 'emotive' words. He told the class to 'put your right hand up if it is the first word; put your left hand up if it is the second' (in demonstrating this, the teacher indicated that one example of such contrasting headlines was: 'Fire at School' or 'School Blaze'). The students mainly sat silent and unmoving. Few hands were raised.

In the second lesson there was the same absence of interaction and low level of activity. The students were asked to draw a grid indicating differences between the tabloids and broadsheet examples they had been given. For many pupils drawing this grid took up most of the lesson. Towards the end of the lesson the teacher remarked: 'You've spent far too long drawing the chart, and not enough on content. You've got five minutes left now, and you need to make sure that by the end of this time you've written at least two rows.'

Resistance takes many forms, refusal to engage being one of them. In interview with the project researcher, the students from this class were lively and engaging. Yet in class, over the whole unit observed, the students showed – by their posture and gaze – that they were disengaged from the teaching that took place. They leant back, avoided eye contact with the teacher, spoke without expression, sometimes stifling yawns, with the girls casting glances and smiles at one another if nominated to speak, as if in a conspiracy of non-participation.

In his struggle to make contact, to elicit a reaction, and to get through the (his) set curriculum, the teacher broke the teaching into smaller and smaller 'learning chunks', as we have shown above, filling the time slot with busy work – drawing the grid, filling in worksheets. In interview he said he felt forced to narrow the curriculum:

> I know well the ideal would be that of course you open things up, and the more you open things up the better they can do. But that of course depends on the students you are dealing with and the context that you are teaching within, and we haven't got the students [in this class] with sufficient cultural capital for us to be able to say 'well you have got all the basics so we can open up the text'. We can't do that really.

Bernstein (1990) has argued that education for 'low-ability' groups appears to focus on 'facticity', not on critical reflection or on cultural connectedness. He suggests that the classrooms of those not 'selected' as 'able' are the site of an austere cultural regime where the meanings, ideas and values of learners find few points of connection. However, we argue later in this chapter that this approach to those perceived of as 'low' in 'ability' can also take place in 'mixed-ability' classrooms, though in a subtler form, with different input – both in mode of communication and in content – and feedback still constructing 'sheep' and 'goats'.

Constructing ability in a 'mixed-ability' class

Here we demonstrate the process of constructing ability in a 'mixed-ability' class by focusing analytically on two episodes in one English lesson with the one class in which a teacher, Susan, works consecutively with two groups of students, in Springton School. Focusing in detail on two (typical) episodes of small-group work – of about six minutes each – we show how the teacher's conception of English varies in relation to the two groups, and how different groups therefore receive very different versions of English, even in the same classroom.

Susan's decision to organize her class into small groups for much of the time in her lessons configures the interpersonal relationships between teacher and students in the English classroom in a particular way. It suggests that English, in the context of Springton, is not intended to be a subject produced (solely) by the teacher and transmitted to students in a didactic form. Rather, English is intended to be produced through the interaction of peers, through their engagement with previous knowledge and 'out of school' cultural understandings over a text, with the teacher having more the role of facilitator. As we showed in Chapter 3, this arrangement of the classroom is a sign of this (interpersonal) process of producing English, with the students grouped around the tables facing each other rather than the teacher. However, as we showed in that earlier chapter, spatial arrangement alone does not determine the specifics of the kind of English actually produced. In our study we encountered, in different classrooms, the use of both small-group work and whole-class work, and found that of themselves neither of these allowed us to predict the particular kinds of English that were produced there. For example, in Irene's classroom we found a quite formal arrangement of the furniture, but this did not produce what it might have been expected to produce in terms of social relations.

Before offering a detailed description of these two episodes we first give an overview of the lesson in which they occurred, and show how in each case the National Curriculum frames the lesson. Springton, like the other schools in our study, is an inner-city school with a diverse ethnic population, a high proportion of students from working-class families, and a high percentage of students with English as an additional language – a significant number of whom are refugees. Standards in English overall are well below the national average in all forms of assessment at Key Stages 3 and 4. Susan is an experienced teacher and has taught these particular students over nearly three years.

Government policy at the time of our study promoted differentiation through setting into different classrooms by 'ability'. Springton's decision not to 'set' students for English was mentioned as a cause for concern in the school's most recent Ofsted report, which stated 'The very wide range of attainment within mixed-ability teaching groups makes it very difficult for teachers to ensure that all students are making appropriate progress'. Student ability, and the pedagogic strategies thought to be necessitated by ability differences, were raised by Susan in interviews. For example:

> I mean, that class does have quite a range of students and there is quite an able group at the top I think, which in some of the classes you don't have as much, I don't think. So I think I probably, I am not sure how, that definitely does influence how I teach, I think, and I know there are students that will explain things, so although I do try to get them to feedback into the classes, I tend to do a lot of group work. I think that helps students learn and I would do that with any group. Even with a group that found it difficult I would persevere because that's … where they learn.

And later:

> I think they need quite a lot of support and you couldn't just say 'do this' with any task. Every task has to be broken down – you do lots of tasks to build up

what you want to do. Maybe in a different type of school I think you would approach – you might get to the text more quickly or something like that. I think you have to engage their interest before you even get to the text.

The lesson that we focus on here is the seventh in a series of twelve lessons, over a month, on the poems featured in the NEAB anthology section 'Hearts and Partners'. The subject of the lesson is Andrew Marvell's 'Letter to His Coy Mistress', the only compulsory poem in the examination syllabus, for this unit. That fact gives it a central place in the curriculum, and in our analysis of English here.

The lesson objectives reflect the National Curriculum requirements for reading – the need for students to be able to 'read for meaning' and to 'understand the author's craft'. Specifically, successful students are required to extract meaning beyond the literal; to explain how the author's choice of language affects meaning; to analyse and discuss alternative interpretations and how emotions and ideas are portrayed. These competencies will be assessed, of course, and Susan feels the added pressures of teaching assessment strategies as well as literature, as she said when interviewed: 'I suppose at Key Stage 4, unfortunately, it is quite exam orientated. I mean that is what those lessons are about really and I want them to know and understand the poems that they are studying and to be able to kind of also know what they need to do in an exam.'

The students are seated at tables in groups of three or four; dictionaries are handed to each table. Following a whole-class teaching episode in which Susan models the process of 'textual analysis' for the whole class – the kind of textual analysis required by the examination syllabus – Susan hands over the poem in the form of a one-page hard copy to the students. Each group is given one stanza of the poem to 'analyse', an activity that appears to include, in varying degrees, basic explication, interpretation and response. It is what happens in this part of the lesson that is the focus of our analysis.

When first watching the video of the lesson we were immediately struck by the difference in the teacher–student interaction between two groups she worked with consecutively during this group-work section of the lesson. Group 1 consists of two girls and one boy, all of minority-ethnic-group background. Group 2 consists of four boys, of mixed ethnic origin; in that second group the teacher interacts with just one boy directly, Tony. Our analysis is a multimodal one, in order to 'get at' the difference in the two interactions, to explore what it is that is being produced as English for different pupils, and how this is done. Gender and ethnicity are not our focus here, even though it would be possible from the data to make comments. In this specific context, it is not the social categories of ethnicity or gender that are salient in constructing the different forms of English, but that of 'ability'.

Our analysis demonstrates that both students and teacher are active in the construction of forms of subjectivity through their interaction. That is to say, given the social constraints and possibilities that are at work in this classroom, it is both the teacher and the students who act, even if very differently, and with different means and resources. We want to insist that students themselves are involved as active agents in their own positioning in relation to English, and therefore also to the category of 'ability', although their choices of ways of acting may not be to their own long-term advantage. The episodes are co-productions involving all participants.

A comparative multimodal description of two instances

As we have argued throughout this book so far, semiotic resources (modes) such as movement, body posture, gaze and gesture are as much part of the making of English as are the linguistic resources of speech and writing, which have customarily attracted the attention of researchers. Here we examine the orchestration of semiotic resources in the work of the teacher – including movement, body posture, gesture (including gesture with objects), gaze, speech and writing – in the context of the spatial arrangements of the classroom. We begin by looking at modes other than speech or writing by which English is constructed. We then analyse ways in which 'official' written texts – parts of the poem, the dictionary – are deployed. Subsequently, we attend to the written texts and to utterances produced by the teacher and by students. Of course, in the classroom all these resources are simultaneously in use. We focus on them separately for analytic purposes. In our conclusions, we refer back to some of the wider contextual factors already raised in Chapter 2, and occasionally elsewhere in the book. We want, after all, to keep to the forefront of our attention that it is the multiplicity of social factors that shape the manner of their combination in the realization of English.

The multimodal construction of 'ability' in Group 1

In this classroom, both the teacher and, to a much lesser extent, the students can move in the space of the classroom. They position themselves in relation to one another, and in relation to the furniture and objects in the classroom. As we have argued, these positionings and the resultant interactions contribute to different realizations of English for different pupils, with implications for how students see and feel themselves as learners of English.

In this first episode the teacher walks up to a group around one of the tables. By placing herself at one side of the table (a space not occupied by a student), the teacher effectively locates herself within the group, as if she were one of the participants, for the time of her presence (see Figure 6.1).

Her position provides a specific potential for engagement with this group. She leans across the table, opposite to one girl, whom we will call Sofia, making her, through positioning and gaze, the main focus of the interaction. A little later the teacher moves from her initial position directly opposite to Sofia to somewhat more to the side of the table, producing a shift in her relation to the group – maybe that from *member* more to *observer*, and, thereby invites a shift in the manner of engagement of the three students from *listeners* to *performers*.

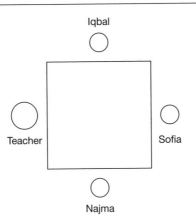

Iqbal

Teacher

Sofia

Najma

Figure 6.1 Springton School, Group 1: position of teacher and students

Her movement allows the three students to see the whiteboard previously obscured by her body. This also marks a shift, from the authority of the teacher herself to a focus on the authority of (what has been written on) the whiteboard. In this way the teacher's *movement* as a semiotic resource becomes a sign of some of her expectations *vis-à-vis* the students, namely expectations about forms of interaction, and serves to frame the teacher–student interaction.

Susan's initial positioning of Sofia as her major interactant, through the position she assumed at the table, is also realized and reinforced through her *gaze*. Throughout, Sofia and the teacher engage in direct eye contact. By contrast, Iqbal (to the left of the teacher) and Najma (to her right) hardly make eye contact with her at all, nor she with them; rather they make eye contact with Sofia. Their gaze confirms Sofia's central role as representative for the group. Sofia herself uses *gaze* to indicate requests for teacher response, reassurance and help, without verbalizing her needs. Throughout the episode teacher and students use *gaze* to draw the text into their interaction.

Although there is a chair at her end of the table, the teacher chooses to stand throughout the interaction, or to lean rather, across the table – into the group, in changing postures. Initially, her upper body and arms are stretched almost horizontally across the table. This posture brings her head much closer to the students than if she had remained upright, or had been seated; her outstretched arms link her to the group. Her posture, her smile and her laughter signify casualness, informality, friendliness, being relaxed. By remaining standing she suggests the temporary nature of her visit and the interaction – as if she had merely 'dropped in', casually, for a pleasurable conversation. The body-posture of the students is also relatively open and expansive. Sofia leans back and stretches her hands behind her head, as does Iqbal later. The students sit relatively low in their chairs, and throughout most of the interaction Iqbal rests his gently folded arms on the table. These embodied signs both shape the interaction and provide a frame for all aspects of them. At this table, they are the material-bodily expression of a construction of English as the pleasure of engaging in discussion over a text.

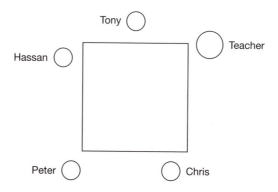

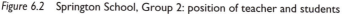

Figure 6.2   Springton School, Group 2: position of teacher and students

The multimodal construction of 'ability' in Group 2

Leaving Group 1, the teacher walks over to the second group of students, and without hesitation sits down at a corner of the table, next to one student, Tony, on her right (see Figure 6.2).

During the episode she does not alter her basic position, signalling 'permanency' by seating herself there (rather than 'dropping in' as she did with the other group). This impression is very clear, despite the fact that both interactions last for the same amount of time. In a seeming paradox, at Table 1 (where she has merely 'dropped in', so to speak) her position signalled membership of the group; here, where she is seated, she is an outsider. Placing herself where and as she does also seems to suggest that she is preparing to work just with Tony, rather than engaging with the whole group.

Once seated, the teacher immediately leans forward to pick up a pencil. She then draws Tony's copy of the poem towards herself, putting her left elbow on the table and supporting her head on her hand as she starts to read the first line of the poem. Her upright, angular and tense body-posture contrasts with the almost horizontal posture adopted by her in the interaction with the first group. In the earlier episode she leaned in toward the students; here she leans in toward the poem. The position of her arms and head over the text close her off from interaction with the other students at the table; it is a posture that does not invite interaction. Whereas in the previous episode the teacher's posture actualizes a sign of shared pleasure, here her posture, together with her appropriation of pencil and text, actualize a sign of authority and of directed instruction (or work).

As the teacher asks the students specific questions, her body posture changes. She leans back from the text, shifting her hand to rest on her left hip, an attitude we had already observed as her stock posture in managing whole-class teaching interactions, of gaining and controlling attention. Her posture is now entirely upright, still angular and tense. Throughout the episode the teacher moves between these two postures of *leaning in toward the text*, and *sitting upright* in her chair. Through her first posture she models 'doing English' as work, an individual engagement with the text. Through her second posture she shifts back to a 'teacherly' role, checking students' understanding.

As with her movement, positioning and posture, the teacher's use of *gaze* differs between the first group and the second. With Group 2, the teacher spends most of the episode looking at the poem/text, focusing attention on the text, her head down, reading, and annotating the text. When she looks up at the students to ask a question, her look is brief, wavering, and it quickly drops back to the text. The text, not the students, is the teacher's dominant object of gaze, and attention to the written text is the purpose of the sign of this interaction. At the same time the students gaze downward at the table in front of them, rarely looking at the teacher, even when the teacher is talking. Unlike Sofia, Iqbal and to a lesser extent Najma, these students do not use gaze as a resource for engaging with the teacher.

Throughout this episode, Tony sits with his arms either under the table, or folded across his chest. His posture is closed. The body posture of the other students at the table is upright and stiff, which can be read as signalling a form of resistance. They shift their posture only when the teacher asks them to look up a word in the dictionary. They do this, leaning forward, flicking through the pages. As the teacher then reads the excerpt, Tony leans backs and yawns, a sign of disengagement. The stiffness of the posture of the students and of the teacher is in marked contrast to the openness, 'looseness' and fluidity of the participants' posture in the first interaction.

The teacher's eye contact with the text signifies her focus in her work with Group 2. The teacher is not intent on the work of producing interaction and debate, and the students are not engaged in the work of producing meaning. The lack of exchange between the teacher and students indicates a lack of co-production of interpretation and meaning in this episode.

'Ability' groupings and interaction

When we viewed the video-recording of this interaction, the difference between the two was striking, both in the modes of interaction, but also in the kind of English teaching that characterized each. At this point we turned to interviews with the teacher, and noted that Group 1 is perceived by her to be a 'high-ability' group. She sees its members as capable of responding successfully to the demands of the curriculum and the examination syllabus. For them English is configured, at least in part, as conversation, in which dialogue, informality, the students' perspectives and expertise are all valued – though valued only in part. As we have seen, the teacher's position and posture was aimed at soliciting from them an articulation of their response to the text. But at the same time, aspects of the teachers' talk, those aspects of her gaze and gesture that involved – even at their table – the dictionary, the whiteboard and its instructions, tend in another direction. At this point there were clearly discernible tensions between the students' interests in exploring the meanings of the poem, and the teacher's urges, which were more directed towards the kinds of reading and response that are valued in terms of the National Curriculum. To some extent the latter constrains the responses that she might otherwise have allowed herself to evoke or to follow up – those of a historical, social or culturally inflected kind, but which in the context of the demands of the official curriculum she perhaps felt could not, seemingly, be foregrounded.

As we have shown, the situation is very different for Group 2, whom this teacher does not recognize as able. Our analysis of the video-recording reveals that in Group 1 the teacher's *gaze, movement* and *posture* produce a sense of English as that curriculum subject in which the text is the point of departure for engaged discussion, for personal involvement, for pleasure. In contrast, the same teacher's use of the same modal resources with Group 2 produces a kind of English that is about closure, about instruction in which the authority of the text, the teacher and the dictionary as producers of its meanings are paramount.

We will now extend our analysis of these differences, looking at the modes of *gesture, talk* and *writing*.

Gesture

In Group 1 the teacher and students both use *gesture* during their interaction, realizing their own constructions of the meaning and purpose of English. In this group students gestured at the poem, the dictionary, and at their body, indicating the focus of interest or term of reference of the gesture. The move from gesturing towards the poem to gesturing towards the body marked a shift in reference from the poem-as-text to their personal response to the poem. Sofia's gestures toward her body – trying to find acceptable words for 'sexually aroused', for instance – relate the emotions and motivations of the female character in the poem to her personal response and emotions. Her gestures that were directed towards the text focus on the meanings of the words of the text. Through gesture she embodies the text.

Open gestures are expansive. Sofia opens and waves her arms and hands to express 'sexual excitement' (a gesture that Iqbal fills in verbally with the word 'horny'), and later she makes a sweeping gesture over her shoulder to express 'the past'. Similarly, when the teacher opens her hand and moves it in a circular motion as she asks 'what is he trying to say there?', she is making an open gesture, which in this instance seemed to be a sign 'making an opening' for the students, asking for their explanation or response – their offering to the interaction.

While both the teacher and Sofia directed gestures at their body and the text, Iqbal's gestural repertoire was different. At one point, while the teacher and Sofia discussed the text, Iqbal, himself not speaking, accompanied their conversation with a set of sinuous hand movements. These seemed self-referential rather than directed towards the poem or the conversation – and to represent a quotation from 'non-schooled' forms of behaviour, associated, we thought, with dance and 'body-popping'. We interpret Iqbal's gestures at this point as indicating a contesting of the value of the conversation between teacher and Sofia, and the counterposing of a (male, unschooled) gestural repertoire to a (female, schooled) one. This interpretation fits with his verbal dismissal of the poem as 'rude' and as outside of the realm of the literary. By contrast, the gestures of Najma were directed solely at the text, suggesting a focus on meaning located 'within' the text, rather than as a personal response to the poem.

The teacher's gestures were primarily directed at the dictionary, which throughout the interaction was deployed as a text second in importance only to the poem itself. While the modes of *gaze* and *posture* invite the students' personal responses, her gesture, by contrast, indicates and reminds the students of her pedagogic intentions, of the job in hand. The teacher's holding of a page, finger pointing to a specific place while a student talked, was a sign of her listening whilst maintaining her pedagogic agenda. By contrast, continuing to flick the pages of the dictionary as a student talked served as a sign of the teacher's desire to change the analytical focus from the personal or sociocultural back to the textual.

Pointing at the text served to bring elements of the text to the fore, whilst linking text and person. At one point in their co-produced analysis, the teacher is pointing at the word 'transpire' in the dictionary while Sofia is pointing to the same word in the poem; the teacher then leans and points to that word in the poem.

In contrast to the shared use of gesture in Group 1, with Group 2 it is primarily the teacher who gestures. As the episode begins, Tony points to a place on the poem/ sheet in response to the teacher's request to know where they are 'up to'. When the teacher puts her own finger at this place, Tony removes his finger. The whole episode ends with Tony placing a finger on the text as if he were 'taking it back'. In between Tony's initial and final pointing with his finger, no student holds or touches the poem. Gesturally, the text of the poem remains with the teacher throughout the rest of the episode. With the exception of Tony's opening and closing gestures, the students do not use gestures in this episode. They gesture neither towards the poem nor towards the dictionary. Nor do they indicate their personal response to the poem by gesturing toward themselves, as the students in Group 1 had done.

With the second group, the teacher's use of gesture is similar to that in the previous group, although used with lesser frequency. She makes several 'opening up' gestures, offering the text for analysis as she asks 'what does it mean?' and a number of more closed gestures, indicating lexical items. However, whereas in the previous episode the teacher had held the dictionary, here she holds a pencil. This use of the objects dictionary and pencil positions her differently in relation to the analysis of the poem. The use of the dictionary in the previous episode had made her into one of the group, jointly deferring to the authority of the dictionary. The use of the pencil in Group 2 separates her from the group, as someone who acts distinctively, controlling the pencil and thus channelling the focus of attention word by word on the reading of the text, rather than inviting the expression of personal experience.

Throughout the episode with Group 2, the teacher keeps control of the poem through her posture of leaning over the piece of paper, her body acting as a barrier to the students on her left, her gaze directed nearly exclusively at the poem, talking *for* the students as though speaking on their behalf, and scribing the talk that she has herself produced (though on their behalf), maintaining a near-constant gestural contact with the copy of the poem, through its physical proximity to her. This is in stark contrast to the 'handing over' of the text in her interaction with the previous group of students, in which the students were able to share access to and even at times have control of the text.

Writing

Here we are particularly interested in who holds the pen in the work of writing. For the lesson, students had been asked make annotations on the meaning of the poem, and this was the only writing expected during the group session. Throughout the interaction at Table 1, writing was a mode used by the students, not by the teacher. Sofia wrote throughout, Najma wrote towards the end of interaction; and Iqbal did not write at all during the episode. In Group 2 likewise much writing was done. The difference here is that it was the teacher who did the work, appropriating Tony's pencil.

Throughout the interaction with Group 2, the teacher writes on the poem-sheet; none of the students writes themselves. The teacher underlines and writes single words and simple phrases on the poem-sheet (for example: Ganges = river; Thou = you; Flood = Noah's flood; Conversion of the Jews = ancient history and bible stories).

At Table 1 the students shared one dictionary. When the teacher joins Group 2, there are four dictionaries on the table, three of which are open at the start of the episode, although one student closes his dictionary as teacher sits down. The teacher had distributed the dictionaries earlier in the lesson, at which point she apparently decided that four were needed on Group 2's table, and just one on the other. This distribution of dictionaries itself suggests the teacher's expectations of each group's capacities in relation to the task in hand – clarifying the meaning of the poem. The dominant presence of the dictionaries on this table suggests that she regarded them as an essential resource for this particular group, indicating her different understanding of the pedagogic task of making sense of the poem for these students. Each of them is to undertake the work of finding words in the dictionary; it seems that the task that the teacher regards them as capable of doing is this mechanical one in which the dictionary is the essential support. For Group 1, the task seems different, so that the role of the dictionary becomes a different one: here the teacher facilitates discussion and speculation, and she herself quickly looks up words for them herself.

Halfway through the episode with Group 2, the teacher taps on one of the dictionaries with the pencil, and instructs the students to 'look up *vegetable* in the dictionary'. The students pick up the dictionaries and – in a desultory manner – flick through the pages. While they do this, the teacher silently reads the poem and underlines *empire*. She asks the students 'What's an empire?' One student, Peter, responds: 'It's like a big kingdom'. The teacher leans forward and writes on the poem-sheet. However, one could not say that the teacher is simply acting as a scribe for the students, for while some of the meanings of words were offered by the students or co-produced with the teacher, nearly half of them were provided by the teacher directly, without attempting any interaction at all with the group.

At Table 2, *writing* interacts with other modes to signify the teacher's continuing possession of the text. With this group the teacher sees it as her role to write *for* the students, in contrast to her role in the previous interaction, where she looked up words in the dictionary for the students while allowing them to focus on relating the poem to their own experience.

Talk

If we look at this in bare numerical terms, we note that in Group 1 the teacher made 34 contributions, mainly focusing on the meaning of words and phrases. Sofia spoke almost as many times (33), largely concerned with the sociocultural context of the poem and the emotional motivation of the female character. Iqbal spoke 16 times, again focusing on the assumed extratextual context. Najma spoke only 3 times, again on the motivation of the woman in the poem. While Najma contributes little more than any of the students in Group 2, the sort of English to which she has access at her table is of a different order to that constructed in the other group.

In Group 2, the numerical distribution of utterances is very different, with the teacher, at points, conducting a dialogue between herself-as-teacher and herself-as-spokesperson for the students. The teacher asks far fewer questions of the students here than in the previous episode. The students do not ask the teacher any questions. This lack of questioning is paralleled in the lack of eye contact between teacher and students.

With Group 2, the teacher spoke 22 times, focusing on the meaning of specific words. She asked 11 questions, with Tony answering 10 of them, Peter answering 1 and Hassan and Chris answering none, all in response to these direct questions on vocabulary. The teacher and the students are involved in an entirely teacher-led interaction. The students do not express ideas about alternative or shared meanings about the poem, and the teacher does not invite a dialogue that goes beyond the barest requirements of the official curriculum. Towards the end of this episode, as the last three lines of the poem are 'discussed', the teacher and the students are all looking at the text, although it is the teacher who writes, reads the poem, and offers a response to the poem. She appears to be modelling 'doing annotating a poem' for the students.

> SUSAN: 'An age at least to every part'. Erm, an age, that means like a sort of, a sort of, well I think he means there … like a period of time, like a generation or something. Yeah. 'And the last age should show your heart'. So that's actually her revealing her love. 'For lady you deserve this state, nor would I love at lower rate'. OK, so that's just basically how much love … yeah

As in the appropriation of the pencil in writing for the students, here the teacher also speaks for the students. Yet what she models for the group is atomistic, a starkly simplified version of 'comprehension', and one unlikely to help them achieve more than a basic grade in their GCSE assessment.

Conclusion

In Group 1, the teacher and the students talk about the poem and are involved in a discussion about its meaning; the students ask questions and offer responses. One of the students writes throughout the episode, and reads the poem aloud. The students' and teacher's use of *gaze* and *gesture* expresses their response to the poem, including *gestures* that link the poem, their body and the dictionary. Throughout, the students interact physically with the poem. Through this use of modes the teacher and the students are involved in a genuine dialogue, and what is produced is 'English as discussion', in which text relates to extracurricular knowledge and their lives.

In Group 2, the students' take-up of modal resources is completely different. The students do not gesture during the episode. Indeed they do not touch the poem itself, but engage with the dictionary ('Look up the word *vegetable*'). They hardly speak, and when they do it is in response to the teacher's questions. The students do not read the poem aloud or read from the dictionary. Nor do they write. They hardly look at the teacher and the teacher's gaze is primarily directed at the poem. The teacher reads parts of the poem aloud, and writes on the poem-text. The poem-as-text is foregrounded by the actions of the teacher; the students-as-people are backgrounded. The stark inequality of the modal resources used by the teacher and the students produces a sparse notion of 'English as comprehension through instruction'. They are left to their silent response of resistance and disengagement, expressed through *gaze*, *posture*, and *gesture*. This is a striking similarity with teacher–student interaction in the 'low-ability' class in the streamed school described earlier in this chapter.

It seems clear to us that English is produced in different ways with different groups of students. That is, what the original designers of the National Curriculum called 'the same broad and balanced curriculum' takes on deeply different meanings, even within the same classroom. For us what produces these different kinds of English is the combination of many factors, but importantly it is high-stakes testing, and demands for performance, which sets a classroom agenda where teachers want to achieve at least some minimal level of success for all of their students. Alongside this is a highly specified National Curriculum, which seems to allow for little local inflection in response to local needs and interests, and particularly so where teachers are anxious about the 'ability' of their students. Another important factor is the decreasing autonomy of teachers to make decisions about pacing, content, values and, importantly, the continuation of longer-standing discourses and practices relating to differentiation on grounds of assumptions about fixed and innate levels of 'ability', which act as sorting mechanisms for both overt and covert social sifting.

In this chapter we have attempted to show how these different entities are produced socially, and given their actualization multimodally. They are not so much embedded in the curriculum's formal content as enacted in classrooms, with teachers and students deploying a range of semiotic resources to make, and to contest, forms of English.

The social production of character as an entity of school English

Introduction

In the previous chapter we looked at different versions of English, produced as a result, we suggested, of different conceptions of 'ability' held by teachers about their students. We concluded, perhaps too pessimistically, that one – among others – factor in this might be the diminishing autonomy of teachers under the 'new dispensations'.

In this chapter we turn our focus somewhat differently, to look at one example of how what we call the 'curriculum entities' of English are produced in different classrooms. By 'curriculum entity' we mean those curricular 'objects', 'processes' and 'relations' that constitute that which is the curriculum. Entities are the abstract concepts that we use to think with in different subjects. In this sense they constitute the subject as a school subject. In school science there are entities such as the water cycle, blood-circulation, electrons and wave-forms, which make up that curriculum, and there are processes which establish how these entities come about, and how they relate to each other and to the world (Kress *et al.* 2001). So in English, too, there are entities having broadly the function of constituting the school subject English: the significant literary and non-literary *genres*, the technical terms whereby we understand meaning and the world (*metaphor, simile, analogy*, for example), the modes for making meaning (such as *speech* and *writing, texts* and the entities of texts), syntactic and grammatical entities such as *sentence* and *clause, noun* and *verb, subject* and *object*, as well as the means for dissemination of meaning, the media such as *book* and *screen*, and so on.

In examining the entities of English, we are also focusing more directly on a different and for us crucial question, namely the question of the degree of 'movement' or 'play', of freedom or autonomy that might still remain with agents of different kinds – schools, students, parents, teachers and others – in shaping English. As we said in Chapter 2, all this is set against the background of a quite clear political, social, economic and pedagogic movement. This background is encoded in the National Curriculum, but also in other policy moves, such as the Key Stage 3 Literacy Strategy, which, in changing the curriculum profoundly, have also had the effect of changing the relations in institutional education, and, as just one example in the case of English, of making the English curriculum much more 'explicit'. One way of seeing this is to think that the aim is to make the English curriculum much more like the science curriculum in terms of explicitness, by setting out clearly what the entities of the English curriculum as well as their relations to each other are.

In this chapter, we focus on one such 'entity', the entity *character*. We want to show how such an entity (as an example of how this would be with *any* entity) is actually produced in the English classroom, and how the social and organizational arrangements of the school and of its environments in all senses affect its production. We focus both on the attributes and features that are ascribed to *character* in the National Curriculum, and on how this is produced, 'inflected', differently in the classrooms that we observed. Through the analysis of classroom data, of interviews with teachers, and of school policies we develop our argument that the conditions for developing different potentials for English are always more than a matter of an individual teacher's philosophies or teaching style. Nonetheless the agencies of the teacher, of departments, of students and of schools remain significant in telling ways. We argued for instance in Chapter 6 that aspects of certain pedagogic discourses such as notions of 'ability' held in the school develop in relation to such specific matters as the admission policies, and the streaming and setting policies of schools, which closely link to that. We describe how *character* appears differently in the different schools that participated in the research, and we focus in detail on two schools: Springton School and Ravenscroft School.

We go beyond simply documenting how an entity appears, in order to show how the particular shape of a curriculum entity, such as *character* – though we might have chosen others – impacts on the *potentials for learning*. We provide a detailed multimodal analysis of the realization of *character* as seen in the teacher–student interaction we found in two classrooms. We conclude that the social relations of the school, the subjectivities of the learners and the form of English itself are intimately connected with the realization or actualization of curriculum entities; they provide one means of access to an understanding of the production of the subject itself in a school.

'Character' and the English curriuclum

The entity *character* is central to English in its relation to literature. It is highlighted in the history and development of English as a school subject, emphasized by its prominence in the National Curriculum, as in the classrooms we observed. English Literature as an academic subject (as opposed to the 'classics') began in the working men's colleges of Britain. The emphasis was on the transmission of moral values through literature to the working class. That had been an essential part of the ideological project of English advanced by the work of, among others, F.H. Bradley and F.R. Leavis (Eagleton 1983). For Leavisites, as for others – Marxists for instance – literature and society were intimately bound together. In such approaches the very stuff of ideology is seen as reflected in (great) works of literature. Colleges and schools encouraged a close engagement with literature to enable the communication of strong moral values through its texts. Such literature, it was thought, offered the potential for students to discover a spiritual home, and ultimately to discover the self through reading it: '[to] know how they came to be as they, very idiosyncratically, are' (Kermode 1979: 15). Throughout the twentieth century, the traditional notion of the study of *character* as a means for knowing oneself has underpinned an oblique form of moral education in British schools.

The residue of this legacy persists in the current (official, though in many cases, also unofficial) English curriculum. In its broadest sense this legacy is embedded in the National Curriculum's focus on 'promoting pupils' spiritual, moral, social and cultural development through English' (DfEE 1999: 8). More specifically, it is realized through the inclusion and exclusion of particular authors and texts, as we discuss in Chapter 10. The study of set texts is a central element of English. GCSE English coursework and examination includes the demand for responding to a set text by recommended major authors. The English National Curriculum programme and assessment schema both highlight 'character' as a core entity. Understanding *character* is explicitly specified as central to a critical and creative response to a range of texts. Students are expected to demonstrate how *character* is constructed through an author's choice and style of language. They are assessed on their ability to make comparisons between the characters in a text and their role in the narrative, and to demonstrate the motivation and behaviour of a character through the analysis of a text (DfEE 1999).

In Ravenscroft School the importance of *character* is enshrined at the level of school policy. For example, policy on teachers' assessment lists key skills that should be developed and assessed in English. These include the 'ability to write stories that portray and develop character' and to 'take on the persona of a character' as well as to 'be able to understand and analyse characterization in plays and critical writing'. The concept of *character* provided a strong framing focus in the lessons that we observed, although it was produced in many different ways.

We think it is important to understand how an entity is produced because the modal realization and the communicational form that curriculum entities are given are key dimensions in the shaping of knowledge. In turn this shapes the potential for students' engagement with texts; and that potential has its effects on possibilities for learning. In other words, curriculum entities, how they are produced and realized, provide different kinds of resources for the production of knowledge and subjectivity in the English classroom.

While the curricular entities of English may be set out in policy documents, they are produced in the social domain of the classroom. Hence how the entity *character* is constructed – what is 'brought (in)to it', what features and attributes are ascribed to it – depends on which social domain rules the classroom: Is it that of the everyday of the students, for instance, as in one of the schools (Wayford) described? Or is it that brought by teachers as their (explicit or implicit) conception of English? Or is it that of policy, made somewhere away from the locality of the classroom, away from the ethos of departments, the professional formation of teachers, away from the demands and needs of the social environments of schools (as in Springton perhaps)? In other words, one deciding factor in this production is *which* world and *whose* cultural capital rule in its formation – to use the terms of Pierre Bourdieu and Basil Bernstein. We said in Chapter 3 that the social relations of the school are expressed in the pedagogy of the classroom, but they are expressed just as much, if differently, in the form of the curricular entities that are produced in the classroom.

The entity *character* is a part of the (official and unofficial) curriculum and is at the same time not at all fully determined by it, in the sense that it is actually very weakly specified in and by either official or unofficial curricula. In terms of modes, we can ask: is it *talked* about, *acted* out, *written* about, *shown*, or *drawn* in cartoon-strips? Epistemologically, we can ask: is it naturalized into an everyday realism, does it have a larger metaphorical effect, a moral or ethical function, does it have a theoretical force – is it strongly linked to and dependent on the social relations that obtain in the classroom?

This is one point where official policy and local practice can – and in our data often do – part company. Policy is general; classrooms are local and specific. The National Curriculum is an attempt by government at establishing a common, unified, social constituency; the *actual* constituency, however, is very much that which is on the ground. What is on the ground, especially in urban contexts, is *difference*, the effects of the multitudinous forces described under that broad term 'globalization', for instance (see Beck (1992) and others). It is at this point that the school's and the department's policies enter into the picture to mediate national policy. Here, especially, policy around admissions and streaming becomes crucial.

While we base our discussion in the rest of this chapter on two main illustrative examples to describe how *character* was realized in two classrooms, one taken from each school, at times we will draw on examples from other classrooms. Among other things this will allow us to show just how different the productions of the 'same' entity are in different schools. For example, to show how each fits into what school English is in the different classrooms and what kind of student work is demanded and enabled – or ruled out. Or, how character is shaped as performance through the use of space, and movement in space – whether in the classroom, in the amphitheatre or the drama studio – and the other modal resources that the teacher stipulates or the students bring.

The multimodal production of character

Here we shift to a description and analysis at the micro-level of the production of the entity *character* in two schools. Taking one English lesson from Springton School and Ravenscroft School in turn, we analyse the way in which character is produced through teacher–student interaction. The discourses about character that are active in the construction of this English curriculum entity are apparent in the quite different modal realizations in each of the two classrooms. We examine what features of English are emphasized through the interpersonal relationships configured by the teacher's organization of classroom interaction; we focus on the position that students are offered by forms of English in each lesson. We explore how National Curriculum, exam syllabus, and son on, are inflected in encounters between teachers and students. Finally, we comment on how the work of the teachers is shaped (and generated by) their attempts to relate the forms of knowledge and subjectivity encoded in English to the interests of students, via the complex demands of the National Curriculum, official policy, school tradition, and the teachers' 'formation'.

Through our analysis we are led to conclude that the admissions policy of selection and of ability streaming at Ravenscroft School produces a classroom in which a social domain is established for teacher and students in which the teacher's values are dominant. The teacher transmits her view of English to her class as a whole. In a seeming paradox, as a result, the teacher is able to incorporate (or subordinate) the *official* curriculum version of English into her own approach to English as a school subject. Here, the teacher constructs *character* by fluidly moving between her knowledge of the social domain of the students' everyday experience of the school as an institution, and the teacher's world; between her version of the curriculum and the official version. Yet the social and epistemological domain is hers. The official curriculum is mediated through, even subordinated to, the teacher's values.

This is quite different in Springton School, which operates without a policy of selection or ability-based streaming (see Chapter 6). Here, where the students are seen as a diverse group with diverse needs, the official version of the curriculum is dominant. The teacher does not put forward her 'own sense of English'. Rather, her attempt seems to be to mediate the official curriculum to the students, but, also paradoxically as it seems, by moving it onto the grounds of the social domain of what she thinks is the *students'* experience. Hence it appears that student experience is used to mediate official curriculum. Ravenscroft, having adopted a policy of selection, can be confident that students have come to the school knowing that to be an achievement; the teachers in the school can respond by confidently offering school knowledge as valuable. In Springton that knowledge and hence that confidence is absent; the value of the school's knowledge has to be achieved by some other means.

Springton School: character – Romeo and Juliet

We have discussed this school already in some detail, in Chapter 6. Here, the activity of 'reading' is used as a means of understanding and actualizing what *character* is. In general, *character* is seen as an entity that is 'just there', as it were, in the text: it is realized via performance, in voice and gesture, and by other means. It is available as an experience. *Characters* have their place in a play, and are presented by the teacher as something unproblematic, to be performed; it is the actualization of *character* that is the crucial aspect of the performance.

In this classroom *character* is not a problematic entity, relatively speaking. It is not a matter so much of establishing what this notion might be; instead, the focus is on producing the entity in and through action, via the use of the modes and the material forms that need to be involved: of *voice*, (facial) *gestures*, the *body*. The understanding of character is related to a quite immediately available level: characters are (like) 'persons'. So the teacher informs the students that they will be assessed on 'how well they put the feelings of the characters across'. This takes it as given that *character* is 'there', and that a character 'has' specific feelings. The task therefore is to actualize what these feelings are, to show 'the feelings'. What the larger or deeper meanings of these feelings might be is not the issue here. That *character* might be a construct, a potential to be used and shaped, to be transformed by the students in their actualization of this potential-for-meaning – these are not questions. Rather, the question asked by the teacher, Julia, is 'what *is* the motivation, what motivates them, what's pushing them forward?' Students are encouraged by the teacher to 'try and see behind the character – why they are doing what they're doing', 'what you think each *person* is thinking and feeling and what actions you think they might be doing or what tone of voice'. A second(ary) task is then to annotate the script with this information, which might then be 'right' or 'wrong', depending on other evidence found in the text.

Character is and remains a concrete entity; it is not presented as a construct, an artifice, it is not a metaphor for something other or larger or deeper. Hence the text as written is central, although the move in teaching about character is away from writing and towards action. Here English exists as the performance of written text. The students are involved in realizing the character multimodally, but they are not encouraged to reflect on the function of *character* in a larger, a more abstract sense: understanding remains at the level of the surface of the play/text.

So in Springton, character is produced as an explicit and quite concrete entity. Rather than teacher and students working collaboratively to construct this concept, the teacher, Julia, presents it to the students as a ready-made set of features and attributes. The task of the students is to 'fill in' these features provided by the teacher. Their task is to bring character 'to life' through their performance, to 'make the character real' through their engagement with, and performance of, its emotions and motivations. *Character* is realized as a discrete 'unit' of the play; so the question of the function of character in a play is not a part of its construction in this classroom. The separation of the entity character from the (meaning of the) play as text is heightened by an exclusive focus on one scene of the play – *Romeo and Juliet* (Act I, Scene v).

The students are not asked to read the whole play, rather they work with a photocopy of the text of this one scene. This fragmentation of the play in the lesson mirrors the modularization of the curriculum – Shakespeare is there as a culturally iconic figure; yet his texts exist simply as 'fragments of text', to be mined for the technical purposes of the curriculum. In this classroom the dominant realization modes for character are *movement*, *body posture*, *gesture*, *facial expression*, and *speech*; in the classroom we discuss below, in Ravenscroft, the dominant realization modes for character by contrast are *speech* and *writing*.

After the students have read the scene, the teacher enquires how many of them 'understood the text': her own initial estimate and suggestion is 'about 20 per cent'. The assessment of what constitutes 'understanding' is seemingly straight-forward enough to be quantified. Beyond this, the teacher does nothing with the idea of understanding. The students are being encouraged into becoming assessors of 'understanding' themselves.

We wonder why the teacher turns the comprehension of English-as-performance into a competition? There is no doubt that she is concerned to ensure that the students should have an 'understanding' at this level by making links to 'the world outside'. For instance, she by takes the word 'pilgrimage' out of the text of *Romeo and Juliet* and, taking it entirely literally, she gets the students to define what the word 'pilgrimage' means via their own experiences, from knowledge gained outside the school.

TEACHER: Can anyone tell me what a pilgrim is?
STUDENT: Yeah, that's a Haj thing.

A student offers the term 'Haj' and the teacher accepts it, but she does not then encourage the students to contribute their own understandings of what a Haj or pilgrimage might mean to them, and how this might illuminate the text. The concern in Springton School is 'by what means can I get the students to satisfy – even if mini-mally for some – the requirements of the National Curriculum?' This often comes down to cursory, superficial definitions of vocabulary, as in the example of 'looking up' the word 'vegetable' we saw in the previous chapter. The text is and yet is not linked into the out-of-school lives of the students. The glossing of the word 'Haj' comes from the world outside; but nothing more is done with that other knowledge. In this way English is produced as a set of competencies rather than as a means for going further, no matter what the textual materials at issue might be.

We have no wish to place responsibility for this on the teacher alone. What we see here is a new conception of English as constituted for the 'less able', in which the aim is the achievement of basic attainment targets; an attempt at satisfying performance criteria. For the teacher, achievement lies in the security of predicting attainable outcomes for her students. These outcomes focus on creating a synopsis of the text at the most basic level; on demonstrating understanding rather than interpretation. There are complex issues here, which circle around notions of equity, and what these might be seen to mean in relation to this school – its student population and its teachers.

Ravenscroft: character, admissions policy and streaming – The Crucible

The collaborative production of *character* in this classroom of Ravenscroft School is a complex process. In order to attain the highest grade in examination, the curric-ulum assessment criteria require that students understand the play, its events and

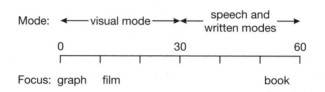

Figure 7.1 Ravenscroft School, representation of modes in use during Diane's lesson

characters as complex signs, to go *beyond* the text, to read *between* the lines; and this is precisely what this teacher expects from the class. While other modes are in use in the lesson, the dominant modes for the realization of character are *speech* and *writing*. *Character* is not performed here; rather, it is talked into being.

Character is never explicitly defined by the teacher, and therefore the sense of what this entity is remains open and somewhat elusive. In the lesson we discuss here, the construction of *character* is used to draw the students into a discussion of the philosophical and political arguments that Arthur Miller develops in *The Crucible*. *Character* is produced as a vehicle that serves the interests of the play; something that 'emerges' through events and dialogue; as a sense that is woven throughout its structure; as a web of references, including references to the students' experiences of life. It is altogether a much more abstract notion of character, not concretely there to be 'read off' the text, but emergent in the play's actions, relations and processes.

In the first half of the lesson the teacher and students summarize 'where we have got to so far'. This 'summary' is a recapitulation of the play, a multimodal reshaping of the play via the multimodal medium of film – in *speech, enactment* and *image* – to produce a shared version of the text-as-meaning, and the entity *character* as a tool in relation to issues around the planned coursework. (The coursework took the form of an essay discussing the character John Proctor in relation to a comment by Miller: 'It takes an individual conscience to stop the whole world from falling'.) In the second half of the lesson the teacher works to establish the framework for this coursework. Here the modal realization is entirely through *writing* and *speech*.

Represented as a time-line, the dominant modes and focuses of the lesson are schematically indicated in Figure 7.1.

Multimodally, *image* is foregrounded in the first half of the lesson, which contrasts sharply with the modal foregrounding of *speech* and *writing* in the second half. This shift in modal realization can be understood as a shift in the pedagogic concern and framing of English in the lesson, from 'English-as-pleasure' or entertainment – based on a much more sensory approach – to English as technical or theoretical competency and skills, with an examination focus. Here there is a much more technical, instrumental approach. In the first half of the lesson the play and its meaning is foregrounded; the demands of the curriculum remain in the background. In the second half, the reverse is true. The shift to curricular concerns demands a shift from English as abstract and a matter of elusive sensibility, to English as specific and concrete. This entails a shift from reading and interpretation to production for the examination.

'Plotting' character

The lesson starts with the teacher asking the students to consider what 'the play might look like as a graph'. She draws two axes on the whiteboard, and labels the vertical axis 'hysteria' and the horizontal axis 'as the acts progress', that is, what is mapped is a theme – intensity of emotion – against the chronology of the play. She marks discrete units on the horizontal axis: 'Act 1', 'Act 2', 'Act 3' and 'Act 4'. The teacher then asks the students 'Where would you have me draw my line – "hysterical"being right at the top?' and moves her pen, hovering, up and down the vertical axis.

STUDENT: Down.

TEACHER: Down [*she moves her pen down the line*]. About here?

STUDENT: Yes.

TEACHER: OK. And as the play goes along where would you want me to draw it?

STUDENT: Up, up [*teacher starts to draw line*].

TEACHER: Continuing up?

STUDENT: To boiling point.

TEACHER: Continuing up to boiling point, which is about there [*teacher draws X on the graph and then draws a vertical line down from the X to the horizontal axis*], the end of Act 3. You could say that for it to continually rise and maybe you'd say there's some ups and downs...

The teacher's use of a graph to represent features of the play is, we think, epistemologically noteworthy. It moves the forms of analysis from the domain of the literary, humanistic, subjective to the domain of the mathematical, scientific, objective; from the modes and genres of speech – such as *talk, conversation, debate* – to the modes and genres of the visual – such as *graph, chart, diagram* – outside the usual genres of English. The teacher's choice of a visual genre leaning on the scientific or technological – a *graph* – to represent the development of the action of the play can be read as a visual marker of a suggestion for the students to stand back, to generalize and to 'objectively' analyse the play in terms of 'empirical evidence'. The abstract character of the graph enables specific events within the play to be 'plotted', in this case the relation of emotion (hysteria), against the progress of the play over time – much as one can plot rainfall or temperature. In this way the abstract entity 'dramatic structure' is brought into existence in a very specific way, and in a very specific domain, not traditionally that of English, around the character John Proctor. Traces of a scientific syntax and genre are present in her speech – for example, 'level off' and 'variables' – and, as we will point out, in visual-gestural form.

TEACHER: Then we are at the Proctor's house again, aren't we? [*The teacher points at the graph with her pen at the section of the line above Act 2.*] Act 2, so it kind of does level off here [*draws a horizontal line*] where we see the home life. But even that has variables in it [*teacher draws a wiggly line over the horizontal line*] because we see the sort of difficult relationship between Proctor and his wife.

Figure 7.2 Diane's graphic representation of *The Crucible*

Drawing on (and pointing at) the graph (see Figure 7.2) the teacher visually places her (and the students') verbal account of specific events in the larger context of the play as graphed.

The teacher's iterative movement between the abstract generalized representation of the play as *image* on the whiteboard and her verbal account of concrete events actualize *character* as a multimodal sign of the complex relationship between themes realized in events and structure in time. Her activity indicates that *character* both needs to be understood within the structure of the play as a whole and at the same time as a part of the *processes of the construction* of the structure of the play. The teacher asks the students a series of questions that focus on signification: these highlight what the teacher considers to be the importance of particular passages and themes in the play, and explores how they are lodged in and realized through character. This also conveys the deeper curricular message that the students are to understand the events in the play as having meaning beyond the events themselves. For example:

TEACHER: Can anyone remember something John Proctor says to, um, what would you say he does, a couple of things he does to show us, the audience, what does Arthur Miller show us, the audience, to show that there's a bit of an uncomfortable relationship between them?

STUDENT: He comes into the house and straight away he puts salt in the food like, and when she comes down stairs she says 'I'm sure it's seasoned well'.

TEACHER: Yeah, they're obviously not communicating very well. She thinks she's cooked him this lovely dinner, taking great – she says she's taken great care to season it properly. He comes in tastes it [*teacher enacts holding a spoon to her mouth*] and goes 'urgh' [*teacher makes a facial expression of disgust*] and puts some salt in it. There's obviously some mismatch of their relationship. What else? Shika?

S: He talks about bringing flowers into the house cos he says 'it's like winter in here' meaning, referring to their relationship – the cold.

TEACHER:: Yeah, yeah, excellent, excellent. And finally, I don't know if anyone remembers but he says 'what about a cup of cider' and she's like 'Oh God I forgot something' [*teacher acts out frustration through gesture and facial expression*] and its like they're really trying to please each other but they have a very strained relationship. And we learn in Act 3 [*gestures at graph*] why their relationship starts to go wrong.

The teacher, Diane, continues with her recount of the play; she selects incidents that establish the centrality of the character of John Proctor. This recount provides a filter for the students who will be watching the film later in the lesson, as well as for the coursework that she is going to set. The recount is established collaboratively – the students supply quotes and extracts from the play to fill out the account. The teacher draws on the students' memory of the play and enacts their quotes through her voice, performative gestures and other movement. In this way the teacher and the students construct an account of the play that is structured around a specific notion of character. At the same time this produces the character and the play as a text with a particular shape. Specifically, the teacher draws on events in the play that highlight the conflict and contradictions within the character of John Proctor. Here the modal realization of character through *speech* allows it to be placed in the domain of 'the past', whereas when the teacher *acts* out the play she acts it out as in 'the present'. The movement between modes is used to produce an analytic process – the shift between tenses (verbally and visually) encourages reflectivity. The performance itself makes the play into 'data'.

The teacher uses her interaction with the students to overlay the graph with specific details of events in the play. *Character* is realized as an abstract entity that exists beyond the particular characters as people in the play. The teacher produces character as a vehicle for the meanings of the play itself. The graph is a visual resource that the teacher uses to mediate between the abstract entity *character* and the concrete character John Proctor in the play. The teacher's iterative movement between the graph and the concrete character realized in the play places *character* clearly within the realm of the abstract, the moral and ethical, and makes it clear that this character has a role beyond the realization of 'just a person, just a man'.

The teacher draws on the personalities of the students themselves in the construction of this entity. When 'casting' the roles in the play, she considered the 'characteristics' of the students and drew on that knowledge in her 'casting'. In doing so, the teacher was drawing on a different notion of *character*, as a sense of being or essence that connects with a sense of self. She draws on the personal experiences of the students as a resource to explore *character*. For instance, to explore the students' understanding of the motivation of John Proctor's wife in lying for him, she asks the students if they have ever lied for a friend. The teacher calls on a student whose name teachers consistently mispronounce in order to focus on the importance of names, and names as a vehicle for identity. The teacher weaves in the school experiences of the students as a resource for their understanding of the character John Proctor. In this way she is using the students' experiences as a resource to mediate the text, and using the text as a resource to mediate the social relations of the classroom.

Film: the multimodal realization of character

When the class watches the film of the play, there is a definite, noticeable shift in seating position and posture, indicating that the manner of engagement has shifted, from 'work' to 'leisure'. There is no note-taking, for instance, and students feel free to sit on desks – the general ambience has become casual.

The teacher continues to develop the notions of 'name' and 'character' as evident through the film version (for which Miller wrote the screenplay) of *The Crucible*. The students watch Act 4 of the play – the court scene, which they had read in the previous lesson. The teacher's selection of two excerpts from the film focuses their attention on the character John Proctor. The teacher mediates the students' viewing by her talk, and the use of the remote control to show 'significant moments'. Through this she is, literally, shaping what they see. The abstract notion of character previously realized in the graph is now instantiated in the realist, filmically shown incidents of character.

Below is a description of the teacher's use of the second excerpt of the film.

The teacher stops the video and stands with her hand leaning on the filing cabinet on which the TV stands, and she addresses the students from there:

TEACHER: What I'm going to let you see just very quickly is John Proctor's absolute fury at the end, which is understandable with all this action. I mean some of you vaguely laughed, some of you kind of go 'God this is ridiculous'. Isn't it obvious that every time someone picks on Abigail she suddenly goes 'Ahhh' [the teacher swivels around quickly and points as if accusing someone] that's her strategy.

The teacher fast-forwards the video tape.

If you look at the end at John Proctor's complete fury at the whole, he says things.

She stops fast-forwarding the tape. On the film at this point the crowd is running out of the town. John Proctor says 'I know this girl she is entirely false'. The teacher continues to fast-forward the video.

T: Now in this in the film version they run off into the sea as if they're going to wash themselves clean. This is where John Proctor really...

The teacher fast-forwards the video, then plays the video. On the film, it is the scene at the sea in which Mary Warren accuses John Proctor of working with the Devil. Throughout the scene John Proctor is framed as separate from the crowd and his accusers – first in close up and as his accusers speak in the distance against the horizon. In response to the accusations he says the lines: 'I say you are pulling heaven down and raising up a whore. I say God is dead!' The teacher switches off the video.

S: [*Groan*]

T: OK.

S: I say God is dead! Is it a demon, ha ha ha!

T: Right, back to your seats quickly then.

The teacher's selective showing of the video structures what sense of John Proctor's character she wants the students to get. The visual realization of John Proctor – through the use of framing, of shot-distance, and so on – literally sets him apart from the mob. The filmic image of him standing alone in the sea, confronted by the hysterically screaming mob is a multimodal realization of the Miller quotation that the teacher later writes on the board: 'It takes an individual conscience to stop the whole world from falling'. The film provides a clear vision of John Proctor as tragic hero, which the written text of the play does not provide quite so starkly. In this way the film provides an interpretative overlay for the students' earlier reading of the play and steers them toward the coursework.

The film offers the students a version of the entity *character* with which they may be more familiar and confident. It is constructed as something realized through performance, involving *action*, *voice*, *set*, and so on. The film further 'fills in' the meaning of the graph – it acts as evidence for the teacher's selective account of the play to produce her notion of *character*, evidence of the emotional and affective, as well as the moral and ethical aspects of *character*. But the students are not expected to produce this version in the classroom. Reading a play is one way of producing character; however, in this lessons the students are not asked to perform the play though their reading – they are not asked to use *voice*, *gesture*, *movement* in their realization of the character. (When the students did bring *voice* as a resource to their reading they were praised by the teacher – however, this had not been made explicit; it had not been a requirement for her.)

The film provides a connection between the students' highly visual textual world outside of the school and the written textual world of the English classroom. But the recontextualization of the film into the classroom is transformative – the film is not experienced in the English classroom as it would be at home or in a cinema. Through the classroom interaction the film is temporarily transformed from an everyday text, from a Hollywood film in the realm of leisure, into a specialized text in the realm of English literature. The film is made an object of study; it is analysed by various means, it is fast-forwarded, it is talked-over, it is discussed as a script, compared to the play. Above all, what is made significant in this work by the teacher is *character*. That is, *character* is produced as an entity that can travel across media – realized in play, film, written text, and even in the students themselves.

Summary

Through the graph, the recounting of specific instances via talk and 'performative enactment', and the showing of the film, the teacher expressed the theme of human consciousness via the entity *character*. The overt theme of witchcraft is suppressed in the teacher's recasting of the play. Her intent had been to produce *character* in quite a different way, beyond the surface, beyond the concrete instance of the 'person'; she did not want the students to come away from the play thinking that it was about witchcraft. She wanted them to see *character* as a means to understanding larger and more profound themes.

Writing character

Halfway into the lesson the rhetorical framing of the lesson changes markedly. The teacher stops the video, turns on the lights, and instructs the students to go back to their seats. She stands at the front of the classroom. The teacher's tone of voice and her use of words are now markedly different to that of the first half of the lesson – she uses short sentences, with an instructional purpose. Now *character* moves into the frame of coursework-writing – a quite new frame. Before this, the overt objective of the lesson had been one of her making: *character*, or *The Crucible*. Now the frame of the lesson has completely changed: this is represented through shift in mode, a shift in medium, and a shift in activity from collective to individual. The work of the students is now to produce a written account, foregrounding the demands of the official curriculum and of coursework:

> TEACHER: This is the part where you need your books. I'm going to write some things on the board and I'm going to say them aloud as I go along and you need to write them down, OK? We are studying *The Crucible* [*writes* 'The Crucible' *on the board*]. This is our twentieth-century drama [*writes* 'C20th drama' *on board*]. Whilst studying our twentieth-century drama and for our coursework we are asked to consider a number of elements surrounding the play. Now on its most simple level if someone said to you from another group what's *The Crucible* about … I want you to quickly brainstorm what you consider *The Crucible* to be about [*she draws a circle with lines coming out of it, with* 'what is it about' *written in the circle*].

This is the first time in the series of lessons that the teacher has explicitly mentioned the curriculum. Although the curriculum is always present in the class-room, it can be foregrounded or backgrounded. Up until this point it has been backgrounded, both in terms of contextualizing the play within the curriculum and in the positioning of the coursework.

The students do the 'brainstorm' and then feed back their comments, which the teacher writes on the board. Moving on from the themes highlighted by the students, the teacher reads aloud a quote from Arthur Miller from an interview, which she has previously written on the whiteboard: 'it takes an individual conscience to stop the whole world from falling'. She asks the students to 'play with it in your head' and to say what they think it means.

STUDENT: It means it can take a single person to like stop the whole world from creating, like war and chaos, and it could like take a single person to like destroy the world. It could take a single person to like create a nuclear bomb.

TEACHER: So the importance of the individual, yes [*points to another student*].

STUDENT: It's like if someone realizes that something is wrong and they speak up about it then other people might also realize that it's wrong, and stop going whatever.

TEACHER: It's got to start somewhere, someone has got to do something, you can't keep waiting for another person to have their conscience pricked other-wise you just go on and on, and on, and on. And it only takes one person … and on the other side, an individual conscience [*looks at quotation*] …

The teacher moves on to link the notion of the individual with the character John Proctor:

TEACHER: John Proctor has a loud voice in his head saying, from the like nega-tive side if you like … look just take your wife just go, just sort yourself out, you're just an individual, you can't do anything, this situation is bigger than you. Then there is another side of him, saying well, look, someone's got to put their foot down and stop it. That line there [*points at Miller quotation*] 'It takes an individual conscience to stop the whole world from falling' is what Arthur Miller truly believed he was doing when he was on trial in the McCarthyism situation in the 1950s with the hunt for the communists …

The teacher presents the character John Proctor as a realization of the themes of the play, in the move from the play as a collection of themes, to the notion of the individual, to the character of John Proctor, to Miller himself. The teacher estab-lishes *character* as a complex web of connections and references that 'hold' the cultural context of the play, the authorial intent of Arthur Miller, and the themes of the play. This enables the teacher to move away from the instantiation of character in the play as a literary phenomenon, and to move the students toward under-standing *character* as an abstract entity – a vehicle for the metaphor of the meaning

of the play. The teacher goes on to discuss the two sides of the American dream –
as potential to achieve, and as blame for non-achievement – as a metaphor for John
Proctor, and introduces this analogy for thinking about the character of John
Proctor. She presents a way of thinking about character as a vehicle for the social
and cultural context of the play:

> TEACHER: So if we look at something with two sides [*the teacher stands at the
> front of the room and holds her hands and arms in front of her like balancing
> scales*]: wonderful promise [*looks at and moves her right hand*], with a fright-
> ening other side [*moves and looks at her left hand*]. If we look at John Proctor
> [*teacher touches the name written on the whiteboard*] he reminds me a bit of that
> himself. First thing I wrote down yesterday, and I'm not going to do it all, [*teacher
> turns and starts to write*] I'm just going to do the first, the first thing I wrote down
> is that he's got these great contradictions or conflict within him [*writes 'conflict'*],
> and I'm going to write contradiction next to it [*writes 'contradiction'*].
> *The teacher starts to walk around as she talks.*
> On the one hand we have John Proctor the wonderful [*clenches her fists and
> moves them down*] powerful man in his mid-thirties. A hard-working family
> man. And on the other hand we have the adulterer, the man who was tempted,
> the man who was weak, but John Proctor is the epitome of not being weak in
> so many ways. Can anyone think of any other contradictions about him,
> anything he says, or anything he does.
> STUDENT: When he says it's cold, it's icy in here like winter, he's like saying
> his relationship is dead. But when they like come to his house and they're
> questioning him on the commandments, he's like, yes we know all of them,
> he's like saying we work as a team together, but then it's like their relation-
> ship's dead.
> TEACHER: Yeah, he kind of switches all the time [*moves her hands from left to
> right*] doesn't he, from being united with his wife, to being critical [*walks
> backwards, in a distancing manner*] in a subtle kind of way.

The teacher draws attention to other episodes in the play where John Proctor
behaves in a contradictory way, focusing on his attitude to God and the Church.
The students offer her their responses and direct quotations from the play.

> TEACHER: There are many many contradictions about what he says, the way he
> behaves, the way he quotes the Bible constantly at Mary Warren – 'remember
> the angel Gabriel, blah, blah, blah' – and then on the other hand he steers away
> from the things that he, he becomes part of the fight, you know, to know more
> about God, he's throws God down and then takes it away all the time, because
> he is a man torn [*holds hands to the side open, as if quartered*] in two. Maybe
> this play is about justice, about revenge, about all sorts of things that give him
> an opportunity to unify himself again, maybe it gives him the opportunity to
> be what he always wanted to be, which was the good man.

The teacher then asks the students to brainstorm their notion of the character John Proctor, focusing on his physical attributes, what is said about him in the play, what he says, and what the students know about him. She hands out the books: at this point the class is about 50 minutes into the 60-minute lesson.

In the move from themes of play, to Miller, to character of John Proctor, the teacher establishes the link between theme, authorial intent, and *character*. The themes of the play and the entity *character* are linked by the sequence of talk, by the activity of brainstorming, and (visually) by the material on the whiteboard.

Conclusion

We have focused on two examples, from two schools and English departments with clear and clearly distinct policies around admissions and streaming. In Springton character is unproblematically 'there' in the play text, waiting to be actualized; in Ravenscroft it is a much more complex notion, to be produced in relation to the deeper themes of a play. In Springton the teacher tries to help her students meet the demands of National Curriculum coursework, without attempting to help them to link their experiences to their understanding of the text, to enact rather than to interpret text. In Ravenscroft, the teacher relied on her own understandings of literature and literary thinking, into which she incorporated as much as was necessary of the National Curriculum for her pupils to succeed in producing the necessary coursework. At the same time, she invited them to make sense of the text in terms of their experience, also taking the insights from their work on character into understanding their own lives.

The different versions of the 'one' entity *character* are founded on and produced in and by quite different pedagogic environments, different kinds of teacher – student interaction and relations, different in content and in their modal realization; different notions of 'ability'; different conceptions of agency for teachers and for students. All provide students with specific resources for thinking, about character, thinking with character, and for thinking much more widely. In Springton School *character* is produced as something to think about, and to perform; it is bounded, technical, and has a limited potential beyond the demands of the official curriculum. In Ravenscroft School *character* is produced as something not only to think about, but to think with in the most general and generative terms. There it is like a 'fly-trap' for every aspect of the play: *character* is a condensation, a distillation of the characteristics, attributes, themes, issues and social and historical events, narrative themes, dramatic structure of the text as a whole. It is a means of distilling ideas about the human condition. *Character* is carried or realized in a social human being; but it is to be understood as metaphorical. *Character* is a vessel in which the issues of the play are collected. How *character* is conceived and constructed in different schools and classroom contexts is, we believe, the result of differently conceived social relations in the school, of school populations, of teachers, students and their potentials for being agents.

Chapter 8

Orchestrating a debate

Introduction

We have, so far, described a range of conceptions of English, and focused either on the means through which they are realized in the classroom, or shown how they are actually produced. At this point we want to document in more detail how English and the 'lifeworlds' of students can be and are brought together in the classroom, by showing a route taken by Irene, the teacher whose classroom at Ravenscroft School we have discussed several times already. Her notion of English incorporates some of the 'traditional' conceptions of the task of school English, and at the same time she is focused quite precisely on the demands of the official curriculum. As far as she is concerned, English has to serve a real purpose for the students who experience it; she is equally clear that English is a subject that can enrich the experience of the students in her classroom.

The literary text is one vehicle for achieving both. Yet, as our multimodal analysis has shown so far, a focus on speech and writing alone misses much that is crucial to the understanding of English. The question is whether this is so with the literary text – that object par excellence which might still be thought to define the subject English. So there are two questions we pose in this chapter. One is a question about curricular purpose – 'How does the teacher bring about the connection of literary text and lifeworld of the students?' – and the other is about our methodology, our 'way of looking' – 'Can the multimodal approach add to an understanding of that curricular task?' Hence we look for the ways in which this teacher builds a fuller sense both of the literary text and of 'the literate person'. The pedagogic purpose, namely seeking and providing criteria and means on which the successful assessment of an essay can be based, is constantly there, forming the backdrop to the teacher's actions: it is the recognition by the teacher of the demands of the official curriculum.

We examine this complex set of aims in relation to one newer and now common *literacy practice* in the school – the shared reading and interpretation of a set text, leading in later lessons to the individual production of an assessed essay.

The newer agenda: 'literacy practices'

Increasing attention has been paid in recent years to the study of literacy practices in informal situations as experienced among adults (Barton and Hamilton 1998; Baynham 1995) and as experienced by young children in the home and community (Gregory and Williams 2000; Kenner 2000; Kress 1995, 2003; Moss 2001; Pahl 1999). These informal literacy practices have been contrasted with the practices of what has been called 'schooled' literacy (Street and Street 1995), 'official' literacy (Dyson 1997) or 'mainstream' literacy (Heath 1983). We are aware that 'things' have moved on since the data for our project was collected in 2001, specifically through the introduction of the 'Key Stage 3 policy' into secondary schools in England. Nevertheless, little attention has yet been given to the study of literacy practices as experienced by pupils at Key Stages 3 and 4 in secondary-school English classrooms. Nor has the role of secondary English teachers or the resources available to them as 'mediators of literacy' (Baynham 1995) to adolescent students been attended to as yet.

This neglect of *literacy practices* in the secondary-school English classroom may have been due to a perception that by this stage of schooling teachers have become so enmeshed in curriculum prescription that there is little to be observed as creatively constructed in the classroom other than what might in any case, and more easily, be gathered from an analysis of curriculum documentation. However, as we have shown so far, even though they are regulated by policy, curriculum and variously approved pedagogic frameworks, English teachers actively construct their subject day by day, *differently* in the settings of the different classrooms. They do so in the materials they use, the ideas they generate, the modes of communication they employ, and the relationships they form (Jones 2003b) as they work with students. On the evidence of our study, we think it is safe to predict that even the most exhaustively regulated educational policies are creatively mediated by teachers; in this their work is shaped by the multitude of factors we have suggested, not least among them their students' responses (Pollard 2002).

So here, working with an example of that common literacy practice observed across the project schools, the shared reading and interpretation of a set text, we begin to examine this practice more closely. As we have said, it aims, in later lessons, toward the production by individual students of an essay for assessment. Our analysis makes it clear that some teachers, while focused on (official) curriculum and examination, have found strategies that give them space to connect texts with the experiences of their students – one of our two primary focuses here. They do so in ways that link English in all its aspects to wider social and ethical issues, drawing on their own and their students' life experiences in order to make connections with the texts studied.

Edwards and Mercer (1987) have argued that it is in the talk between teacher and pupil that education is done or fails to be done – in the construction of 'common knowledge'. But in the process of transmitting academic knowledge and skills, education regulates and positions not only talk but also bodies (Bernstein 1996). Thus it is not enough to examine the use of verbal resources, as the work of

Edwards and Mercer itself shows. That is one foundational reason why, in our research, we turn a 'multimodal' lens on teaching higher-order literacy skills in the English classroom. In our use of the term 'higher-order literacy skills' we refer to the broader conceptual issues of understanding a text itself – the meanings of literary texts, a full sense of the potential of curriculum entities such as *character* and *narrative* – rather than a narrow, sparse sense of literacy as residing in the competencies of using the resources of writing, of syntax and grammar alone. In other words, we understand the teaching of literacy skills as based on a multimodal production, in which speech and writing are just two modes among many in the ensemble of modes involved in the production of English in a specific classroom.

The starting point for multimodal approaches is to extend the social interpretation of language and its meanings to the whole range of representational and communicational modes employed in a culture. Multimodality assumes that all modes have, like language, been shaped through their cultural, historical and social uses to realize social functions. We, along with many others, take all communicational acts to be socially made, and meaningful about the social environments in which they have been made. We assume that different modes shape the meanings to be realized in mode-specific ways, so that meanings are differently realized in different modes. In the example discussed here the resources of gesture – for instance the spatial extent of a gesture, the intonational range of voice, the direction and length of a gaze – are all part of the resources for making meaning. The meanings of multimodal signs fashioned from such resources, like the meanings of speech, are located in the social origin, motivations and interests of those who make the sign in specific social contexts. These all effect and shape the sign that is made. In order to explore the uses of all modes, we turn to the social semiotic notion of meaning functions, derived from the work of Michael Halliday (1985). This allows us to analyse how the modal resources are used to realize both ideational (somewhat too broadly: 'what the utterance is about') and interpersonal (also too broadly: 'how the relations between makers of signs and receivers of signs are represented') meanings as signs. As we have indicated at various points, and particularly in Chapter 3, we think that our theory, our way of looking, provides a range of tools with which to 'prise open' the meanings of the English classroom more fully than a focus on the modes of language alone. We apply these conceptual tools to examine the meanings of the signs and of what Scheflen (1973) calls 'customary acts': acts that happen in a particular context at a particular time and which have an established function.

In the remainder of this discussion we now focus on the 'multimodal orchestration' of a 'whole-class' debate around a text, as an example of our two concerns here.

The context of the classroom

The example discussed in this chapter is drawn from Ravenscroft School. The social origins of signs are deeply implicated in the (multimodally realized) meanings created, and so it is important to note the teacher's own social postioning.

Irene is a Black African-Caribbean woman, an ethnic background shared with a significant number of her pupils. In interviews, she expressed a strong interest in the impact of cultural difference on learning; she has a powerful commitment to raising students' academic attainment. Her aim, she says, is to provide students with a framework within which they will be able both to succeed academically and to read real life critically. Irene is able to create a particular relationship with her Black students, such as those participating in the incident we shall describe here, by sharing some of her own life experiences as a Black woman with her class, at points where this has relevance. Conversely, the students told us in interviews that in English lessons 'We voice our opinions ... We are allowed to talk and say what we feel'; 'we feel we have got respect'.

The focus of this lesson is on drawing out and establishing, in debate, dialogue and interaction, the construction of gender, both as it is in the text and in its meanings for the students in the class. This shared cultural, ethnic and social positioning, and the relationship of trust established by the teacher with the students over time, we think underlies and makes possible the specificities of this particular event.

Rhetorical orchestrations

In the lesson we focus on here, Irene is working at mediating a text to the students as part of the Key Stage 4 National Curriculum requirements for 'wider reading'. The text she has chosen is a short story by William Trevor, *Theresa's Wedding*. It examines the relationships among an Irish Catholic family and their friends and partners, as revealed at a wedding reception. The teacher's *curriculum objective* is to develop students' skills in providing evidence from the text to justify their interpretations of these characters, their feelings and motives.

At the start of the 'critical incident' that we have chosen to analyse here, the teacher has changed her position in the classroom, and her posture has altered. She has moved from a formal posture and position (seated in an upright posture at a desk at the front-centre of the classroom) to an informal one (sitting on the edge of a desk at the front-left side of the classroom). This marks and, we argue, makes possible and produces a significant change in discourses adopted from then on by both the teacher and the students. We try to show how the teacher rhetorically 'orchestrates' the students, drawing on them as a resource in the analysis of the text that she wishes to construct jointly with them. We can see the teacher deploying her knowledge of her students' lives to construct a seemingly simple framework that they can use in a successful interpretation of the text for the purposes of meeting assessment requirements.

Simultaneously she uses the text to ask students to reflect on their own lives and their social positioning. In this case, the students are asked to focus on gender relationships – on the construction that she offers: 'And you boys will need to examine sometimes how you behave towards girls, even in school as well. Yes?'

Women | Men

Figure 8.1 (Representation of) the teacher's diagram on the board

Creating a framework for text analysis

In the first stage of the sequence the teacher sets up a framework for the critical analysis and debate of the text through her use of the resources of the photocopied text of the story, through *talk, gesture, drawing* and *writing* on the board. She employs the modes of *gaze, gesture* and *posture* to focus on the text, subduing her own and the students' bodily movement. She stands at the front of the classroom and instructs the students to 'find the page' where the revelation that 'Theresa has slept with Screw Doyle' is revealed. She then moves away from centre, moves a little to the left, to perch informally on a table in the far-left corner of the classroom, expressing her own difficulty in making sense of the reaction of the male character in the story as she is moving across. Her move away from the centre opens the floor for debate to the students, while her request to 'find the page' positions the text as the ultimate authority in critical reading events. The teacher then draws a diagram on the board (Figure 8.1).

Through her talk and gesturing in relation to the 'diagram', she produces an analytical device, or frame, for the discussion of the text, in which gender is the single category. Visually, the diagram polarizes 'women' and 'men', literally dividing them as two elements. In the visual semiotics of Kress and van Leeuwen (1996) it is assumed that where an element is placed in the framed space is a matter of compositional *choice*, and its position is therefore meaningful. They suggest that the direction of written scripts has shaped how people come to 'read' and 'produce' images, and that as a result particular meanings (information values) are associated with the spatial position of an element. In societies where people read from left to right the information value of *given* ('what we know or take to be the case') is associated with elements on the left, and the information value of *new* ('what we assume to be new information') is associated with elements that are positioned on the right of the space. In the diagram shown in Figure 8.1, the element 'women' would therefore have the value of 'given (and 'known') (the teacher is, after all, a woman), while 'men' is compositionally associated with the value of 'new' (and therefore 'not known'). The separation of 'women' and 'men' is emphasized by the teacher's repeated gesturing at the two sides of the diagram. These gestures are accompanied by her comments that 'this is the men now' and 'we're looking at how men act', in the context of her discussion of the author's placing of male and female characters in different settings in the story. While talking about the story the teacher makes several circling gestures around the diagram; these gestures link the diagram and its meanings into the debate that follows.

The story itself acts as a resource in that each student has the actual text of *Theresa's Wedding*. (We might draw comparisons here with the treatments of texts in Springton and Wayford School that we discuss in other chapters, particularly where students were given no direct access to texts or only to small extracts from them.) These students are used to using a full text; they look through it, they find and agree on the page at issue, and they read the passage. The teacher deals with the text at the more abstract level of a 'theme', in this case that of gender relations. The diagram and her gestures in relation to it have already linked the 'text as abstract theme', 'text as literal story' and 'text as material object'. The diagram remains as a visual backdrop throughout the lesson, serving as an abstract schema onto which the teacher can map (constantly varying) aspects of the text itself, the classroom interaction and the analytical theme for the assignment.

In the second stage of the sequence, the teacher opens up the text (as object) to begin to elicit the students' own response. The text is read and then the teacher asks 'All right. Would ... what's wrong with that? What makes you feel ... what is wrong with Screw Doyle telling Artie on his wedding day?' The students begin to respond and the teacher then starts to orchestrate the often very lively debate that ensues.

In the third stage of the sequence the teacher sets up a debate between the students on the basis of their gender, calling first on the female students and then, separately, on the male students. At this point the teacher's talk changes. She adopts a wider pitch-range, and a more emphatic rhythm, which we take to be signifiers of heightened emotion (see van Leeuwen 1999). Her choice of vocabulary changes from the formal to a less formal: for example, 'Ah. All right! Hold on to that!' and later 'Ah, I like that, inequality. Who takes responsibility for this?' The teacher's gestures change from being infrequent, slow, small-scale hand movements close to her body, to more frequent, more rapid, larger gestures, directed away from her and at the students. This shift in *voice* quality, in *vocabulary*, and *gesture* points to an intensification of energy, and represents a shift across all these modes from a *register* of a formal style to a *register* of one that is less formal. We think that this intensification in the teacher's communicational manner is akin to the 'customary acts' (Scheflen 1973) of talk shows, such as those of Oprah or Jerry Springer. In her interview the teacher commented that the students watched these TV debates and that the parlance of the shows had begun to 'enter' the classroom as part of the students' communicational repertoire. During this part of the interaction quite similar changes appear in the students' *talk* and *gesture*. For the moment, the focus shifts away from written text to student experience. The teacher is, literally, orchestrating the discussion *through her gestures* – 'shushing' and holding her hand up to stop boys from talking, waving the girls to respond. The girls and the teacher together 'fill in' the women's side of the diagram. Both through her *gesture* and her *talk* the teacher constructs the diagram as an analytical framework for examining both the text and the social relations of the classroom. The female side of the debate ends with the question 'Who takes responsibility for this?' and with that question the debate is now opened up to the boys.

In the fourth stage of the sequence, the teacher opens the debate with the boys by asking 'How would you have felt? Put your hands up, as males in this room, if it had been your wedding night, Christopher, and somebody had revealed that about your bride?' Here she draws on shared knowledge, as both she and the class know that Christopher had recently been involved in a physical confrontation. Again the pitch, tone and volume of her voice are higher and more variable than at other points during the lesson. There is a noticeably less formal use of language by the teacher and the students. The teacher gets up from her seat and paces across the front of the room. Her earlier expansive gestures of 'calling in' the girls' responses are replaced with tight, small, pointing gestures: she points and wags her finger 'challenging' the boys to engage in the debate. Christopher smiles and hits his fist into his hand and says, 'You'd be feeling quite angry, init'. Peter volunteers 'I'm going to feel angry, coz I know if it was way before the marriage, yeah, I simply wouldn't have gone through with the wedding, because, that's, that's...' Peter's and Christopher's comments on their imagined anger and the gesture of 'mock violence' serve to sketch in a content for the 'men' side of the diagram.

Through talk and gesture Irene has placed the male and the female students in a different relationship to the text. The teacher does not ask the girls to place them- selves in the position of Theresa, the main female protagonist; perhaps she assumes that they will automatically do so. Rather, the focus is on 'men', and the girls are asked to comment on 'how men act' and 'why men feel free to talk about their conquests'. By contrast the teacher asks the boys to respond directly (and emotionally) to the situation described in the text, rather than to engage in a more distanced analysis of the text itself.

The literary text as evidence

In the fifth stage of the sequence the teacher brings the text back to adjudicate in the debate, by asking a female student to read out a relevant passage. The girl reads the part of the story where the bridegroom's friend, Screw Doyle, reveals that he had slept with the bride some years before, arousing the anger of the bridegroom towards the bride, rather than towards Screw Doyle himself. The teacher's use of the text here achieves two things simultaneously. Firstly, it negates the male response of Christopher and Peter. They, like Artie the male character in the story, have 'not listened to the facts'. Secondly, it reminds the class of the curriculum objective, the need to ground their personal responses in the evidence of the text.

The first battle won, the teacher returns to her position on the left of the class beside her diagram on the blackboard, smiling, her posture relaxed and her voice calm (low volume, even pitch and tone, and regular rhythm), and again now using formal vocabulary. The transcript below shows both the modes used by the teacher and her drawing on the characters in the text, to link the responses of the students in the classroom with the wider issue of gender. (We have used the transcriptional convention of (McNeill 1985), in which the *underline* shows the temporal placement and extent of the gesture in relation to the speech.) Throughout this episode the teacher sits on a desk to the left of the board at the front of the classroom.

(1) SPEECH: So you see how men then draw a – a kind of – you know
GAZE: *At Lizzy*
GESTURE: *Right hand in air – pointing brings hands together, palms flat fingers touching [to form a line]*
POSTURE: *Sitting on edge of desk, one leg on floor, back upright – angled towards Peter*
(2) SPEECH: There's a line between male and female
GAZE: *At Peter*
GESTURE: *Moves right hand few inches in front of left, palms flat, moves hands away from one another and back again*
POSTURE: *Sitting on edge of desk, one leg on floor, back upright – angled towards Peter*
(3) SPEECH: It seems, because the men,
GAZE: *At diagram on board*
GESTURE: *Holds right hand – palm flat in front of her, moves, stretches out left arm, places hand on board and touches the 'men' side of the diagram – holds it there*
POSTURE: *Sitting on edge of desk, one leg on floor, back less upright – body angled toward Peter*
(4) SPEECH: You know, because the men –
GAZE: *At diagram on board*
GESTURE: *Left arm stretched out, palm flat against 'men', taps 'men'*
POSTURE: *Sitting on edge of desk, one leg on floor, back less upright, body angled toward Peter*
(5) SPEECH: Some men … might possibly would have become violent towards Screw Doyle
GAZE: *Around classroom to places occupied by male students then directly at Christopher*
GESTURE: *Drops and sweeps right hand/arm away from body out toward the classroom; takes left hand from 'men' on board and keeping it stretched sweeps it out around the classroom; moves left arm back again to touch the 'men' side of the diagram*
POSTURE: *Bends forward – leans in toward the class*

Through her gesture the teacher transforms the diagram on the blackboard into an analytical grid for use on the text. Augmenting the 'line' acting as a division between 'women' and 'men' on the blackboard, the teacher gestures with her hand to create a barrier in front of her body between herself and Peter. As she does this she says: 'there's a line between male and female it seems….' This gesture serves to realize the 'line' between men and women as a physical, material one. She gestures back at the line of the diagram, and by so doing she links the line on the board with the physical barrier she has created between herself and Peter: she *embodies* the separation of men and women. In this way the teacher places herself and Peter on either side of the line of the diagram, and of the structure of the text more generally. Momentarily she has re-framed the power structure of 'teacher and student' into one of 'female and male'.

Sitting on the table, she gestures at 'men' written on the board, and as if lifting this generalized term from the board, she sweeps her arm around the room as she says 'you know, because the men … Some men might possibly become violent towards Screw Doyle'. She gazes directly at Christopher, who had earlier in the discussion made a punching gesture in response to how he might feel in the character's position, and other male students. Here, we think, the teacher is drawing the social positions and the responses of the male students into her quite abstract discussion of the thematic of the text, as it is realized in the diagram. Her *gesture* and her *gaze* make comments at the same time both on the men in the text and the young men in the classroom. However, the comments on the men before her and the men in the text happen in different modes: the teacher's comment on the young men *in the classroom* is made through her *gaze* and *gesture*, while her comment on the *men in the text* is made in her talk. We might say that in a traditional analysis it would be said that comments in *gaze* and *gesture* might be felt as implicit, and that comment in *talk* as explicit. In a multimodal analysis, we might say that comments made via *talk* are immediately available for overt debate, for rejection or negation (as of course for acceptance also); and that comments made via *gaze* and *talk* are not. If that is the case, then the teacher has made her points more potently, for the students cannot directly challenge, contradict or reject them.

Throughout the lesson the teacher uses *gaze* to nominate, and she uses *gesture* to restrain the students for the rhetorical purpose of the lesson. For instance the teacher used *gaze* to nominate female students to talk and to associate Christopher visually with her comment on some men's potential violence. Earlier in the episode, she had used *gesture* in order to orchestrate a debate along gender lines (holding her hand up in a 'stop sign') to subdue male students from talking. Through her *gesture* and *gaze* the teacher defuses aspects of this highly charged debate, as she did not have to *say* 'I don't want to hear from the boys right now', she was able to stop them as 'individuals' without referring to gender. She was also able to carefully select which boys contributed to the debate. Theoretically and methodologically we might comment that she uses mode in a highly apt manner in relation to her purposes; ideologically of course this opens a different potential debate, one about the (seeming) covertness of her rhetorical strategy.

Although the teacher herself has 'drawn the line between the sexes', and gestured it into existence in the classroom, she attributes the production of the separation of 'men' and 'women' to men. Of course, she could have attributed the line to herself as an analytical device for looking at the theme of gender in a text; or to William Trevor, the author of the text, as a literary device; or to the position of the girls and herself as women. However, she attributes it to the attitudes (and potential actions) of men in general, to the male students in the classroom and to the response of Peter and Christopher in particular. In doing this she links the text with men as a group and with the male students in the class in a particular way. Through her *gesture*, *talk*, and use of the diagram-*image*, the teacher and the students whom she has selectively nominated to contribute to the debate collaborate in producing the text as a reflection of social reality.

Without the diagram the teacher would have had to *talk* the abstract notion of gender into existence and to link the behaviour of the male students directly to the characters in the story and to men in general. To *say* such things would both take time and, as we have said, be highly contentious. The diagram enabled the teacher to establish the divide as a 'fact', and to do so quickly and without debate. Her gesture with the diagram enabled her to make a visual link between the characters in the story, the students, and 'men' in general. This enabled the teacher to elide the move from literary fiction to the lived lives of the young men in the classroom. It also enabled her to treat them as a homogeneous group in the category of 'men': whether the young Black men in the classroom or the young Irish men in the story. It enabled her to introduce the concept of gender, to isolate it descriptively and to simplify it as an analytical tool.

Talk show

Throughout this concluding sequence of the episode the students are at their desks and the teacher is seated on a desk, at the front-left of the classroom. The teacher stands up and asks 'So, why wasn't he angry with his friend?' As she does so her gestures emphasize her question and her negative evaluation of Artie's behaviour. As the students all begin to respond simultaneously, Peter says 'Because' and puts his hand up. The teacher does not respond immediately, but then does look directly at him and nominates him: 'Peter'. He now has the floor, and 'takes off'. Lizzy and Christopher, the teacher and Darcus join in.

Peter

(1) SPEECH: What I was going to say is
GAZE: *Smiles, looks directly teacher*
GESTURE: *Holds left hand high in air finger pointed*
POSTURE: *Leans back in chair, body angled toward teacher*
(2) SPEECH: He ... probably could, true, it is different between men and women.
GAZE: *At teacher*
GESTURE: *Holds left arm high, wags finger up and down at teacher/moves arm to point at Lizzy, then back to teacher, wags finger*
POSTURE: *Leans further back in seat*
(3) SPEECH: But also, a friend – yeah, he's been his friend for years. Her, he didn't even love her too much.

GAZE: *At teacher*

GESTURE: *Holds left arm high, hand pointed, wags finger up and down*

POSTURE: *Leans back in chair*

(4) SPEECH: It's not a, it's <u>not a proper relationship</u>.

GAZE: *At teacher*

GESTURE: *Lowers arm, brings both elbows to side body, opens arms apart, palms open*

POSTURE: *Sits forward, shaking head from left to right*

Lizzy

(5) SPEECH: It's his <u>pride</u>, it's his pride. He's damaged his pride.

GAZE: *Looks at Peter, then at teacher*

GESTURE: *Hands clasped on lap*

POSTURE: *Leaning right arm on desk, facing teacher (back to Peter)*

(6) SPEECH: 'Cos it's a <u>male thing</u>, 'cos he doesn't really care.

GAZE: *At teacher*

GESTURE: *Holds hands apart, fingers spread moves to and way from her body*

POSTURE: *Facing teacher (back to Peter)*

(7) SPEECH: <u>What</u>, if he doesn't love <u>her it doesn't</u> really matter too much!

GAZE: *Turns to look at Christopher*

GESTURE: *Stretches left arm, palm open, sweeps out directed at Christopher, then drops arm and hand to rest on her lap*

POSTURE: *Leans back onto desk – moving away from Christopher*

Christopher

(8) SPEECH: <u>He probably</u> thought <u>if she's having my baby I gotta marry her</u> – religious as well. That's why he married her –

GAZE: *At Philip, then at teacher*

GESTURE: *Rubbing hands together on desk and moves hands apart, moves left hand in front of and away from right hand, then clasps them*

POSTURE: *Leans to right (towards Philip)*

(9) SPEECH: finds out she been having <u>sex with the best man</u> – <u>mixed emotions</u>

GAZE: *At Philip – then at teacher*

GESTURE: *Holds hands open and apart, swings both hands towards Peter, holds hands to side of head, makes soft circular motions*

POSTURE: *Leans back slightly in seat faces front*

Teacher

(10) SPEECH: <u>So men can behave in a certain way</u>? <u>That is acceptable</u>. But a woman can't? He was cross with Theresa. Didn't even want to sit next to her, on the bus. Do you remember?

GAZE: *At Peter and Christopher*
GESTURE: *Makes slow circular movement on knee with left hand*
POSTURE: *Leaning back on right arm stretched to side, legs crossed, head up back slightly, and tilted to the left (in direction of Peter)*

Darcus (off camera)

(11) SPEECH: No – where does it say that?

Teacher

(12) SPEECH: Look at your story.
GAZE: *At Darcus*
GESTURE: *Holds up left hand, points slowly moves arm up and down*
POSTURE: *(as before)*
  [Students look for place in story]
(13) SPEECH: Didn't affect his relationship, friendship, with Screw Doyle.
GAZE: *Looks at Peter*
GESTURE: *Waves left hand right and left in front of face, fingers spread*
POSTURE: *Turns to face Peter*
(14) SPEECH: That's a men thing. And you boys will need to examine sometimes how you behave towards girls, even in school as well. Yes?
GAZE: *Turns to look at Christopher then around the room*
GESTURE: *Nods head, holds up left arm with opens fingers, cups hand and flicks open fingers, drops hand to knee. Nods head.*
POSTURE: *Leaning back on right arm stretched to side, legs crossed, head up and back slightly, hand on knee*

Peter's jabbing, pointing gesture, his laid-back posture, the increased volume of his voice, his varying pitch and rhythm as well as his use of 'colloquial language' combine to shift the style of interaction back to the genre of the talk-show debate. Peter wags his finger at the teacher, in an echo of the teacher's earlier gesture that had negatively evaluated the response of the male character Artie (and Peter). He gazes directly at the teacher as he gestures, and his body is turned toward her. His gaze and gesture direct his words at the teacher (and at one moment at Lizzy). He acknowledges the teacher's (and Lizzy's) earlier point (that men and women might be different) but directly challenges her interpretation of events. He offers an alternative view of male behaviour (Artie's behaviour): it is not that men don't listen, but that long-term friendship is more valuable than immediate and potentially false 'love'. This can be read in different ways, perhaps that men are more reliable than women or that you can depend on long-term friendships more than on sexual partnerships (the latter of which may be true for many young people).

The teacher does not comment, leaving the floor now to the students. Lizzy responds initially; she looks at the teacher, echoing the teacher's usually more restrained body posture, open gestures, calm voice to suggest authoritatively that it is Artie's 'male pride' that causes him to be angry with Theresa instead of with his friend. Peter's response is to change his body posture: he turns away from the teacher and Lizzy, his gestures change to a wide open surrendering movement, as if giving up. He puts his hand to his mouth and turns to face and talk to Christopher. Through body posture, gesture and position, Peter physically 'withdraws' from the debate.

Lizzy then shifts her body posture and position in order to address her own comments also to Christopher. Her voice quality changes, her voice becomes louder, more high pitched – both indicators of greater energy/intensity and therefore of heightened emotion; her gestures are bigger as she leans back and points into the air towards Christopher: 'What if he doesn't love her, it doesn't really matter too much!' Lizzy, through her *talk, posture, gesture, gaze,* and her talk of love, continues the 'talk show' genre. Through their *posture, gesture* and *gaze* Lizzy and Peter make Christopher the focus of the debate: he is the person whom both are trying to convince of their argument. However, Christopher does not side with either Lizzy or Peter, although he does try to appease Peter through leaning toward him, looking at him and gesturing at him. But Christopher also looks at the teacher, his clasped hands echoing the earlier gesture of the teacher. He shifts the discussion back to the text: 'He [Artie] probably thought if she's having my baby I gotta marry her – religious as well.'

Although Christopher introduces the issue of religion, the teacher chooses not to pick up on this alternative reading. Indeed, when she speaks, she does not comment on what Peter, Lizzy or Christopher has said. Following Christopher's lead, she returns to the text to show how men and women seem to be expected to behave differently: 'Didn't even want to sit next to her, on the bus. Do you remember?' In this way she uses the text as *evidence* of the wrongness of Artie's (and Peter's) 'male' response. The students start to look for this line in text. As they are examining the text for the evidence of Artie's behaviour toward Theresa, the teacher says 'And you boys will need to examine sometimes how you behave towards girls, even in school as well. Yes?' As she says this she looks first at Christopher, and then around the classroom. Through her *talk* and *gaze* she directly links the examination of the text with the examination of self.

The boys' comments offer an alternative reading of Artie's behaviour – as a matter of friendship, time, trust and religion, rather than of gender. However, these 'alternative' readings unsettle the analytic frame of 'marriage and gender equality' that the teacher is working to establish for the students to use in making their assessed written response to the text. Hence the teacher's refusal to acknowledge alternative views is not simply a response to gender relations in the school and society more generally, not just the insertion of a piece of social and ethical instruction into the English lesson, a distraction from curriculum objectives. On the contrary, the issues raised, the debate itself, are directly linked to the teacher's objective, to provide an analytical device and frame that the students can then deploy in order to receive good grades in their next essay. Gender provides the possibility of constructing that frame, with the relationships between the distant Irish wedding guests played out in their own classmates' bodies and emotions. Now the students can produce a 'personal response' to the text, as required by the National Curriculum.

Conclusion

A link between text and self, the 'personal response', is a rhetorical stance explicitly demanded in the National Curriculum, and still lodged in the traditions of English. As we said in Chapter 6, the transmission of moral values has been an essential part of the ideological project of English Literature. This position, it was hoped, would offer the potential for students to discover the self through reading '[to] know how they came to be as they, very idiosyncratically, are' (Kermode 1979: 15). The residue of this legacy persists in the official English curriculum's focus on the development of citizens with a sense of moral and spiritual values. It also persists in the now unofficial curricula of a nearly past tradition.

Our detailed exemplification shows two aspects of the curriculum that might seem distinct; how the official curriculum – how literacy and 'being literate' are to be taught and learnt in social interaction in the secondary school – is to be linked with the social construction of the 'personal response', which is also required in that curriculum, demonstrably so for assessment purposes. In our example, the literary text is used very deliberately to construct particular understandings of social identity. These were then reflected back onto the text in order to construct a workable framework for its critical analysis, a framework that could then be deployed by the students in successfully accomplishing the forthcoming *literacy demand*, the 'assessed essay' of a comparison of two texts on the theme of marriage and gender.

We see all these aspects of the curriculum, whether 'personal response' or literate activity, as the result always of multimodal 'orchestration' rather than purely spoken dialogue or written performance. We are clear that in the process of teaching and learning English, whatever the skills, teachers and students are required to choose from, to engage with and in the process transform, the representational and communicational affordances (Kress and Bearne 2001) of all the modes available to them in the classroom. The teacher in the classroom here is involved in the choice and *designed* orchestration of a range of modes to actualize her specific purposes. Even when speech is foregrounded as often in this lesson, the teacher also uses *image, gesture* and body *posture*, both her own and that of her students, to construct meaning. In fact our example shows that the uses of *gaze, gesture* and *image* are crucial for her accomplishment of her rhetorical task. On the one hand, to look only at language overlooks and denies the meanings carried in other modes and the complex interplay between modes; on the other it actually mis-describes the accomplishment of the production of English in the classroom. Many of the the essential meanings and connections made in this lesson were carried in modes other than language; and no matter the degree of trust established between teacher and students, they would have been too contentious to verbalize. By expressing these meanings within the realm of the 'unspoken', through *gesture*, *gaze* and the *image* of the diagram, the teacher brought the issue of gender clearly into the debate while keeping the discussion relatively uncontentious, focused and concrete. Here a multimodal analysis has enabled us to examine the ways in which 'that which cannot be easily spoken' is realized in the English classroom. The unspoken meanings are as potent as those that are spoken.

Acknowledgement

A version of this chapter appeared as a paper by J. Bourne and C. Jewitt, 'Orchestrating debate: a multimodal analysis of classroom interaction' appeared in *Reading: Literacy and Language* 3(2), and we are grateful to Blackwell Publishing for copyright permission to use it here.

Chapter 9

Only write down what you need to know

Annotation for what?

Introduction

The annotation of texts of all kinds is a key practice in English. An annotated text can be seen as a direct pedagogic link between the actualization of English in the classroom and its official (re)production via an examination. We analyse two examples of annotation in two classrooms in two schools in order to describe how the teachers' deployment of annotation constitutes what the text comes to be, through notions of 'textual meaning' developed largely implicitly in that practice. That meaning in its turn positions students (and teachers) to English as a subject. Both examples are from lessons focused on 'wider reading', at the end of which students write a comparative essay on two short stories. In both our examples issues of student agency and curricular control are explored, and the link between annotation and examination is made apparent. In this way 'annotation of texts' becomes another lens through which we view the central question of this book 'How does English come to be as it is in a specific classroom?'

Through our analysis of the two lessons, one drawn from Wayford School and the other from Ravenscroft School, we offer a description of what it is that the teachers and students are engaged in when annotating a text. This description enables us to pose yet again the question what the teachers are hoping for and attempting to achieve, and what view of literary study they are attempting to construct.

Annotation is a device that teachers use to shape their students' responses to a text. In as far as it also elicits their responses, it is a means to bring students' 'private thoughts into public words' (Hackman 1987: 12) leaving 'a trace on the page of the sense you have been making of the text' (Northedge 1990: 41). In this way annotation is a means for reflection, in which a reader responds to what they find significant and meaningful. The marks that students make on the copy of the text as they work around and with it can be seen as signalling a sense of the text as an object (Hackman 1987). Annotation, and more general note taking, is seen as one way of making reading an active process and focusing the readers' attention on the text.

Annotation as it appears in the classroom is embedded in historical practices of textual analysis that go beyond school English:

> If you ask annotators today what systems they use for marking their books and where they learned them, they generally tell you that their methods are private and idiosyncratic. As to having learned them, they have no more recollection of having been taught the arts of annotation than of how to fasten a wristwatch. If you listen to their accounts of what they do, or if you are allowed to examine their books, however, you find (with very, very few exceptions) that they reproduce the common practices of readers since the Middle Ages. These are traditional practices culturally transmitted by the usual tacit and mysterious means – example, prohibition, word of mouth.
>
> (Jackson 2001: 5)

We will discuss the tacit character of annotation later in the chapter. In our first example, what annotation means is relatively unregulated and implicit: the teacher rarely instructs the students in 'how' or 'what' to annotate. For her, annotation serves as a more general device for developing 'reading', seen as a major tool for learning; she sees the need to read critically and to gather information as requiring the students to be able to excise judgement on a text, to modify, reject or develop views of the text (Lunzer and Gardner 1979). By contrast, in our second example the teacher makes the actual signs and devices of annotation explicit. As we have said, both teachers directly link the work of annotation to examination.

The English GCSE examination procedures (AQA 2002) offer a very specific definition and regulation of annotation. The NEAB anthology can be taken into the examination room and may be annotated; and the AQA stipulates what is included and excluded from the term annotation for the purposes of examination:

> Annotation means brief handwritten marginal notes, underlinings, hightlightings and vertical lines in the margin but not continuous prose. Additional notes, 'post-it' notes or loose inter-leaved sheets of paper and prepared answers are not permitted.
>
> (AQA 2002: XX)

Dymoke (2002) comments on the limiting effect the NEAB poetry anthology has had on the study of texts, as students learn to concentrate and focus on annotation rather than on creative engagement, as they are anxious to cover all potential examination questions. She argues that a focus on annotation and examination 'produces kids who can produce responses rather than kids who can write poems' (Dymoke 2002: 88). Our data similarly shows that teachers and students can become both fixed on and successful at attending to the tasks of examination rather than on the meaning of the literary texts. Of course this raises serious questions about what English is in this area. Protherough (1986: 39) warns with some alarm that a line-by-line exegesis of a text can 'degenerate into an alternative text'. While

we would not echo this way of posing the problem – annotation of any sort necessarily produces a new text – we share the sense that practices of annotation can
work to close down certain possibilities of interpretation and response. Annotation
is one practice – maybe *the* practice, where the pressure of exams is most clearly
apparent. There is much general evidence of the incredible pressure of examination on teachers, students and schools, with the impact of 'failure' on each of these
being so high (Elsheikh and Leney 2002). This pressure can lead to the teacher
handing over – and students accepting – ready-made readings of a text. Such pre-
packaged interpretations by-pass the need for students to develop their own skills
in (critical) reading and the time required for repeated readings. In this scenario,
played out in example two here, the response of individual students becomes
redundant: response to the text is no longer the issue; rather the point now has
become 'getting it right'.

Annotation in the English classroom

Our first example focuses on a series of lessons on William Trevor's short story
Theresa's Wedding taught by Irene in Ravenscroft School (see also Chapter 8).
The teacher works with the students, focusing on the theme of marriage and
gender. The second example draws on data from John's classroom in Wayford
School, in which he works with two short stories: *Superman and Paula Brown's
New Snowsuit* (Plath) and *Kiss Miss Carol* (Dhondy). Here the theme established
by the teacher is 'the loss of innocence'.

Annotation in Irene's classroom, Ravenscroft School

This teacher has two aims when dealing with annotation. The process of annotation was clearly linked to preparing the students for examination, as the excerpt
from her interview below demonstrates. However, for her it is also a device to
support the students in developing an understanding of a text and to give them the
ability to relate the literary text to their own life experiences. As Irene commented
during her interview:

> Every time you teach something you feel that it is where the child is going that
> you will have to be taken, so you are teaching annotation. Finally [it] is the
> exam. How will that child make sense of it? Will the child just start answering
> the question or will the child be reflective, go through the steps? There is a key
> word here and reading through and making notes. Because they will come out
> with a better exam result. We try hard to get them a bit of exam technique and
> there are all these things we have to consider and annotation is important
> because when the child first encounters a passage and then decides to structure
> a response – they have read all the questions yet sometimes they are not
> reading at the heart of the text – they are missing those critical points and so
> annotating is bringing a wealth of experience … This is analysis; before that it

is retelling so annotation empowers them to be more analytical and see beyond. It is always beyond. What we want is for them to make what they are reading match to real life – do you know what I mean? There is a story that is purely for enjoyment: what are the author's intentions? And in annotating they realize the writer is possibly saying a or b and whether they are wrong or right, if they can give evidence, then you have to say 'well, that is their perception' and they can back that up.

For Irene, annotation is a part of the process of reading as deep engagement with a text. Perhaps unsurprisingly then, her focus is on the meaning of the text, and annotation as technical process in the terms set out by the exam board is less prominent. On several occasions she tells the students what to write, but she does not tell them 'what to think'. By contrast, in our second example, from Wayford School – discussed later – it is the process of annotation that is foregrounded: the places where marks should be made, and how they are to be written and symbolized, are all made explicit.

Throughout Irene's lesson the teacher and the students sit at their desks; the story as text is in front of them, their pencils in hand or on the desk. Their attention is on the printed text; it is held, and gazed at; students run their fingers and pencils across its pages, underline sections and write on it. They constantly return to it; it begins and ends every exchange. Sitting at her desk, holding the text, the teacher starts the lesson by clearly framing the purpose of re-reading and annotating:

> We've read the story and now we're looking at the issues arising in the story. So you need a pencil to annotate. Remember what I said – when it is comparative writing you need to be aware of the various issues that arise so that you can group similarities and differences in order to write a valid response.

Throughout the lesson the teacher works to establish that 'the story' is a general comment on marriage, rather than on this specific wedding. The lesson is structured, at this point, as a series of rhythmic, cyclical movements across sections of the text, as discussions between teacher and students, and as acts of annotation. The teacher does not offer the students a specific reading: she does not interpret the text for them. Rather, she offers a conceptual lens – namely 'marriage' – through which to read the story, and she offers them analytical tools such as symbolic inference and close textual reading and invites their responses. She instructs them on what kind of 'reading' they should engage in: 'You need to scan now, when you've read something already and you're looking for information, you scan, you're scanning now, just going through quickly, looking for where things are…'

In return the students offer their opinions on the text, on the motivation of characters, and on marriage. They discuss the characters' feelings, the respectability that the characters attribute to marriage, the assumptions that 'people' in general make about marriage and happiness, and so on. The teacher weaves the students' responses back to the text, reminding them of the need to ground their response 'in' the text. The students are involved in the work of interpretation, discussion, annotation, and finding textual evidence. The following excerpt in which the teacher focuses on the character of Agnes, sister of the bride Theresa, is typical:

TEACHER: How does she [Agnes] feel about the marriage?

LINDA: She doesn't approve.

TEACHER: Find the line that confirms…

Students, heads down, reading or scanning texts.

LINDA: 'It sickens you a marriage like that.'

TEACHER: OK, so 'sickens you' – underline, 'a marriage like that'.

Students underline their texts with pencil.

TEACHER: Loaded statements. Does she like Artie?

STUDENTS: No.

TEACHER: How does she feel about this place?

MELINDA: She don't like it.

LINDA: She left, didn't she? Left it.

TEACHER: But how does she refer to it? 'She'll be stuck in this…?'

STUDENTS: Dump!

TEACHER: Tells you about her feelings, so you're looking for feelings as well, what the writer feels.

LIZZY: She wants, does she want her sister to break out of, she wants her to marry a more successful person so that maybe they can have more choice in their future and they can move out if they want to.

TEACHER: OK.

KERRY: Like I don't think she's happy.

TEACHER: You don't think who's happy?

KERRY: Agnes, even though she's married.

TEACHER: Yes, and we are told somewhere – where are we told that [*students start looking at story*] Agnes isn't happy? Although she is in a marriage that appears to be successful we've learned somewhere in the story that she's not happy.

LINDA: I just think she feels stable, in some way stable.

TEACHER: OK find it. You can't… [*taps on the copy of story on her desk*] it has to be here. You must find textual evidence to justify your point. So where in the story could you say this is implied if not stated explicitly? OK scan now, do not read in detail, just scan please.

PAULA: Page 57, paragraph 4.

TEACHER: Read please.

PAULA: She says [*reads the story*] 'She'd met George Tobin at a dance in Cork and had said to Loretta that in six months' time she'd be gone from the town for ever. Which was precisely what had happened, except that marriage had made her less nice than she'd been. She'd hated the town in a jolly way once, laughing over it. Now she hardly laughed at all.'

LINDA: It's a purpose I suppose, it was a convenient way to get married rather than for love, it was more a convenience to escape I suppose.

TEACHER: Yes, you see you learn that now that she is married she is not a nice person any more … page 55.
Students all turn to page 55.
MELISA: She's turned sour, hasn't she?

From this more general discussion, the teacher returns to the text and the question of annotation and says 'Annotate that please, put your square bracket, the reader learns that Agnes got married to get away from the place that she hates'. The text is a constant presence, and the cyclical rhythm of the lesson serves to foreground the interpretative and discursive work of the students alongside the teacher; the teacher – while certainly taking a leading role – does not deliver ready-made interpretations of the story. This 'collective' way of working is reflected and embodied in the shared resources of the teacher and students – the story itself, as a material text, and a pencil. During this part of the lesson, the teacher did not use the board, nor did she did offer the students dictionaries, and she worked with her own copy of the text, a fact whose significance becomes clear when we compare Ravenscroft with Wayford. Both the teacher and the students sat at their desks throughout the lesson; they had adopted the same basic body posture and gaze, leaning on the table looking down at the story, and in their discussion they adopted broadly the same tone of voice.

Annotation in John's classroom, Wayford School

Our second example is a lesson from a series of lessons in which the teacher, John, is working with two short stories – Sylvia Plath's *Superman and Paula Brown's New Snowsuit* and Farrukh Dhondy's *Kiss Miss Carol*. The teacher is working with the students and the *Superman* text, using a mixture of whole-class and small-group work.

If 'shared practice and resources' characterized the last example, here annotation is used to establish an authoritative set of relationships between the teacher, the students and the text. As before, examination provides the background.

The first quarter of the lesson is used to give explicit instructions on how to annotate and how to draw evidence from the story. During this time the students are seated at their tables in small groups, each with an anthology opened at the story, and pens or pencils in hand or on their desks. No student speaks, and the teacher only demands a raised a hand as a 'yes' in response to his questions. The teacher stands at the front of the classroom; unlike Irene, he does not have a copy of the text. He writes on the board, and he talks. These differences in posture, position, and in his relation to the text signal him as 'expert' in relation to the text and its meaning. We might say that these features are signs that 'the text is in him', that he is 'above the text'. He outlines the module, indicates the homework, comments on the use of quotations, gives instructions regarding examination, talks about 'evidence', describes how to annotate, and gives instructions on how to address specific questions, for example on setting and on character, which he has written on the blackboard. The teacher's focus is on evidence, annotation and examination, but it is unclear what the content is that is to be evidenced, annotated and examined. The focus is on 'rules of technique'. Students are urged to: 'find the evidence', look for clues, 'make sure that your notes are sufficient that if I asked you to talk to the next lesson you can', and 'don't write down what you don't need'.

John starts the lesson by instructing the students to look for connections between the two stories:

> You're going to go through the story and with a pencil you are going to be looking for things. You're looking for how the story is told, you're looking for quotations you can use in your exam. Now the exam question is going to be a general question comparing two stories and the two stories are *Superman* and *Kiss Miss Carol*. As you're going through *Superman* you're automatically looking at how does it fit together, how does it connect with *Kiss Miss Carol*?

The tasks set out for the students – 'look for quotations', look at 'how things fit together' or 'connect' – tend to be inexplicit and rather difficult. It is unclear what criteria the students might use to select a quote or decide what might be a valid connection. But the task of quote selection is foregrounded by the teacher and held up as a kind of organizational structure for responding to the stories: 'That's the most important thing you should have done, find the quotations first. You don't work out what you're going to say and then find the quotes. You find the quotes first because the quotes are actually where your answers come from.'

Thus John suggests that selection of quotation precedes analysis – that students have to know what they're looking for before they have made any organized sense of the text. This, he conveys, is what the examination demands: 'May I remind you that over here [*points at poster of curriculum assessment criteria on wall – described in Chapter 4*] is the assessment criteria. Yeah?' And to meet these requirements students must produce copious annotation: 'I want you to find lots of cfs, yeah I want you to have [*writes on board "cf: KMC"*] yep? And if you're really smart you'll have a number there [*points below the "cf: KMC"*] which is the line. Yeh? So you might have cf: KMC 204 okay? So you need a pencil and whizz through the story.'

There are difficulties here. Students are encouraged to learn a technique that seems not to depend upon prior analysis, nor on the kind of exploration of textual meaning that conversation might enable. They are urged to do so in the name of GCSE assessment criteria that seem accessible enough, yet detached from textual exploration will remain entirely inscrutable. The new explicitness seems in this respect to be as opaque as older, much-criticized implicit pedagogies, in which students were meant to imbibe method as invisibly as they absorbed the capacity to make judgements about literary value. And the movement between the reading of the text and the writing of an answer is left underexplained.

During the next twenty minutes of the lesson the teacher organizes the students into groups of four to discuss the text. This accounts for half the lesson time. The discussion is framed by a series of questions that the teacher has written on the board:

1   Who tells the story – how do you know?
2   What happens in the first paragraph? How is this a beginning? What clues to what will happen – foreshadowed?
3   What is the setting – place, time – evidence?
4   Paragraph 2 look at the description – what is described? Why is it described? Use of colours?

The students sit, pencils or pens in hand, they work a bit, then talk about music, football, television, downloading music; they flick through the story-text, rolling pencils across desks; they read the questions on the board. There are uncertain gazes, much pencil fiddling and looking at the text; there is little or no talk. John moves around the groups and intervenes, writing in pen on the students' texts.

The students' lack of conversational focus and involvement in their written suggest that they know, perhaps, that they can rely on the teacher to supply the interpretation that they are not inclined or enabled to produce. Certainly, when the lesson turns towards interpreting the text, and towards the opportunity for students to feed back their own ideas, there is more evidence of the teacher's interpretive involvement than that of learners:

TEACHER: Francis, can you tell me some information please, that your group have got from the first paragraph?
FRANCIS: She talks about the past.
TEACHER: Yeah, how long ago in the past?
FRANCIS: 1942.
TEACHER: How old was she in the story?
FRANCIS: Fifth grade.
TEACHER: Yeah, but how old was she? Information you can possibly deduce, how old she is.
STUDENTS: 10 or 11.
TEACHER: What war is it? World War Two; I know this because I know the story is American; America got involved in 1942. How many people had that?
    Some students put hands up, teacher counts them.
TEACHER: How old was Sylvia Plath when she wrote the story?

What is expected in this instance is information not interpretation, and what seems to be developing is a curriculum of facticity, what the students can pull out from the text in the most direct way, rather than what they might 'make of' the text through an act of interpretation.. The students' contribution to this curriculum is to say yes or no It is difficult to find evidence of response in the older sense of the term – that is of a motivated engagement – and the lesson does not give us reason to think that different responses to and interpretations of the text are in play. The emphasis falls instead on the teacher's interpretive work:

Then she has this really complicated bit about a kaleidoscope … It seems to me that there is something symbolic here to do with how you look at things. And maybe it's something to do with how you see the world when you're 10 and how you see the world when you're 23. When you're looking at the same thing … it seems to me that this idea of kaleidoscope goes right through the story in terms of colours. Now we've talked about light and dark that goes through all these stories. Dark is ignorance, dark is fear; light is knowledge, light is safety and in this one we've got other colours as well.

In the lesson, generally speaking, the students are called on more to listen than to participate in a conversation., There are exceptions, but even here the 'balance' of conversation tends to be in several senses unequal, shaped by the teacher's strong sense of the incapacity of students, their inability to enter the mysteries of textual interpretation:

TEACHER: What else is mentioned in the title?

JIM: Superman, a fictional character with special powers.

TEACHER: Is Superman going to come into the story in a significant way? How?

JIM: I think it's going to be that that's what the snow suit is like.

TEACHER: You haven't read the story.

JIM: Yeah I have, I've read a bit of it.

TEACHER: Oh. Homework four weeks ago was reading a four page story!

JOANNE: Flying.

TEACHER: Some one's saying something about flying – can we leave that bit! Superman is in the title, therefore it seems to me that Superman is important. Superman is not in the story therefore Superman must be symbolic? Do you think you need to write symbolic next to Superman at the top, unless you already have? How many people were going to say symbolic to me?

Some students put their hands up, including Jim.

TEACHER: About four? Well no, James, you didn't say symbolic and you had your chance!

Of course, questions of individual teaching style and experience are important here, in shaping the teacher's way of addressing the class. But it is difficult to over-look a wider set of influences, which relate to the distance between many students in urban schools and the demands of the formal curriculum. The sorts of expectation that John reveals could be read as signs of a familiar and well-established relationship between urban teachers and students, in the context of a long history of working-class academic failure and disenchantment. In the *Superman* lesson, they serve to underpin a curriculum presented to students as something beyond their reach. In this context the do-able routines of annotation come to stand in for those more conceptually orientated activities of which students are led to believe they are incapable.

Discussion

We can organize our sense of what goes on when annotation is being done through a number of connected categories and issues. First, there is that of agency – what kinds of capacity to act and to make meaning are available in the English classroom, and to whom are they available? In what ways do practices of annotation relate to forms of agency? Second, there is the question of the text – What notion of text is produced in the different practices of annotation and what consequence do they have? There is, third, the idea of a pedagogic practice and its immediate purposes – Does pedagogy take as its main objective the preparation for examinations, an accumulation of skills, or some other collection of purposes related to intellectual or moral or cultural development? Fourth there is the question of knowledge – What counts as knowledge? With whom does knowledge reside? With the teacher as authority? With the class understood as a group-in-dialogue? And, fifth and last, there is the question of the larger pedagogic and educational purposes of English, the question, to put it starkly: 'What is English for?'

The two classrooms show distinct approaches to questions of agentive capacity. In the one, students are encouraged to participate in the production of the meanings of the text, and the text is subject to negotiations between teacher and students. In the other, the 'rules' of the classroom suggest that agency lies with the teacher: he is the authoritative source of access to the text, and the students are relatively unskilled. The status of the text also varies from classroom to classroom. At Ravenscroft it is the centre of a process of enquiry and 'cross-referral' between story and world. In Wayford, the text is not so central to discussion. Its meanings are not matters for discussion, only for teacher interpretation. It supplies more a series of facts that, at best, can serve as the basis for an effective examination answer. To put it another way, the text is something to be mined. And what the text-as-mine affords is the valuable ore of 'quotes'. The value of the ore lies in achieving the real purpose of the text, namely allowing students to succeed in the examination. This utilization of the text is closely allied to the issue of annotation as pedagogic practice. Allied, too, to the issue of classroom knowledge, either as the product of a collective labour, or of the lonely work of the teacher, with annotation as the record of one or other of these processes.

Which brings us to the question of the pedagogical and educational purposes of English, the question: 'What is English for?' In the first example, English consists *inter alia* (the *alia* including the meeting of examination requirements) of the making of meanings that connect in exploratory ways the text with the world. It aims to offer in addition the tools that are necessary to record and elaborate these meanings, in this case the tool of close reading through annotation. Our other example provides a sparser view of English, although it rests on an appeal to certain kinds of sophisticated textual expertise. English, it turns out, is like other subjects, a means for passing or failing, except that the tools for success are largely left implicit, and are difficult for students to access.

Chapter 10

The textual cycle of the English classroom

Introduction

In this, the last descriptive, 'empirical' chapter in the book we look at the 'textual cycle' of the English classroom – that is, the selection of texts, their presentation and re-production to and for students, and the teacher's production of new texts. The question 'What is an appropriate English text?' has been and remains a highly charged one. It has been asked and answered differently by successive governments since the beginning of the 1990s. The literary texts that are brought into the curriculum constitute the cultural, social and ethical material with which the teacher and the students will need to engage, and they come to form one important element of what English can come to mean. We focus successively on moments of this cycle to show how the larger-level social relations of education work to position teachers and students in this respect, and how they create particular versions of English. The position of media studies in this respect is a case in point (Buckingham and Sefton-Green 1994).

The National Curriculum for English now stipulates what kinds of texts and authors are to be studied in the English classroom. What texts enter the classroom and what is done to and with them is therefore a political decision, in at least two ways. First, there is the larger public domain and controversy within it about textual inclusion and exclusion. An example of this was the controversial effort of the Conservative government in the early 1990s to drive texts of popular culture from the English curriculum and to restore 'pre-1914' literature to Key Stages 3 and 4. Second, there are micro-political decisions, taken within the framework established by policy, where a preference for one text rather than another can still be exercised, even though the space for such decisions has shrunk (see Jones 2003b).

In this chapter the inflection of English through different kinds of texts found in classrooms is explored. Through our analysis of teacher interviews we examine the reasons why texts are selected – or not – and made available to students as their experience of English. These texts form a crucial resource in the production of school English. As the official curriculum makes it compulsory to study a Shakespeare play, the second part of the chapter focuses in some detail on how *Macbeth* is introduced and studied over a series of lessons in one school. In particular we try to 'track' how 'formal' texts such as *Macbeth* are transformed into 'informal' texts – texts made by teachers – and how these two kinds of texts relate to one another.

Texts at the level of the National Curriculum

The question 'What is an appropriate text for English?' was in the past answered by English teachers in the context of the examination syllabus. At the time of writing, however, it is answered (if not fully determined) by the National Curriculum. Before the Cox Report (DfEE 1989), the texts to be studied for English were not prescribed. The Cox Report itself, implemented in 1990, is not prescriptive about the texts to be studied. It specifies the range and genres of texts to be studied, and focuses on teaching methods and how to approach texts in the classroom.

> There is, however, no consensus on which works should be chosen from the vast riches of written English and given a privileged status in the classroom. Formulations of 'literary tradition', 'our literary heritage' or lists of 'great works', however influential their proponents, may change radically during the course of time. It would be wrong, therefore, for us to prescribe a list of set texts. There is such a variety of good literature available for inclusion in syllabuses that we want teachers to have the freedom to make their own choice of suitable books within the broad guidelines indicated
>
> (DfEE 1989: section 7.14)

These broad guidelines indicate that programmes of study should be constructed so as to give all pupils the opportunity to work with a wide range of literary forms. The list included short stories, novels, plays and poems, biographies, autobiographies, diaries, film or TV scripts, works from different parts of the world and pre-twentieth-century writing. The Cox Report also states that 'In particular, every pupil should be given at least some experience of the plays or poetry of Shakespeare' (DfEE 1989: section 7.15).

In 1992 the government reviewed the curriculum recommended in the Cox Report, and in 1993 a new National Curriculum was implemented on the basis of that review. While the scope and range of texts remained relatively stable, the National Curriculum became increasingly prescriptive in character specifying the range of texts and a list of authors whose writing should be studied. During Key Stages 3 and 4 students were expected, as a minimum, to read one play by Shakespeare, a drama, some fiction published before 1900, a range of other fiction by 'reputable writers', poetry by two poets published before 1900, and poetry by three other major poets. 1993 also saw the introduction of SATS (Standard Attainment Targets) alongside the National Curriculum, which included testing on non-fiction or 'informational' texts as well as Shakespeare. The curriculum was revised again in 1995, although this was considered to be a basic 'tidying up' of the previous version.

The version of the curriculum in operation during the period of our study demonstrates that since the early 1990s there has been a merging of the curriculum and of examinations, leading to the production of restrictions and prescriptions of texts. The National Curriculum (DfEE 1999) stipulates which kinds of texts and authors are considered appropriate to be studied in English. Despite the prescriptive character of the official curriculum, the list nevertheless adds up to approximately 5,000 books, short stories and poems, leaving teachers 'overloaded with unrealistic choices' and the work of finding 'ways of taking the imposed oath without perjury' (Preen 1998). Indeed, in the case of poetry, examination boards have responded to the National Curriculum by the production of poetry anthologies that mediate curriculum and examination requirements. The increasing control of the selection of texts by central government via policy serves to heighten the political nature of the role of texts in English, and bears on notions of 'access' and 'equity'.

The National Curriculum provides 'guidance' on the 'knowledge, skills and understanding' that students are expected to develop in reading at Key Stages 3 and 4 in the form of competencies that students 'should be taught'. These 'competencies' are presented under the sub-headings of: understanding texts; English literary heritage; texts from different cultures; printed and ICT-based information texts; media and moving-image texts; language structure and variation. This policy framework positions texts as the material for the development of 'knowledge, skills and understanding'. In the process the entity 'English text' is constructed in a number of ways: as meaning; as a sign of authorial intent; as heritage; as (popular) culture and tradition; as informational resource; and as knowledge about language. To this extent, the meaning of 'text' has shifted decisively away from that of text as a literary concept. The analyses of work with texts in classrooms that we have shown decisively demonstrate that.

As our chapters so far suggest, however, the relationship between policy and how it is realized and inflected in what 'actually happens' in the classrooms is a complex one, with a range of diverse social forces in operation. In other words, schools, teachers, students and others are involved in the re-inflecting and transforming of national policies in their appearance in particular sites (Ball 1990).

Texts at the level of classroom

During the data-gathering part of our research, we observed teachers and students working with a wide range of texts. Media texts that were used in lessons included newspapers, film trailers, and the opening sequences of television programmes (such as *The Simpsons*, *PJ's*, *ER* and *Buffy the Vampire Slayer*). We observed three classes working with plays, two with Shakespeare plays (*Macbeth* and *Romeo and Juliet*), and one with Arthur Miller's *The Crucible*. Two modules of work focused on 'wider reading', comparing in one case the short stories *Theresa's Wedding* (William Trevor) and *Three Sisters* (Austen), and in the other *Kiss Miss Carol* (Dhondy) and *Superman and Paula Brown's New Snowsuit*

(Plath). One of the classes that we observed was studying poems from the 'Hearts and Partners' anthology.

The teacher's selection of texts is seen by some commentators as primarily a choice based on their understanding of the function of literature and the meaning of personal growth, cultural heritage, skills based learning and the transformatory view of literature (Marshall 2000). By contrast we view the texts that appear in the classroom, and how these are worked with, as reaching beyond the teacher's personal philosophy of English. Indeed these texts can, as we will show, stand in stark contrast to the teachers' expressed philosophies. Like others (such as Sarland 1991) we see a range of factors shaping teachers' selection of texts. These include the resources available in the school, the teacher's perception of the literary quality and status of a text, their perception of students' interests and ability, and the characteristics of the student intake of the school, in particular students' ethnicity, culture, language and religion. These underpinned the teachers' and departmental principles for the selection of texts, and shaped the sense of what makes a text relevant for students.

Texts in Springton School

Springton School is situated in a locality made up of a wide range of different ethnic communities; the norm of most inner-urban London schools. When interviewed, Anna, a teacher at the school, described the school's student population as follows (this matches official information on the school):

> It is quite a deprived school. It is in one of the ten most deprived areas of the country and it did have 70 per cent free school meals but I think it has gone down slightly, just under 70 per cent now, and it was 50 per cent Bengali but again I think that may have fallen just a little bit, I think it is about 45 per cent and there is 20 per cent of the school that are refugees and there are a lot of Somali kids as well and there is a disproportionate number of girls to boys so I think it is 40 something girls to 50 something boys.

There is, and has historically been, considerable tensions between the ethnic groups in the community that the school serves, tensions that are realized along racial and ethnic lines in the form of street violence. In response, the ethos of the school, and of the English department more specifically, is to attempt to harmonize the fractures (along racial and ethnic lines) within the local community. This desire to harmonize emerged in interviews with each of the three teachers. The Head of the English Department, Susan, commented in interview, for example, that:

> I think one of the things that is great about the school, there are issues and conflicts that go on outside school. There is quite a gang culture outside school, there [are] tensions between various racial groups as well. It doesn't generally spill over into what happens at school. Although you have some of

the posturing generally you don't have anything too... it never boils up particularly and I think one of the reasons is because they see school as a calm place.
In the Ofsted report it was described like an 'oasis of calm in a troubled area',
which I think is the best way of describing it

This teacher's comments suggest a polarity between the 'inside' and 'outside' of
the school, a perception that was echoed by the other teachers at the school. In the
English classroom this polarity is realized (at least in part) as a separation between
the students' lived experiences in and of the world outside of the school, and the
'stuff' of the classroom. During the lessons that we observed, the teachers did not,
for instance, refer to or draw on the students' experiences, beliefs or values; nor did
the students offer these in the classroom. Instead the teachers' and the departmental focus was on the production of English as a subject with a clear body of
knowledge for examination: 'when they go into maths or science they are learning
things that are new to them and they can tangibly feel that and they like to feel that
in English that it is something they wouldn't normally encounter' (Susan).

The students who were interviewed did not, however, view English as compar-
able with these subjects; also, they emphasized the school–society connections
rather than their separation (as this excerpt from a group interview with students
from one teacher's (Julia) class shows):

KALEEM: ...what you are being taught from a science teacher is different from
what you are being taught by an English teacher 'cos you are learning about
the outside world, the things that happen with animal cells, human organisms
and that, space. In English it is very different.

INTERVIEWER: If you learn about the outside world in science, what do you learn
about in English?

K: The inside I guess, about society and culture.

When interviewed by the project researcher, some students spontaneously
connected their community knowledge of arranged marriage with the text they
were studying, *Romeo and Juliet*. This is a move that neither they nor the teacher
brought to the classroom despite there being a high percentage of students in the
class who are Muslim, who are therefore likely to have communal knowledge of
'arranged marriage', and access to a range of cultural notions of love. One teacher
(Julia) commented:

I think partly because although all of our students really share or are bi-
cultural, they do live in London and they straddle their two or three cultures
sometimes very successfully and I know in the past, especially the humanities
for example, if all the examples you give are 'oh, this is in Bangladesh' or 'oh,
this is development in Africa' and you hope you are going to reach out to the
students. Actually they get a bit fed up with it so I think the idea has to be
good-quality literature and examples so that the themes, because they are
going to be universal, because that is what literature is, they can relate to those
and sometimes, I suppose you have to create an ethos in the school where it is

fine for everybody to talk about different cultures and if you are looking at a book written by a different author, a non-British author, then it is going to be fine. But we do poems from other cultures as part of the GCSE but I have not noticed that people make any comment on that.

The teacher's genuine desire to 'reach out to' the variety of cultural experiences of the students could have led her to turn towards a position of 'cultural hybridity' rather than one of 'universalism', and of literature as ways of overcoming cultural polarities. The departmental notion of literature, embedded in the notion of classic texts, appears to be more closely connected to the universal. However, the teachers' regard for the stability that the National Curriculum provides has its effects here: at the very least, elements of contentiousness around the meanings that can be made with literary texts are removed from the work of the teacher.

The students' comments suggest that 'cultural hybridity' is a position that at least some of them have adopted. When interviewed, the Muslim students spontaneously related *Romeo and Juliet* to their family culture as opposed to their own transformed 'British culture', and drew on both these sets of cultural experiences to explore the play, as shown in this excerpt of interview transcript:

HANEEF: The interesting thing is he [Shakespeare] talks about the human nature – his things are based on it – it is all happening now, this, isn't it? In Muslim religions if you are going out with a girl or boy, it's not allowed basically, unless you really really love them or something, but that is where hatred and conflict comes in between the two families, and he talks about, Shakespeare writes about it, and he puts his knowledge in the book. It is very interesting.

NAJMA: Because you know in our culture, Bengali culture, and the Muslim thing you are not allowed to go out with boys and girls, and girls usually get married young, init, and that is where Juliet comes into the thing.

MAHMOOD: Yeah, that's the Asian culture. There is laws and stuff. The fighting between two families, that still happens in a lot of places and the love story.

KAALIM: It's one of my mate's brother, he love this girl but he couldn't get her.

INTERVIEWER: Because she didn't like him?

K: Her parents and family, they disapprove and he got kind of mental [breakdown] … It is really strange when you see films based on this stuff, because in our family something has happened and you watch a film with all these things happening – it certainly happens to your family. You end up feeling, you know.

In Springton School we have established that the teachers work with texts in what we think of – at least at one level – as 'universalist' terms. By contrast, the students interweave their reading of these texts with their own cultural experiences and knowledge. However, the students find it difficult to bring their cultural readings of these texts into English as it is realized in the school classroom. 'Universalism' conforms to the teachers' aspirations for social relations in the school; by contrast, the students with their informal policy make the connections between (their meanings of) the texts, and their world.

The 'universalist' character inflected in the choice of texts for English in this school fits well with the rhetoric of 'equity and access for all' that is embedded in the National Curriculum. The choice of text and the English department ethos are closely interrelated, through the ways in which this department's ethos inflects and shapes the teachers' mediation of texts in their teaching of English. Canonical literature, such as the texts featured in this school, can be taught in a way that recognizes the positions that different students may have to them, while not making them foregrounded and potentially problematic. A teacher may set out to bring out all that they know and assume about the valued community cultures of their students. Alternatively, a teacher may teach the same literature in an attempt to 'replace' student culture with a dominant culture of 'Englishness'. Or an English teacher may choose to work with texts that in their terms reflect the range of cultures in the school.

Texts in Wayford School

Despite the lack of a coherent departmental ethos in Wayford School, and the many differences between the teachers' realization of English in the classrooms that we observed, there are shared principles that underlie the teachers' choice of texts. These reflect the department's particular stance to the student population and English, mediated by notions of culture and of the social as central to the production of English. The teachers' choice of texts was actively informed by their perceptions of the culturally shaped experiences of students' lives outside of the school, experiences that the teachers drew on explicitly and implicitly in their teaching. The texts were contemporary, or mediated – as film, for instance – to relate to contemporary experiences and issues. They dealt with themes of poverty, innocence, class and race. The teachers commented on the need to relate texts to the cultures of the students.

For instance, in one series of lessons taught by John, the short story *Kiss Miss Carol* was the text for study. It explores the school production of *A Christmas Carol* through the eyes of Jolil, a Bengali boy who lives in London's East End, in particular his father's response to Jolil's role as Tiny Tim. The teacher (John) commented when interviewed:

> Um, *Kiss Miss Carol* [Farrukh Dhondy] we do because we are a multicultural school. Thirty-five per cent of our kids are Bangladeshi. There are kids here who are refugees, who are private school kids from Afghanistan. There are kids here from Somalia, or whatever, who went to private schools and there are kids who come here who are essentially peasants, no sense of schooling at all, who have never been to school and are 16 years old, so there is a huge range.

The teachers in Wayford (John, Lizzy and Stephen) commented on the need to relate texts to the representational forms that inform the life-worlds of the students, a focus that is also realized in the classroom displays of this school discussed earlier in Chapter 3. When interviewed, Lizzy said:

> For a kid like Joseph for example, whose older brother is now applying for a course to become an animator, so there is a real audience for it and Joseph can express himself very well through pictures and respond to Manga comics, Manga videos, in a way he won't respond to anything else and there is precious little opportunity for that.

John gave the following reasons for selecting *Kiss Miss Carol*:

> I like it as a story. I think it is charming and I think it brings up quite interesting things because the main thing we deal with through the stories is to do with relationship between parent and children or adults and children and there is another theme that goes through the other stories to do with becoming an adult, realizing what the world is like, kind of thing ... you can look at class. I touch on coming from another country is equivalent to what happens in *Sons Veto* which is working-class girl marrying a middle-class man and coming to London. It is different cultures. I tend to use the word culture for class, religion, etc.

Later during the interview John commented further on his view of 'culture':

> I always have a broad range of reference things. I talk about culture before we do culture and traditions. I will say, I don't say 'God' so much as I will say 'Our Buddah' or whatever. There is always a broadness of it. I always link, like when we are talking about Bangladeshis, you can cross out the word Bangladeshi – this is any culture that comes here and I am in that category as well. In a different easier time, as an Australian, I come in I don't know these things.

John's comments on culture and his selection of texts suggest that for him, as a teacher, there is a homology between certain kinds of story and certain kinds of student experience. At the same time, he defines culture as a broad category in opposition to the dominant English culture and Christian religion. In doing so, the teacher negates race and ethnicity as key factors thus enabling himself to join the same category of 'cultural other' that he understands his students as occupying. The students who were interviewed identified their social class and 'race' as key factors in shaping their educational, work and general life opportunities, as one student, Benjamin commented:

> I think class and race is one of the biggest issues of the day. Class makes you know where you are going to go like if you go to a private school it is much

more likely you are going to get to University and get a better job. Here it is more likely [a student] from [a local independent school] is more likely to get a better job than I am.

Several students contested the teacher's (John) notion of culture and his mediation of it via the use of the text in the classroom. The following three episodes offer examples of the students' resistance to the teacher's interpretation of the events of the story through their own cultural readings both of the text and the teacher's positioning of himself and them. These also show how some students, both 'White' and 'Black', acted to diffuse the potential for different interpretations of culture to come into conflict.

Episode one

JOHN (TEACHER): Is there anything anyone wants to say? Anything about Jolil's relationship with his father?'

MADI: They're always together.

SUNDI: He's always telling him things about how White people are bad.

T: [to Sundi] Do you think things like that?

S: No.

T: Good boy. Why did I say that?

BENJAMIN: [quietly] 'Cos you're White.

JIM: 'Cos he's a boy, and he's good!

M: 'Cos it means he's [Sundi] not racist.

T: Thank you – yes.

Episode two

TEACHER (JOHN): Khalil [Jolil's brother in the story] is in front of the mirror, doing 'being a good Bangladeshi boy': shoes with buckles, striped trousers, black shirt.

NADEEM: [mutters] 'Oh God, sir!'

T: That's what they tell me, my Year 7 Bangladeshi girls: that's being a good Bangladeshi boy!

N: [mutters] That's looking smart.

Episode three

TEACHER: I've watched programmes on television and because I used to work in the East End I used to see them – little kids, particularly people new to the country, get paid next to nothing, if you haven't got the English you end up doing exciting things like sewing loops onto belts and you get paid by the thousand. The way to get somewhere is to work. That's why he [Jolil's father] doesn't want him to be in the play because school is about work not about fun.

NADEEM: He doesn't want him to be in the play 'cos he didn't want his son to play a beggar!

T: Just write it down.

Through the study of the text the teacher, John, positions culture as central to English and language as central to successful participation in the dominant culture; in this, English has a mediating potential for his students to succeed. He comments when interviewed:

> That language is power and knowledge is power – able to use language will get you power of the broadest possible sense – it will get you what you want when you go to a meeting or see somebody – being able to go to a library and use it. Being able to speak in the right way at the right time to get your jobs. It comes down to that. Power is the main thing. That is what I teach. How to get power ... In a psychological sense I think it [English] matters. In a social sense and an economic sense, an educational sense, English is the only thing at the moment that really focuses on the nature of how to get anywhere in society – it isn't a question of just getting a grade.

Lizzy and Stephen, the two other teachers that we observed at Wayford School, worked to enable the students to bring their 'own' experiences as mediated by social class and race into the classroom via the texts they worked with, rather than teacher perceptions and interpretations of the students' cultures. Nonetheless, all the teachers that we observed at Wayford School selected texts that both mediate the curriculum and foreground cultural themes. Within this school, we argue that the selection of texts mediates the purpose of English as being for life not for examination. As one student (Madi, a refugee from Kosovo) commented when interviewed:

> Basically, these stories they aren't for English people. I ain't being racist or anything, but it isn't for people that live in England. It is basically for people who come here. Like if a Bangladesh person comes here and reads that story, he is going to know, because that story is, basically, it is not your story. Like a Bangladesh person is going to know how to adapt to England and it is basically for them.

Texts in Ravenscroft School

There is a strong departmental ethos in Ravenscroft school, in contrast to the last, and this ethos informs the process by which particular texts appear in the English classroom: the teachers share, discuss and select the texts and ways of working with the texts collaboratively. As Irene, the Head of the English Department, said in interview:

We talk about 'owning things' and it is to do with team work as well, pooling together all of our ideas, deciding what we think will meet the needs of students best. Somebody might have information from another quarter that this is a good text, so what we tend to do is bring in all of our ideas, review books, talk about what this has to offer and then we agree, looking at all that we have, which books would be best to use to achieve the aims and objectives.

The texts that we saw being taught draw on the list of the official curriculum, authors such as Jane Austen, William Trevor and Norman Mailer. Some of the texts selected for study were rather obscure. These were meant to offer the students access to cultural and social themes that the teachers perceived as relevant to the students' interests and lives, and to the 'best' of literature. Irene again:

I am always looking back in order to look forward because time has gone by when the children weren't that engaged, the texts weren't interesting maybe, didn't reflect their experiences possibly and so children didn't see themselves in the situations which we were bringing into the classroom and so that was something we had to address. How to engage these students and so look carefully at the text as I said and decide 'this is an exciting story'. Has it got substance? Has it got mileage? Because you can't [just] give them this excitement, has to have some meaning, some substance to it, so at the end of the day you are contributing to their learning experience.

When I first arrived [in 1985] I had the experience where in the department Shakespeare wasn't taught ... I thought 'Shakespeare is supposed to be the best writer, and if he is why are these children not exposed to the best writer?' It didn't matter what I might think and there are texts lying in the stock-cupboard collecting dust. I decided that I was going to try out *Macbeth* with my two Year 11 classes. They did well and after that we decided 'yes, all children should have access to the best'. Always give them the best that is on offer.

This teacher, and the English department in Ravenscroft School more generally, value literature as offering a framework as a resource for the students in their lives; as a 'life experience' for the students; 'a window' through which to view the social world: marriage, gender, religion, culture and human nature.

You see because they [students] are not able and they are of a young age to participate in the things they are reading about, it gives them some insight. It is personal development and intellectual development as well. ... Therefore we are trying to prepare them, something for that world, something that they possibly might encounter later in life. It might be that they look back at some experience in the classroom and they say 'I've come across this before'.

(Irene)

The departmental focus on classic authors and the 'best' texts, on literature as a window on the social world, positions English in this school against a current in English teaching in which 'everyday' texts are brought into the classroom (as in the case of Lizzy in Springton School).

Choice of texts across schools and classrooms

Plainly, in one sense the texts that were studied in the classrooms we observed were there because teachers had chosen them. However, the teachers are institutionally positioned, so that for example exam constraints steer them towards particular texts (Sarland 1991). They are also discursively positioned, and it is on the basis of their positioning that they make their choices of texts.

In Springton School, 'classic' texts were chosen, and they were positioned by teachers as both having universal and high status for students and parents, and constituting the main body of knowledge for examination. The potential of these texts to relate to 'human experiences' was not a tool used by the teachers to draw in the diversity of the students' experiences. During the lessons that we observed the students did not articulate the links between the texts and their own lives that they made very articulately in the interview. The location of the school in an ethnically diverse and divided community produced the ethos of the school as a kind of 'retreat from the street'. The Head of the English Department (Susan) commented that the school had been described as an 'oasis of calm' in a troubled area in a recent Ofsted report. The boundary between 'in school' and 'out of school' was strongly marked in the classrooms of Springton School by the absence of references and links between the two. The focus remained firmly on curriculum and examination – a different kind of response to the diverse resources of the student body focused on access to linguistic resources and classic texts.

In Wayford School the texts that we saw in the classrooms were contemporary, and had been explicitly chosen to reflect and connect with the 'multicultural life-worlds' of the students. The ethnically and linguistically diverse student population was mentioned by all of the teachers who participated in the project. The need to 'engage' students in school English and in the school more generally was ranked as a high priority by the teachers in a school with considerable truancy problems. Texts were used in English as a tool to mediate social difference and cultural diversity, and in an attempt to engage with the students' life worlds, in an attempt to make English 'relevant'. However, while this may have been the teachers' professed position in the interviews, in the case of the teacher John, it was his perception of the students' culture that dominated the discussion of the texts being studied. The students' comments on the texts and culture were frequently dismissed as 'untrue' or 'incorrect'. In this way, the notion of culture itself became a 'curricularized' fact within English. Each of the teachers that we observed at Wayford School viewed English as a forum for the development of self and connected to the potential in life, either in relation to work and power or in relation to self-awareness and communication.

The teachers in Ravenscroft School speak from yet another position in English teaching, that of working-class and Black students having a right of access to 'the best'. Their position is produced at the intersection of particular ideas about high culture, and the experience of urban schooling. Institutionally, what gives further weight to this position is the nature of the school with its mix of elements of selection and many Black 'high achievers', and the nature of the National Curriculum and the priority that it gives to the study of 'Shakespeare'.

Bringing the text into the classroom: *Macbeth* in Springton School

The selection of texts for English is only one part of the 'textual cycle'. In the remainder of the chapter we focus on how texts are brought into the classroom. In particular we show how this process is shaped by the demands of the curriculum, by the teachers' perception of the students' interests and ability, and by the resources of the school. We discuss how the teacher Anna in Springton School brings *Macbeth* into the classroom and 'prepares it for examination' over a series of twelve lessons. We attempt to draw out how what happens to texts in the classroom often stands in stark contrast to the teacher's ideas of English expressed in interview, and how the text itself is produced in ways that provide students with different resources for making meaning, and, ultimately for learning.

The text of *Macbeth* takes some time to 'appear' in the classroom. In the first two lessons the teacher, Anna, does not tell the students that they are going to be studying *Macbeth*: the play is introduced in the third lesson. The series of twelve lessons focuses on five broad areas of work, and in each of these areas the text *Macbeth* is realized differently modally and features in a different way. The first of these areas, the focus of lessons one and two, is the social and historical context for *Macbeth*. In these lessons the text is quite literally not present for the students. These first two lessons provide a context that later will allow the teacher to connect *Macbeth* with her sense of the students' interest in witchcraft and superstition. She sees it as 'a way into' the text for the students that relates it to the National Curriculum and to the coursework requirements.

The second area of work, the focus of lessons three to five, is the analysis and 'deconstruction' of Act I, Scene i of the play. This is achieved in the first instance through a reading of the scene as written, and then through watching and analysing two film versions of the scene, one of which is an animated film. The third area of work can be described as the students' construction, through performance, of their own version of the scene in lesson six. In the next two lessons, seven and eight, the students move on to study the plot of the whole play, not through the script of the play, but through a film version, and through images of key moments in the plot. The fifth area of work, attended to in the final four lessons in the series, focuses on the coursework essay on *Macbeth*, its planning and writing. Below we discuss the way in which the text is realized and features in relation to each of these areas.

Creating a context for the text – creating the text?

Since the early 1990s there has been a marked shift in the teaching of Shake-speare. This is epitomized in the currency of Rex Gibson's (1998) approach to the teaching of Shakespeare. It has led to the publication of the Cambridge School Shakespeare series in which pages of Shakespearean text alternate with pages of practical, activity-orientated approaches to exploring the meaning of the text. The imperative for taking these 'active approaches' to the teaching of Shakespeare is derived from ways of studying Shakespeare that have been made compulsory for students in the lower years of secondary school, which culminate in a standard-ized test for fourteen-year-olds. This has demanded an approach that attempts to engage the interest of younger students through involvement in practical activity. These approaches have percolated through into the study of Shakespeare for public examination at the age of sixteen and into advanced study after that. These moves have reconfigured the teaching of Shakespearean text.

The central argument of Gibson and others is that the key to making Shake-speare accessible is the vividness and energy that is to be found in Shakespeare's language. This energy is said to hold universal appeal to students, if teachers can find ways to immerse students in the text. Such 'immersion' can be encouraged by allowing students to play with the language and accompanying action and, through this, to experience the sensory and sensual nature of Shakespeare's text. The underlying view of the Shakespearean text is that rather than treating it as a 'sacred text' to be approached intellectually, the plays should be experienced as 'living' text for performance. Playfulness is seen as a 'point of entry' into the text, 'inhabit-ing' the text and, through this, motivating the students towards more traditional scholarly approaches to textual interpretation, through practices such as close reading and annotation. The sensory nature of word play in Shakespearean text, its rhythm and rhyme, rich imagery, all serve to aid an active animation of the text. Such an approach has been lent support and given academic and dramatic credi-bility through historical and experimental approaches to 'playing' Shakespeare developed by such organizations as Globe Education and Shakespeare's Globe Theatre. Many London teachers and school students have had access to workshops at a centre such as this. These facilities can be seen to be a real resource supporting teachers' attempts to convince students that studying Shakespeare can be 'fun' and relevant as well as being a compulsory requirement of the curriculum. To 'inhabit' Shakespearean text through such active approaches renders the text less remote as a canonical object of study, and closer to students' lives.

Lesson one focused on the issue of 'witchcraft'. The lesson started with a whole-class discussion of witchcraft and the students' expectations and associations with witches, and their knowledge of the crimes and accusations associated with them. The teacher instructed the students to make a poster of a witch to show 'what witches look like' and to answer the questions 'what they have' and 'what they do'.

Lesson two explored the 'historical context' of life in the seventeenth century. The teacher asked the students to imagine and write about what life in 1603 would have been like, with no formal state, no modern science, technology or education, a stronghold of religion and superstition. As Anna said when interviewed:

> I am quite interested in witchcraft anyway and one of the things I really love about English and what I always try and do when I am teaching something is to set it in an historical context, because I think it is really important, and how our responses changes as the context changes so I knew I wanted to set up where they had a strong understanding of the context.

The next task Anna set for the students was to match five pictures on a sheet to five written characteristics that 'define' witches, such as 'They can fly through the air, and can make themselves invisible at will'. The teacher gave the students an information sheet on witchcraft that she had made from information on the Internet and a series of questions to answer on it 'in full sentences'. Questions included, for example, 'What is a "sabbath"' and 'What was thought to take place at one?', 'What is heresy?', 'Who passed the first act (law) against witchcraft?', 'When?' and 'Why was James I so "terrified" of witches?' The students' homework was to do research on James I and witch-hunts.

During these two lessons the text to be studied is not foregrounded; indeed, it is not mentioned until the end of lesson two, and then only to indicate what the next lesson will focus on. These two lessons ostensibly focus on providing a 'social and historical context' for the play (as outlined in the teacher's lesson plan and a requirement of the National Curriculum). Alongside this, however, Anna's comments when interviewed suggest that the focus on witchcraft is a strategy for engaging the students with the text via this theme.

> I didn't tell them for a while what we were doing. I don't know if you were here for the first few days, when I set it up. I didn't tell them we were doing *Macbeth*, I just got them to think about what life would be like then, and that did seem to catch them a bit, catch their imagination and get them to think about witchcraft and they also respond quite well – if you give them something complicated, something new they have learnt, I don't know if I have shown you this – this sheet which is all about the history of witchcraft at the time and they really respond to that because it is something completely different, something they don't know. That always seems to have a kind of calming effect on classes.

It also reflects Anna's strategy, shared by the other teachers in the English department of Springton School, to break down work in English into manageable chunks. This strategy and the elements it breaks English into clearly reflect the teachers' sense of the demands of the curriculum. In the process it produces English as a set of facts, and learning as a matter of knowledge of the play: a curriculum of 'facts'. As Anna commented when interviewed:

They always go 'ugh, not History' and things like that when I do that sort of stuff but I don't generally have classroom problems when they are doing stuff like that. They get on with it and also, because it is a kind of comprehension, they are quite straightforward questions and they like comprehension a lot and it is almost like a closed task; they can see the ending. They can see what they have achieved.

This 'breaking down' of the process of study, and of the text *Macbeth* itself, reflects the teacher's perception – and as we showed in Chapter 5, construction – of the students' 'ability'. It is also the teacher's response to the classroom management issues that she is faced with in Springton School.

The analysis of Act I, Scene i

The second area of work, the focus of lessons three to five, is the analysis and deconstruction of Act I, Scene i of the play. In the first instance, this happens in relation to the written text of the scene, and then through watching and analysing two film versions of the same scene in lessons four and five.

In lesson three Anna gave the students a worksheet that she had made: the top half listed a series of questions directed towards a scene analysis, and the bottom half presented a photocopied version of the scene. The worksheet also instructed the students 'This piece of work must be at LEAST one side of A4 long'. The questions on the worksheet are as follows:

Explain what takes place during the scene – what happens?
Pick out interesting images or language used and explain what effects are being created.
Does this scene give the audience any clues to the important themes of the play?
Does this scene prepare the audience for future plot development?
What effect might this scene have on the audience?

These questions can be seen as Anna's mediation of the examination requirements. The combined effect of these questions on the scene is to present *Macbeth* as a kind of worksheet, in which the scene is dislocated from the play as a whole. This fragmentation of the play is a material consequence of the examination requirements, and possibly of Anna's perception of *Macbeth* as a text that the students will find difficult, which is also suggested by her comments during the interview:

I decided this year, because they do find it so daunting, I decided just to do the first scene and get them to focus on that in a lot of detail, and I thought it was something they could get a handle on and they could get to know it really well, and understand it well, so it should make writing about it easier, but yes, I am not sure about whether they actually understood the whole story of *Macbeth*, because of the way we did it, because we did it afterwards.

Throughout the series of twelve lessons the students are not given access to the written text of whole play, nor to any other acts or scenes. This reflects the particular focus on examination in the lessons, and of the Springton English department more generally. Anna commented when interviewed that:

> I don't know whether they actually understood the story so well, but then really, for what they were actually being asked to do for their coursework, they didn't actually have to. It is a kind of shame, because I think, it is a real shame not to teach the whole play, but from past experience I know they actually find that really difficult, and they would have switched off and not written the essay or not written them so well. The other thing I do is to make sure everything I teach them is quite short. Because their attention and the amount of enthusiasm and interest they can show is very limited.

While Anna's rationale for focusing on one scene within the play is clear it stands in stark conflict with her understanding of the educational purpose of English. Certainly, Springton School's focus on 'student ability' in relation to the demands of the curriculum, does not enable Anna's philosophy towards the texts of English, professed in her previous comment and the following one, to be realized in the classroom.

> Where I am coming from with English is because I have a real passion for reading, that is what I really want to get across to them, maybe sort of encourage them to read a little bit. I want them to achieve and do well in their exams and things, although I think it is a shame that so much is structured around exams, because it does change how you teach. Sometimes that is quite good because it keeps the pace up, but the way you teach the text, you can't just, well you have to learn how to teach and you can enjoy it. This year I really think they enjoyed a lot of it, because my attitude wasn't like 'we have to do the whole play', kind of picking out bits and teaching those bits, and it is the same with *Macbeth*, picking out one bit, but I do think that is a shame that they don't get to read the whole.
>
> … As they go, so when they sit an exam, to give them a fair chance you have to teach them quite a lot of exam technique, teach very much towards the exam, which is a shame, because I think at Year 9 there is a lot of other things you could be doing

As we have pointed out, the degree to which examination and the official curriculum feature in the classroom varies between the schools in our study. The fragmentation of the text here does not happen in Wayford and Ravencroft Schools (as discussed in Chapter 6). In those schools, the curriculum is mediated through different concerns of the teachers, whereas here the relationship between the National Curriculum and the actualization of English in the classrooms is much more immediate. As we have insisted, teachers make decisions as to how to mediate and transform the curriculum, and the choice of text and ways of dealing with texts reflect this.

Lesson four centred on the viewing and analysis of the representation of the scene in a contemporary film of *Macbeth*, made for television. Anna and her students watched the scene five times, and at each repeat viewing the teacher focused the students' attention on a specific aspect of the representation: the setting, the appearance of the witches, how they spoke their lines, the mood and atmosphere created. The students commented on the visual depiction of the witches, mentioning their 'ugly, crooked noses', 'warts', 'dirty, bad teeth' and 'raggy clothes'. The use of the voice – rather than the language of the lines themselves – to 'stretch out' words, as well as the witches' 'itchy', 'scratchy' voices, was commented on by the students. They talked about how the film's setting of the scene, a battlefield in a foggy valley, created an 'evil' atmosphere. The students were set the task of responding, in writing, to questions on each of these aspects (for example, 'How is the setting depicted?'), and to evaluate the representation of the witches in the scene.

In lesson five the students are offered another representation of the scene, an animated film version. Using the same questions as in lesson four, the students analyse the scene as they repeatedly watch it. In addition to this they are asked to discuss 'What can you tell about the action of the play from this scene?' and 'What questions about the rest of the play do you have?' The teacher addressed these questions by showing them the rest of the film version of *Macbeth*, stopping the video at the end of each scene, summarizing characters and plot, and clarifying names, places and details of the play. Although Anna does not tell the students what their coursework will be, she comments, 'To do your coursework you need to understand what happens in the rest of *Macbeth* – so no talking while the film is on'. The homework set by the teacher involves the students in evaluating the images of witchcraft in the film and in the animated versions of the scene, and discussing which version they prefer. Anna commented on her choice of film during the interview:

> I showed them the video, the beginning of the animated version, and they had to analyse that. We have done quite a lot of media work, sort of analysing images, and they tend to quite like that, and the boys like anything that involves TV, so that is always a good plan … a lot of them while they will be fazed analysing the scene, and they wait for others to forward their opinions, but when you get them to talk about television they can come out with really amazingly intelligent things, and even though it is just in a different form, I always find it quite fascinating that they are really good at analysing the television … I think they are just not frightened of it, because they understand it, whereas where they have like an unusual language in front of them, their

confidence goes and they can't understand it, also it is just too much effort. Obviously I am generalizing massively.

The making of a new text

By this point in the series of lessons Anna has introduced the students to the written scene and two realizations of it on film. In the lesson that follows, lesson six, she sets them the task of performing the scene in the class. The lesson centres on the students' construction, through performance, of their own version of Act I, Scene i. At this point in the series of lessons the textual realizations of *Macbeth* analysed in the earlier lessons become a resource for the students' production of the text.

Anna introduces the lesson by saying: 'Right, what we are going to do this morning is work on how you can make this an effective scene.' Working with the whole class, she allocates three students to read the lines of the three witches and one student to read the stage directions. The students read through the lines without using a 'performance-voice', stumbling over the words, and speaking out of time with one another; the rhythm of the lines is lost. The teacher asks them to read through the scene one more time and asks if the students have any questions. The students' questions refer to the meaning of the words (for example, 'ere' and 'hurly burly'). This is the first lesson in which the meaning of the lines is focused on.

The teacher informs the students that she wants them to stage the scene in an 'innovative' and 'imaginative' way. She asks them to draw on the film versions of the scene they have watched, and to think what resources they could use in the staging of the scene. The move from the film representations of the scene to the students' performance of it in the classroom illustrates the teacher's strategy of starting with a medium (film) and mode of distribution (television) that the students are familiar with, and moving to one that is unfamiliar to many. The students suggest that they can use the resources of voice, body movement and facial expressions in their staging. The teacher demonstrates how to use voice to slow down a line for emphasis.

The teacher then asks the students to organize themselves into groups of four: three students are to take the roles of the witches and the fourth the role of director. Several of the students in each group arrange their clothes, coats and scarves and hooded tops, to form cloaks and to cover their faces as a way of representing the witches. In several groups the students use the space of the classroom as a resource to create rhythm in the performance of the scene. For example, one student said: 'First you come in, then me, then eventually we'll all be in a circle, then we do our spell and we look up, OK?' The students walk round in a circle as they read the spell and in doing so they 'create' the central cauldron. A group of three girls working together devise a kind of 'dance routine' in which they mirror each others' movement, creating a sense of the witches all working and conspiring together. They use a range of voices, changing the pitch, tone and pace of their voices to create the different characters of the witches. In one group, drawing directly on a scene from the film version they watched in an earlier lesson, the 'stage director' lies still on a desk and the witches lean over him and pull at his clothes and jewellery. In the same group the students memorize the lines and speak them with the broken rhythm of a rap track: 'foul/is/foul/and/fair/is/fair'. As the students develop their scenes through the use of voice, movement and 'props', they search to find a way of representing thunder and lightning, and decide to turn the classroom lights on and off, and bang the side of a filing cabinet.

Throughout the performances the groups frequently break into laughter, and comment on their lack of ability. For instance, one student said: 'Miss, man our group's stiff' and 'See look at them, you standing there like saying lines in monotone, look at him: big head – no brain', and another said, 'I can't act; this boy can't act and this boy can't read'.

Each group 'performs' the scene in front of the class. At the end of each the 'audience' of students spontaneously claps. The teacher then asks them to assess the performances by offering 'good comments' and 'targets for making it better'. Comments about the use of voice, the clarity of the lines, the importance of making sure that the audience can see what is happening and so on are offered. The teacher praises all the groups and emphasizes her pleasure that 'so many of you have learnt the lines'.

Anna commented in her interview on the importance of the students' performance of the play:

> With Shakespeare particularly I think it is important for it to come to life in front of them. I don't think that they necessarily ... you can talk about it, and you are going through lines and say this means this, and they will talk about it, and they will even come up with quite interesting perceptions, but I don't think they get a handle on the whole scene and how, unless they actually see it performed, or act in it, and I think it gives them an understanding. Like you talk about it in the class and then unless they actually think about, OK, they've got to say this, and how should they say it, and how should they move, I don't think they really understand the whole. I think it just makes it more real for them.

Following the performance, the teacher writes a title, 'Staging Act I scene I of *Macbeth*' on the whiteboard and instructs the students to 'explain, describe, account for what decisions you made', and to answer six questions that she writes on the board:

1 What did your group decide to do with the scene? Explain why.
2 What are you most proud of about your scene?
3 What could you improve?
4 What did you learn from seeing the other groups perform?
5 What effect would this scene have on an audience of 1603? How would this be different from an audience of 2001?
6 If you were performing this scene in a theatre how would you dress the witches? What backdrop (setting) would you use?

As the students work on these questions, Anna points at question five and says: 'If you want to hit the high grades, C and over, you need to demonstrate to the examiners that you understand that Shakespeare is to be performed not read ... that the effect is on audience not on reader, and to show you understand the historical context, why would they watch it differently.'

Anna's questions are discursively and institutionally positioned by the requirements of the curriculum, and by the materials on Shakespeare that inform her approach to the text.

The whole text: 'I know this sounds slightly confusing but it will become clearer when you look at the pictures'

At no point during the series of lessons are the students given the complete written text of *Macbeth*; their access to the whole play is mediated visually and multimodally. In lesson seven, in order to 'focus on starting to get to understand the rest of the story of *Macbeth*' the teacher reads a summary of the play and tells the students that they will watch the rest of the television production of it in the following two lessons. As she reads the summary and students begin to ask questions (for example, 'Miss, is Banquo his friend?') Anna says 'I know this sounds slightly confusing but it will become clearer when you look at the pictures'. The pictures that she refers to are a set of 14 images with captions that portray key moments in the plot. The students' task is to arrange these in a sequence that reflects the plot of the play. In this way the narrative is broken up and visualized, and plot takes on a contextualizing function for the coursework.

Planning and writing: from multimodality to writing

In lessons four through to seven, *Macbeth* is produced as a multimodal text. Anna starts lesson eight by writing the coursework title on the board, saying 'this is your coursework title', and reading it out aloud. 'Imagine you have been asked to direct *Macbeth*. Explain how you would stage Act 1, Scene i to engage a modern audience's attention and prepare them for the rest of the play.'

In this way Anna is 'retextualizing' the students' retextualization of the play, back from the multimodality of film, image and performance, to a written commentary. She walks around the classroom distributing dictionaries and thesauruses to the students as they copy the title into their exercise books. She asks students 'What is the first thing you do with a title?', to which the students reply 'underline the key words' – a means of preparing for examination. 'What does "direct" mean?' For the students it means something to do with film; for the teacher it relates to theatre, to 'look, setting, costume, act, how speak, move'. Other words underlined in Act 1, Scene i are 'imagine', 'explain', 'audience', 'attention', 'engage', 'prepare them', 'stage'. Working in pairs, the students 'brainstorm' the title. The teacher draws on the result of the 'brainstorms' to write a plan for the essay on the board; though she orders and rephrases these elements to produce a clear structure.

In this lesson all the work of the previous lessons is transformed into a resource for writing the essay: 'preparing us for this essay'. So far, the teacher's essay plan has been matched by the unfolding structure and sequence of the lessons.

The essay plan written on the board and copied down by students was:

1 Introduction – Introduce the main points of your essay (purpose); no more than 30-word description of the plot of Macbeth.
2 Historical context – Why was it written? How was it received in Shakespeare's day? What effect would it have had on the audience?
3 Look at stage directions: Setting – effect on audience; atmosphere created sound effects; costumes – how they enter.
4 How the witches speak and move – body language.
5 Would this be a good representation of witches? What do we expect witches to look like?
6 Conclusion

Anna tells the students to refer back to their notes in their exercise books and reminds them that they have already written about each section of the essay. She links the previous work on historical context to the essay-structure and to the grading criteria: 'This is a major part of your coursework grade – you must refer to historical context to achieve a higher grade'. She tells them that when writing the essay they 'must use the language of the question in [their] answer'

The teacher breaks up the task of writing for the students. Literally, she numbers the paragraphs, orders them, sets time limits on the writing of each section, and as they write each paragraph she asks some of the students to read out their paragraphs to the class. She breaks up the amount of time they write for into manageable 'chunks of time'. She provides them with tools that further structure, chunking the text into manageable units. She has 'helpful props', for example a poster on the classroom wall that reads 'MUD: Make a point, Use evidence, Discuss'. Anna says: 'So you're making a point, using your evidence, and you're discussing it afterwards'. This 'tool' demands a high degree of specification in relation to the texts that the students are to produce, as does Anna's commentary: 'Every single paragraph, every point you make, you're going to refer to how it affects audience attention and prepares them for the rest of the play so that you can show you're answering the question.'

At this point, Anna works individually with the students as they write their introductions, she reads, writes and corrects them, instructing them to 'take out any unnecessary words and repetitions'. This is a frequent role for the teacher; it provides interpersonal support for the students through difficult work. The curriculum itself is not very negotiable and the teacher has to 'work around' it. As homework the students are given the task to write the first three paragraphs of the essay. Lesson ten is taken up with the teacher working with individual students in turn, reading and correcting structure, vocabulary, grammar, spelling, very much a focus on linguistic matters. With some students who have not written much the teacher talks with them to generate ideas for them: 'What do you need to do next?', and then 'Write that down then'. In other cases the teacher and student talk and the teacher writes, clarifying the task, editing, encouraging them to look back over notes, linking their plan to what they have done and written in the previous lessons. Anna is concerned that they are able 'to stage the scene': 'You've already staged the scene – look back at what you wrote and you've seen other versions of the play'. She gives starter sentences 'to help get the scary atmosphere I would…?' Few students work during this time unless directly with Anna, in periods that last between two and six minutes. Many sit with their arms raised waiting for her to come to them. For most of then there is no independent working going on.

In the final coursework, when it is word processed, all the work of the teacher is masked.

Conclusion

We wish to make three points in conclusion, which seem to typify what is likely to happen to English under the pressure of present conditions. The first connects to social relations.

There is a move from the collective process of study in relation to the text in lessons one through to seven, to the 'individual' process of writing in lessons eight through to twelve. The lessons in which the teacher introduces the play – via image, video and performance – rely on collective sharing and discussion of the text. When writing and the coursework are foregrounded the students are working individually – although remnants of the collective character of the teaching method in the school reappear at moments through these lessons, such as the reading out of students' writing, the task of swapping exercise books to get good ideas from others. The teacher's mode of working, and the social relations that she creates when asking the students to write, change dramatically between the lessons focused on the study of the text and the lessons focused on the essay. In the first instance the teacher works in the main with the whole class, or small groups of students. In the second, she works with the students entirely individually. Indeed she comments that it is 'not possible to talk to 30 people at the same time'. This shift in mode has dramatic consequences for classroom management: while the teacher is working with one student the majority of the other students are not working; many are waiting for the teacher to help them.

Our second point concerns the curricularizing of English, and its effects on what the subject can be or is becoming. The essay plan developed in lesson eight provides a tight organizational structure that all of the students work with. Many of the students missed this planning lesson (there was a transport strike) and they were given the plan in lesson nine. Throughout the series of lessons that were focused on the coursework essay, the teacher worked with the students to 'fill in' the content of the structure, suggesting opening sentences, reading out and critiquing the students introductory paragraphs and so on. In this way the potential for the students actually to produce a 'personal response' (one of the assessment criteria used to achieve the higher grades) – rather than learning how to *construct* one – is limited. But then, 'personal response' has long since become an entity in the English curriculum, like character and plot. In this sense the teacher's assertion that 'even though an essay is a formal piece of writing you can still be quite creative with it' is both correct – yes you can, there are resources for doing so, and it can be taught; there are explicitly describable resources to produce 'personal response' – and it is also no longer correct: 'personal response' is now a curriculum entity. The thesaurus distributed to the students is one such resource for this realization. The focus of Anna's comments throughout the three lessons, and later on her written comments on the student's draft essays focused on these structures and their use of language, rather than on their ideas.

Our last comment refers to the main point of this chapter, but in a sense also still one of the main points of the subject: the status of *text* in English now. Throughout this series of lessons, Anna and the students worked with a range of modes, and were involved in the task of moving from a multimodally based exploration of texts towards the written assignments. What seemed most strongly marked to us was the disappearance of the text through its fragmentation in these lessons (as in others that we observed); and in that sense that is one of the most interesting factors in the production of English now. In the lesson discussed above, we see this fragmentation as the sign of a loss of confidence by the teacher about the teaching of writing. It is a point we had noted in the chapter on 'annotation', as we had in chapter 6 when we talked about the production of the students as able or as not able. But in a wider sense it is the disappearance of texts as such – whether as literary entities, or as textual entities of different kinds – to be replaced by a focus on text as the site of mechanically performed operations.

As we have shown throughout the book, that is not the case in all the classrooms we visited, but it is one likely response in schools that for various reasons see themselves under irresolvable pressures from all sides.

Chapter 11

And so to some final comments

Throughout the book we have stressed that our aim was not to establish what English was 'then' in 2000 or is now, as we have finished writing 'the book of the project' in early 2004. So if not that, what have we done? We had also set out to answer a question that seemed essential to us: 'Can you understand English if you focus on speech and writing alone?' Here too we can ask what our conclusions might be. And beyond our two aims, there are the broader questions: 'Can we say anything about English that has wider application?' 'Can we say anything that might help in thinking about the future of the subject?'

So the four points we will deal with in this conclusion are:

1 'Have we been able to show how English comes to be realized in a specific classroom, and what are the salient factors in that?'
2 'Is our methodology one that has produced a significantly different way of looking? And 'Have we seen something that would not otherwise have been visible?'
3 'What are some of the implications of our study – for English teachers and for the education of English teachers as well as for policy?'
4 'What remains as shared in the subject across the differences that we have observed?' In other words, is there something distinctive still, in and across the variety of forms of English?

The production of English in its social environment

We have said a fair bit about what English is *now*, not as a comprehensive or definitive account of what it *is* but as an indication of how this subject has responded to the demands and pressures of policy and of the many aspects of the social environments in which it comes to be realized. Whether in the production of 'student ability', in the notion of what a 'text' is, in the manner in which an entity such as 'character' is materialized, as in the many other examples we have discussed, we show how it is the *ensemble* of social factors – realized through the assemblage of modes of representation – that leads to the varying forms English takes in interpersonal interactions as pedagogy and in ideational forms as curriculum in the classroom. Just to stress this point once more: it is not individual factors individually considered, but the ensemble of factors as a whole that leads to the form that English has.

So we think that here we have demonstrated how we can look at any one particular instance of English – whether in the 'production' of ability, or of character, of text, or of whatever – and give a plausible account of the factors that have been significant in shaping that bit of the subject in this way. Because we have focused on the *processes* of the production of the subject – rather than on the description of the subject at a particular moment – we think that our 'findings' remain valid despite changes in policy, for instance those that have been implemented since the end of the period of our data gathering, that is, the introduction of the Key Stage 3 Strategy. In other words, the processes that we describe remain as we have described them even when different curricular or pedagogic issues are introduced.

Our research shows the subject English at an important moment of transition. It is, we have suggested, being moved from being a subject that deals with values-as-meaning into one in which meanings are becoming curricularized as knowledge. Since the late 1980s, schools have experienced a long period of transition from the former state to the latter – a change that is also documented in a succession of policy documents. Admittedly, to characterize English as the subject that is or was quintessentially about meaning is a rough and ready characterization, but here we will nevertheless push it a bit further. We might say that English is the subject that has, traditionally, focused not just on meaning but on the combination of meaning-and-values. Or to be more precise, English is the subject in which *the* issue is the manner by which the meaning of values is established. In terms of the distinction between school subjects focused on knowledge and those focused on meaning it could be held that all the policy changes since the early 1990s have attempted to move English much more in the direction of turning it into a subject dealing with knowledge rather than meaning. English, to put it in sloganistic terms, is being moved in the direction of subjects such as science.

There might be three objections to this at once. The first would be that all school subjects convey or enact values – value production is one of the central features of the work of the school. To this we would say that English differs from other subjects and practices, in that 'values' and 'meaning-making' are closely woven into its ideational work. Second, those who teach subjects such as religious education, for instance, will insist that they are and have always been interested in values. That is no doubt the case; it is our contestation that it is the conjunction of meaning and values – the question 'By what processes are the meanings of these or those values established?' – that had made English different and distinctive. The third objection is a much newer one, one which would say: 'Well, actually, English is not all that different any more; because while English is being pushed in the direction of explicitness in curriculum, subjects such as science are undergoing a move in the other direction'. As science ceases to be the subject that gives access to the discipline for the purposes of becoming a 'scientist', let's say, and is moving in the direction of providing essential information for informed participation in public life – often labelled by the inappropriate term 'scientific literacy' – it begins to deal with matters of ethics, for instance, of understanding the implications of scientific work on matters of everyday issues such as nutrition, health or the environment. There is, it seems, something like a 'crossover' in the trajectories of the two subjects.

We are, as we point out above, aware that we may be overstating the case, but it is nevertheless, we think, a discernible trend. In each case the motivation seems the same: to make the subject fit contemporary social and economic demands – the demands of competent communication in the one case, and of informed citizenship in the other. What differs in each case is the (assumed or actual) starting point in the movement of the two subjects.

To what extent this trend appears in any specific classroom varies, as we have shown; it is dependent on what social factors are in play, and in what combinations. However, what our research shows clearly is that while *direction from above* has effects to a certain extent, and maybe even in partially predictable ways, these ways are predictable not from the contents of the policies so much but rather much more from the mix of social factors to which we have drawn attention: does the school operate a policy of selection?; does it have a policy of streaming?; what kinds of departmental culture does it enable?; how does it perceive its local environment from a number of different perspectives?; and so on. These factors are of course in some senses the outcomes of national policy – a policy that favours 'diversity' between schools and selectiveness within them. In other senses, they are the product of other sorts of histories, experiences and commitments. Their effect is to ensure that English is always 'inflected': they position teachers differently in relation to their local practice in the English classroom, and supply them with different resources, perspectives and constraints. Here, at classroom level, it is the actions of the various agents in the 'mix' that are the telling factors, and the decisions that are made that have real effects on the appearance of the subject. On the basis of such an understanding, which takes into account the interplay of structure and agency, it is now possible to make some predictions on how a particular mix of factors will play out in shaping the subject. These are findings that are significant for anyone interested in policy or in curricular change.

As far as teachers are concerned, it is clear that while there is, seen from one perspective, the threat or even the actuality of deskilling and deprofessionalization, there is, from the perspective of our research, the reality of the teacher as a real agent in the mix. Teachers still can and do make a difference; and while we have argued at various places in the book against an assumption that it is 'teacher-style', or the individual characteristics of teachers in some way or other, which are the telling issues, it is also the case that teachers remain more than merely the 'deliverers' of some pre-packed learning commodity – however much other aspects of education policy may be tending in that direction. We think that the insights from our study can be very useful in reflecting on that issue, and can be applied in any one teacher's reflection on their practice. Understanding their own role in the ensemble of factors, and reflecting on the effects of their actions in all the ways we have indicated – not in any way mysterious and yet also not immediately open to view – will give teachers a clearer sense of possibilities and constraints, and in what directions, in what domains, they exist.

The 'curricularization' of English is going on, and in that process English is being forced to develop more explicit notions of its curriculum. The authors of the book are united in seeing explicitness as essential; we see it as the sine qua non of equitable participation and practices in the classroom. What our research demonstrates, however, is that explicitness as such guarantees nothing very much: resources made explicit can be used for opening up possibilities in all sorts of ways, and can be used to close things down pretty well entirely.

We think that there are other insights to be gained from our research. Yes, it is possible from our perspectives on English to reflect on to other subjects, and may be to understand processes there in ways not otherwise possible – our occasional references to science are a case in point. But it is also possible to extent this insight to other modes and sites of teaching. Consider the matter, ever more pressed on and pressing for education as an institution, of using the facilities of the new information and communication technologies as the main – or at least a major – vehicle for teaching – usually in the name of greater efficiency, effectiveness, of economies of various kinds. What our study allows us to do is to engage in a mind-experiment. English is shaped in specific, describable ways by the range of factors that we have attended to, always acting in particular kinds of ensembles. We have not looked at English outside of such contexts, but we could imagine subtracting factors, one or more, from such ensembles: what would the shape of English be like outside of the insistent teaching of the wall-display? Or without the set-up and layout of a classroom that brings you together with your peers and with the teacher in particular ways? How would the entity 'character' be developed in the absence of a teacher, of peers, of the specific characteristics of the school, of the neighbourhood, and of all of their influence?

Our study, by showing the effects of these various factors allows us to imagine what English – and maybe not just English – would be like learned in the absence of all or some of these.

English and multimodality

English is that school subject which seems to be founded absolutely on the rock of language, spoken or written. Much or maybe most of the research on English until now has focused on the linguistic modes of speech and writing, and in particular on speech-as-talk. We have shown that many of the meanings that 'make English' what it comes to be in particular 'sites' are never articulated in speech or in writing, yet they are very much present nonetheless, and constantly inform and infuse what English is. We have shown these meanings: for instance in relation to what English itself 'is' – whether it is the subject that deals with the life world of the students – in Wayford School; or the subject that brings resources to the students as a means of dealing with significant issues in their world, in

Ravenscroft school; or as the subject that is defined by the National Curriculum, in Springton School; and indeed the others we have met and described. But we have also shown these meanings in relation to what the entities of the curriculum are, what 'text' comes to mean, how 'character' is to be understood, and so on.

The question that arises at this point most immediately is this: if these meanings are so significant, why are they not expressed, articulated, not spoken or written? Our answer might seem paradoxical: they are not spoken or written because to do so would take their force, their power from them. Take the 'suggestion' of what English is which is made by the wall display. On the one hand it is there: all the time, silently and yet insistently, constantly. As it is not spoken it cannot be countered; if it were constantly spoken it would, on the one hand lose its force (or become unbearably tedious, obnoxious) and on the other hand it would articulate meanings that cannot safely be articulated. The 'silent' assertion of what English is makes it constantly present and yet invisible, in the sense of withdrawing it from the possibility of open contestation.

The 'silent' assertion that this or that conception of English is what obtains in this classroom, or maybe even that it is a shared understanding of this subject – whatever the meaning that is asserted – removes it from the possibility of contestation. To speak it would be to state it explicitly in a mode that would make it available for contestation, that would invite objection, rejection, change. It would open the floodgates to the assertion of different claims, about texts and values, about histories and hierarchies of value, about ethnicity and religion, about language, class and gender. It is difficult to imagine what English would become if it were made the explicit issue for debate, in the mode of talk, the mode that most facilitates debate. In the form that it is asserted, a form of English is both put on display, and withdrawn from being the locus of debate.

The same applies to forms of pedagogy: in the discussion on *Theresa's Wedding*, the teacher's use of gesture and gaze allows her to marshal her rhetorical resources as she needs them – without the possibility of being accused of favouring one gender over another – by bringing her position clearly into the debate without actually 'speaking it', and by making it possible to assert *her* position through the voices of the students. To have said, especially to have said several times, 'I don't want to hear from any of the boys at all' would have made the debate impossible immediately. Just as in another of our schools, the teacher did not need to say – what would have been impossible to speak – 'for you, here at this table, English can only have this – much reduced – meaning'.

So our methodology is justified, has stood the test of revealing aspects of English both crucial and central and yet never spoken; it is a methodology that offers an entirely different approach to how, by what means, in what meanings, the subject is realized. Talk alone, or even talk supplemented by an attention to writing, could not have produced the understandings that we have shown.

Implications

And so we come to the issue of implications. We promised that we would say something about this from the perspective of English teachers, and from the perspective of the education of English teachers, as well as from the perspective of policy.

From the first of these perspectives we can ask, in absolutely practical terms: Do our insights, does our methodology offer a way of acting differently? Do they offer a means of reflecting for a teacher on her or his practice that would allow them to change aspects of their practice, should they wish to do so? Our question here is set in the context we mentioned in the Preface: all the teachers who allowed us to see their teaching are professionals whose clear aim is to do the very best for the students in their classrooms, to maximize their possibilities of success in English.

Given that, we can imagine an in-service programme in which we would look, with a group of teachers, at the classroom we have discussed in Chapter 4. Our absolute precondition would be that we would not slip, immediately or maybe at all, into evaluation, but rather that we would describe what we can see in the teacher's interaction with the students at the first table, and analyse what factors have what kinds of meanings, and what factors have what kinds of effects. We would do that for her interaction with the students at the second table and compare the descriptions and our analysis. We would then pose the question: What could the teacher have done, do, differently in her approach to the students at the second table?

We make several assumptions in this. For instance we assume that in making explicit the resources the teacher uses, in linking them to specific social factors, including factors that the teacher might be thought to have held silently, we provide the teachers with resources for reflecting on their own practice. We assume about the students that however much they might actually differ in 'ability', they will recognize very well that the teacher acted differently at the table from which she has just come, and understand the meanings entailed in that difference, even if they might not be conscious of them, or be able to articulate them. These assumptions would then guide the response to the question: 'What might be done differently?' Some things are clearly different: sitting down vs not sitting down; eye-contact vs no eye-contact; taking the piece of paper with the text-fragment vs not taking the paper; asking questions and immediately answering them herself vs asking questions that are left to be answered by the students; and so on.

The teacher works in a school that has adopted a policy of streaming, though not one of selection. That is a policy decision by the school taken as a response to its sense of how best to deal with the pressures that the students experience in their lives in the neighbourhood. However, the English department as such, much against the pressure of the school, has resisted introducing streaming in English classrooms. As we have said, we know both from our observations and from interviews with this teacher (as with others) that she sees it as her aim to ensure that even the weakest students in the class should succeed in terms of their examination performance. That, for her, is a given. She apportions her time at the different tables very precisely – equitably – whether aware or not, at about six minutes of interaction per table.

Now, we can suggest immediately that the teacher could adopt the same practice with all students, at all tables: sit down at each table; not take the piece of paper at any table; annotate or not at each table; and so on. Of course, she has very good reasons for acting differently in each case, though the differences in action immediately change the possibilities for action, the potentials for agency, of the students: not having the sheet means not being able to write or be responsible for writing; answering the questions for the students means not giving them that task; and so on. The students are positioned in specific ways, and these ways have effects on how the students come to see themselves.

Of course, leaving agency to the students has penalties attached: they might not write, and they might not speak. Long silences hold a 'terror'; and long silences are, from the perspective of 'achieving a goal' unproductive. Here our issue of time enters: six minutes is not sufficient time for a change in practice; six minutes per table is linked to the 'achievement of a goal' in the immediate term, as well as to notions of equity. To change practices would require setting the targets in a different time-frame: something like 'over the course of this term, I will attempt to change my practice in relation to…'. And at this point also another consideration has entered, that of the policy environment, the system of time-organization, in which the teacher and the school operate.

In England at the moment, as of course in all Anglophone countries, there are stringent regimes of performativity. The government, in England, expects a constant raising of 'achievement' measured in terms of results in examinations. Schools can be successful or not in these terms, but success, by and large, is defined for all schools in the publicly funded sector in these terms. At this point the success of the school, and the success of the teacher become somewhat blurred in relation to the success of the individual student. The success of the student becomes the necessary prerequisite to the success of the teacher, whose 'performance' is measured in these terms; and the success of all teachers becomes the means for the achievement of the school's success. An unsuccessful school will suffer all kinds of penalties, many of which, in the end, reduce the resources of all kinds available to the school.

The teacher's strategy in this context is to minimize risk: risk for the individual student, by setting an assumed safe goal for each student; and risk for herself and the school at the same time of not meeting 'targets'. In this environment it becomes a high-risk strategy to adopt medium- to long-term goals, or to adopt a strategy that defines success differently, namely in terms of the realization of the potential of each student. We have encountered teachers in the group we met who were prepared to maximize risk (Lizzy in Wayford School); and whose students, as the result of that risk, showed the benefit in terms of consistently better-than-average performance in exams in that school. We have also described teachers from a school that had a policy of selection and streaming (such as Irene from Ravenscroft) where the risk was diffused, so to speak, by the policy of selection, which at the same time changed the school's 'climate' in every way – whether from the perspective of the teacher or those of the students. In short then, 'risk' is an issue always faced in the context of the environment and its potentials, a matter in part within and in part beyond beyond the individual personality of the teacher.

When all of this is set in the much wider and pervasive 'culture of blame' that characterizes contemporary anglophone societies, it becomes possible to begin to see where a start would need to be made in policy in order to begin to change the present situation of designed underachievement. Judging from the results of our study, the present policy climate, is one in which the denial of students' potential has become a design feature of educational policy. It is the paradox at the base of present educational policy and practice, the surface rhetoric of which is about the raising of achievement. It is not – as our study shows – that schools and teachers are powerless in the face of this paradox; it is the case that it makes the realization of the ostensibly proclaimed goals difficult or impossible in many cases.

Lastly, then, a comment on our fourth point, namely what makes English recognizably English, even across these differences. What, in other words, makes it possible for us to say 'this is not history', 'this is not "values education"' or whatever. In subjects in which knowledge is foregrounded, the issue is straightforward: we recognize the subject by the ostensive curriculum. In science, the topic 'states of matter' remains 'states of matter' irrespective of the pedagogy adopted, and irrespective of the teacher's teaching style or personality. The curriculum-entity might be well taught, or badly, but it remains recognizably the same. To some small extent this is true of English, though as we have shown throughout the book it is far less so than it is in other subjects. There is, in English, no matter what the curriculum-entity might be, a constant issue, namely the connection of curriculum and the 'life' or the 'life-world' of students. We have of course seen this overtly in many instances, whether in the discussion of *Theresa's Wedding*, or in the wall-displays in different classrooms. In other subjects this is attempted at times, under the banner of 'making maths relevant', or of 'making science illuminate problems of the everyday'. However, these have remained largely unsuccessful projects, and in general the students have seen through them as facile attempts.

In English, by contrast, the connection of curriculum to life is always present, whether in the attempt at teaching 'literary sensibility', or in the link between the subject matter of a short story and the lives of the young people debating it, or even, in the current context of issues around literacy, where the matter becomes one of 'your forms of spoken or written English' seen in relation to 'acceptable or standard forms of speech and writing'. 'Connection' of curriculum to life-world is as present or maybe even more so in the reality of disconnection – 'this issue, this text, has nothing to say or to do with me' – than in real connection. Where in the science classroom the attempt to connect curriculum and life always becomes a matter of epistemology – 'the everyday world is like the world of scientific explanation' or 'the everyday world furnishes us with the problems that science can answer' – in the English classroom the (dis-)connection is immediate and present.

In our data we have a statement from a group of students from Springton. Asked what they saw as the difference between science and English they said:

> STUDENTS: … what you are being taught from a science teacher is different from what you are being taught by an English teacher 'cos you are learning about the outside world, the things that happen with animal cells, human organisms and that, space. In English it is very different.
>
> INTERVIEWER: It is a really hard question, but if you learn about the outside world in science, what do you learn about in English?

The answer to this 'really hard question' was given by Kaleem, one of this group of students – regarded as being of low ability. We leave to him the last words in this book: 'The inside, I guess, about society and culture.'

References

AQA (2002) *GCSE English*, Manchester: AQA.

Ball, S. (1990) *Politics and Policy Making in Education: Explorations in Policy Sociology*, London: Routledge.

Ball, S., Kenny, A. and Gardner, D. (1990) 'Literacy, politics and the teaching of English', in I. Goodson and P. Medway (eds), *Bringing English to Order*, Lewes: Falmer Press, pp. 47–86.

Barber, M. (1996) *The Learning Game*, London: Gollancz.

Barnes, D. and Barnes, D. (1984) *Versions of English*, London: Heinemann Educational.

Barton, D. and Hamilton, M. (1998) *Local Literacies: Reading and Writing in One Community*, London: Routledge.

Baynham, M. (1995) *Literacy Practices: Investigating Literacy in Social Contexts*, London: Longman.

Beck, U. (1992) *Risk Society: Towards a New Modernity: Theory, Culture & Society*, London: Sage.

Berman, M. (1983) *All That Is Solid Melts Into Air: The Experience Of Modernity*, London: Verso.

Bernstein, B. (1990) *The Structuring of Pedagogic Discourse*, London: Routledge.

—— (1996) *Pedagogy, Symbolic Control and Identity: Theory, Research, Critique*, London: Taylor and Francis.

Blair, T. (1996) *New Britain: My Vision of a Young Country*, London: 4th Estate.

—— (1999) 'Forces Of Conservatism', speech to the Labour Party Conference, 28 September, Bournemouth.

Bourdieu, P. (1973) 'Cultural reproduction and social reproduction', in R. Brown (ed.), *Knowledge, Education and Social Change*, London: Tavistock.

Bourne, J. (1994) 'A question of ability?', in J. Bourne (ed.), *Thinking Through Primary Practice*, London: Routledge.

Bourne, R. and McArthur, B. (1970) *The Struggle for Education: 1870–1970*, London: School Masters Publishing Company.

Bowe, R., Ball, S. and Gold, A. (1992) *Reforming Education and Changing Schools: Case Studies in Policy Sociology*, London: Routledge.

Brown, R. (ed.) (1973) *Knowledge, Education and Cultural Change*, London: Tavistock.

Buckingham, D. and Scanlon, M. (2003) *Education, Entertainment and Learning in the Home*, Buckingham: Open University Press.

—— and Sefton-Green, J. (1994) *Cultural Studies Goes to School: Reading and Teaching Popular Media*, London: Taylor and Francis.

Campbell, J. and Neill, S. (1990) *Thirteen Hundred And Thirty Days; A Pilot Study Of Teacher Time in Key Stage 1. Final Report*, London: Association of Assistant Masters and Mistresses.

Daniels, H. (2001) *Vygotsky and Pedagogy*, London: RoutledgeFalmer.

David, M. (2002) 'Teenage parenthood is bad for parents and children: a feminist critique of family, education and social welfare policies and practices', in M. Block and T. Popkewitz (eds), *Restructuring the Governing Patterns of the Child, Education and the Welfare State*, London: Palgrave, pp. 28–51.

Davies, C. (1996) *What is English Teaching?*, Buckingham: Open University Press.

de Certeau, M. (1984) *The Practice Of Everyday Life*, Berkeley CA: University Of California Press.

DES (1967) *Children and their Primary Schools* ('the Plowden report'), London: HMSO.

DfEE (1989) *English for Ages 5 to 16* ('the Cox report'), London: HMSO.

—— (1998) *The National Literacy Strategy*, London: HMSO.

—— (1999) *The English Curriculum*, London: HMSO.

—— (2001) *Schools Building on Success*, London: The Stationery Office.

Doyle, B. (1989) *English and Englishness*, London: Routledge.

Dudek, M. (1996) *Kindergarden Architecture*, London: E & FN Spon.

Dymoke, S. (2002) 'The dead hand of the exam: the impact of the NEAB anthology on poetry teaching at GCSE', *Changing English* 9(1): 85–93.

Dyson, A. (1997) *Writing Super Heroes*, New York: Teachers' College Press.

Eagleton, T. (1983) *Literary Theory*, Oxford: Blackwell.

Edwards, D. and Mercer, N. (1987) *Common Knowledge*, London: Routledge.

Edwards, T. and Tomlinson, S. (2002) *Selection Isn't Working*, London: Catalyst Forum.

Elsheikh, E. and Leney, T. (2002) *Work, Work, Work!: After the Exams: Students' Perceptions of Study and Work–Life Balance Issues under Curriculum 2000*, London, Association of Teachers and Lecturers.

Englund, T. (1997) 'Towards a dynamic analysis of the content of schooling: narrow and broad didactics in Sweden', *Journal of Curriculum Studies* 29(3): 267–87.

Evans, L., Packwood, A., Neill, S. and Campbell R.J. (1994) *The Meaning of Infant Teachers' Work*, London: Routledge.

Fiske, E. (1995) 'Systematic school reform: implications for architecture', in A. Meek (ed.), *Designing Places for Learning*, Alexandria VA: Association for Supervision and Curriculum Development, pp. 1–10.

Foucault, M. (1991) *The Foucault Reader*, ed. P. Rabinow, London: Penguin.

Franks, A. and Jewitt, C. (2001) 'The meaning of action in the science classroom', *British Education Research Journal* 27(2): 201–18.

Freedman, A. and Medway, P. (eds) (1994) *Genre and the New Rhetoric*, London: Taylor and Francis.

Furlong, J., Barton, L., Miles, S., Whiting, C. and Whitty, G. (2000) *Teacher Education in Transition: Re-forming Professionalism?*, Buckingham: Open University Press.

Gewirtz, S. (1998) 'Post-welfarist schooling: a social justice audit', *Education and Social Justice* 1(1): 52–64.

——, Ball, S. and Bowe, R. (1995) *Markets Choice and Equity in Education*, Buckingham: Open University Press.

Gillborn, D. and Youdell, D. (2000) *Rationing Education: Policy, Practice, Reform and Equity*, Buckingham: Open University Press.

Grace, G. (1987) 'Teachers and the state in Britain: a changing relation', in M. Lawn and G. Grace (eds), *Teachers: The Culture and Politics of Work*, London: Falmer, pp. 193–228.

—— (1995) 'Theorising social relations within urban schooling: a socio-historical analysis', in P. Atkinson, B. Davies and S. Delamont (eds), *Discourse and Reproduction: Essays in Honour of Basil Bernstein*, New Jersey: Hampton Press, pp. 209–28.

Gregory, E. and Williams, A. (2000) *City Literacies: Learning to Read Across Generations and Across Cultures*, London: Routledge.

Grosvenor, I. (1999) 'On visualising past classrooms', in I. Grosvenor, M. Lawn and K. Rousmaniere (eds), *Silences and Images: The Social History of the Classroom*, New York: Peter Lang, pp. 83–104.

——, Lawn, M. and Rousmaniere, K. (1999) (eds) *Silences and Images: The Social History of the Classroom*. New York: Peter Lang.

Hackman, S. (1987) *Responding in Writing: The Use of Exploratory Writing in the Literature Classroom*, Exeter: National Assocation for the Teaching of English.

Halliday, M. (1985) *Language as Social Semiotic*, London: Arnold.

Hamilton, D. (1989) *Towards a Theory of Schooling*, Lewes: Falmer.

Harvey, D. (1989) *The Condition of Postmodernity*, Oxford: Blackwell.

Heath, S.B. (1983) *Ways with Words: Language and Life in Communities and Classrooms*, Cambridge: Cambridge University Press.

Hextall, I. and Mahony, P. (2000) *Reconstructing Teaching: Standards, Performance and Accountability*, London: RoutledgeFalmer.

Hodge, R. and Kress, G. (1988) *Social Semiotics*, Cambridge: Polity Press.

ILEA (1984) *Improving Secondary Schools* ('the Hargreaves report'), London: Inner London Education Authority.

Jackson, H. (2001) *Marginalia: Readers Writing In Books*, New Haven CT: Yale University Press.

Jewitt, C. (forthcoming) *Knowledge, Literacy and Learning: Multimodality and New Technologies*, London: RoutledgeFalmer.

—— and Kress, G. (2003a) 'A multimodal approach to research in education', in S. Goodman, T. Lillis, J. Maybin and N. Mercer (eds), *Language, Literacy and Education: A Reader*, Stoke-on-Trent: Trentham Books/Open University Press, pp. 277–92.

—— and Kress, G. (2003b) *Multimodal Literacy*, New York: Peter Lang.

—— and Oyama, R. (2001) 'Visual semiotics', in T. van Leeuwen and C. Jewitt (eds), *A Handbook of Visual Analysis*, London: Sage, chapter 6.

Jones, K. (1989) *Right Turn: The Conservative Revolution in Education*, London: Hutchinson Radius.

—— (2003a) *Education in Britain 1944 to the Present*, Cambridge: Polity Press.

—— (2003b) 'Culture reinvented as management: English in the new urban school', *Changing English* 10(2): 143–53.

Kenner, C. (2000) *Home Pages: Literacy Links for Bilingual Children*, Stoke-on-Trent: Trentham Books.

Kermode, F. (1979) *The Genesis of Secrecy: On the Interpretation of Narrative*, Cambridge MA: Harvard University Press.

Kress, G. (1995) *Writing the Future: English and the Making of a Culture of Innovation*, Sheffield: National Association for the Teaching of English.

—— (2003) *Literacy in the New Media Age*, London: Routledge.

—— and Bearne, E. (2001) 'Editorial', *Reading: Literacy and Language* 35(3): 89–93.

—— and van Leeuwen, T. (1996) *Reading Images: The Grammar of Visual Design*, London: Routledge.

—— and van Leeuwen, T. (2001) *Multimodal Discourse*, London: Arnold.

—— , Jewitt, C., Ogborn, J. and Chararlampos, C. (2001) *Multimodal Teaching and Learning: The Rhetorics of the Science Classroom*, London: Continuum.

Lancaster, L. (2001) 'Staring at the page: the functions of gaze in a young child's interpretation of symbolic forms', *Journal of Early Childhood Literacy* 1(2): 131–52.

Larsen, J. (2001) 'Contestations, Innovation and Change', PhD thesis, University of London Institute of Education.

Lawn, M. (1999) 'Designing teaching: the classroom as a technology', in I. Grosvenor, M. Lawn and K. Rousmaniere (eds), *Silences and Images: The Social History of the Classroom*, New York: Peter Lang, pp. 65–82.

Luke, A. and Luke, C. (2001) 'Editorial: calculating the teacher', *Teaching Education* 12(1), 5–10.

Lunzer, E. and Gardner, K. (1979) *The Effective Use of Reading*, London: Heinemann Educational Books.

Maclure, S. (1984) *Educational Development and School Building: Aspects of Public Policy 1945–73*, London: Longman.

Marshall, B. (2000) *English Teachers: The Unofficial Guide: Researching the Philosophies of English Teachers*, London: RoutledgeFalmer.

Martinec, R. (2000) 'Construction of identity in Michael Jackson's *Jam*', *Social Semiotics* 10(3): 313–29.

McNeil, D. (1985) 'Language viewed as action', in J. Wertsch (ed.), *Culture, Communication and Cognition*, New York: Cambridge University Press, pp. 258–72.

Menck, P. (1995) 'Didactics as the construction of content', *Journal of Curriculum Studies* 27(4): 353–67.

Mercer, N. (2000) *Words and Minds: How We Use Language to Think Together*, London: Routledge.

Merleau-Ponty, M. (1976) *Phénoménologies de la perception*, Paris: Gallimard, pp. 324–44.

Moore, A. (2001) 'Teacher development and curriculum reform', *Journal of Education Policy* 16(3): 269–77.

Moss, G. (2001) 'To work or play? Junior age non-fiction as objects of design', *Reading: Literacy and Language* 35(3): 106–10.

Northedge, A. (1990) *The Good Study Guide*, Milton Keynes: Open University Press.

Pahl, K. (1999) *Transformations: Meaning Making in Nursery Education*, Stoke-on-Trent: Trentham Books.

Peim, N. (2001) 'The history of the present: towards a contemporary phenomenology of the school', *History of Education* 30(2): 177–90.

Pollard, A. (2002) *Reflective Teaching*, London: Continuum.

Preen, D. (1998) 'Realistic choices among the prescribed pre-twentieth century writers', *English in Education* 32(3): 21–6.

Protherough, R. (1986) *Teaching Literature For Examinations*, Milton Keynes: Open University Press.

Reay, D. (1998) *Class Work: Mothers' Involvement in their Children's Primary Schooling*, London: University College London Press.

Rose, N. (1990) *Governing the Soul: The Shaping of the Private Self*, London: Routledge.

Rosenholtz, S. (1989) *Teacher's Workplace: The Social Organisation of Schools*, New York: Teachers' College Press.

Rutter, M., Maughan, B., Mortimore, P. and Ouston, J. (1979) *Fifteen Thousand Hours: Secondary Schools And Their Effects On Children*, London: Open Books.

Sarland, C. (1991) *Young People Reading: Culture and Response*, Milton Keynes: Open University Press.

Scheflen, A.E. (1973) *How Behavior Means*, New York: Gordon and Breach.

Seaborne, M. (1977) *The English School: Its Architecture and Organisation Vol II 1870–1970*, London: Routledge and Kegan Paul.

Sinclair, J. and Coulthard, M. (1975) *Towards an Analysis of Discourse: The English Used by Teachers and Pupils*, London: Oxford University Press.

Street, B. (1984) *Literacy in Theory and Practice*, Cambridge: Cambridge University Press.

—— and Street, J. (1995) 'The schooling of literacy', in P. Murphy, M. Selinger, J. Bourne and M. Briggs (eds), *Subject Learning in the Primary Curriculum*, London: Routledge, pp. 75–88.

Stuebing, S. (1995) *Redefining the Place to Learn*, Paris: Organisation for Economic Co-operation and Development.

Thompson, E.P. (1991 [1965]) 'Time, work-discipline and industrial capitalism', in *Customs in Common*, Harwondsworth: Penguin, pp. 352–403.

van Leeuwen, T. (1999) *Speech, Music, Sound*, London: Macmillan.

—— and Jewitt, C. (eds) (2001) *A Handbook of Visual Analysis*, London: Sage.

Volosinov, V. (1973) *Marxism and the Philosophy of Language*, translated by L. Matejka and I.R. Titunik, Cambridge MA: Harvard University Press.

Walkerdine, V. (1990 [1985]) 'On the regulation of speaking and silence', in *Schoolgirl Fictions*, London: Verso, pp. 143–62.

Waterhouse, P. (2001) *Classroom Management*, Stafford: Network Educational Press.

Williams, D. (1989) *Making it Happen: Classroom Organisation for the National Curriculum*, Swindon: Wiltshire County Council.

Index

Page numbers in *italics* indicate illustrations not included in text page range.

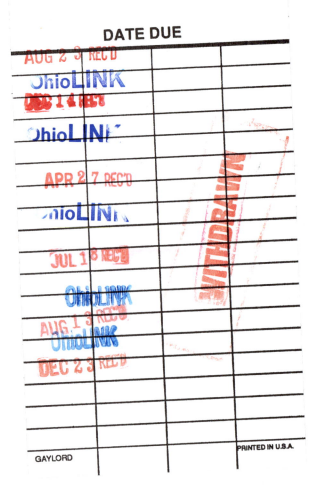